SOJOURNER TRUTH

ALSO BY CARLETON MABEE

The American Leonardo: A Life of Samuel F. B. Morse
(PULITZER PRIZE)

Black Education in New York State: From Colonial to Modern Times
(JOHN BEN SNOW PRIZE)

Black Freedom: The Nonviolent Abolitionists from 1830 through the Civil War
(ANISFIELD-WOLF AWARD)

*A Quaker Speaks from the Black Experience: The Life and Selected Writings of
Barrington Dunbar*
(WITH JAMES A. FLETCHER)

The Seaway Story

SOJOURNER TRUTH

Slave, Prophet, Legend

by Carleton Mabee

with Susan Mabee Newhouse

NEW YORK UNIVERSITY PRESS

New York and London

New York University Press
New York and London

Library of Congress Cataloging-in-Publication Data
Mabee, Carleton, 1914–
Sojourner Truth—slave, prophet, legend / by Carleton Mabee, with
Susan Mabee Newhouse.
p.   cm.
Includes bibliographical references and index.
ISBN 0-8147-5484-8
1. Truth, Sojourner, d. 1883.   2. Afro-Americans—Biography.
3. Abolitionists—United States—Biography.   4. Social reformers—
United States—Biography.   I. Newhouse, Susan Mabee.   II. Title.
E185.97.T8M32   1993
305.5'67'092—dc20
[B]   93-9370
CIP

New York University Press books are printed on acid-free paper,
and their binding materials are chosen for strength and durability.

Manufactured in the United States of America

c   10   9   8   7   6   5   4   3   2   1

Contents

Illustrations

The illustrations appear as a group after p. 78.

vii

Preface

Sojourner Truth was born and grew up a slave in New York State. As a slave, she was called Isabella. It was only long after she was freed that she adopted the name of Sojourner Truth. Under her new name, in the period before and after the Civil War, she became a national figure in the struggle for the liberation of both blacks and women.

Drawing on her faith in God, Truth acted courageously against the folly and injustice of her time. Despite her poverty and illiteracy, despite being black in a predominantly white society, despite the customary pressure at that time for women to remain passive, she significantly shaped both her own life and the struggle for human rights. She became in her time and ours an inspiration to women, to blacks, to the poor, and to the religious.

Myths often grew up about Truth. Because she was so colorful, and because so little precise information about her has been available, persons with causes to promote have often found it easy to mythologize her. Over time, the various myths have served a variety of changing needs, needs that were often psychological or political.

Much that was written about Truth in her time and ours has been written without stating sources, which has encouraged mythmaking. Several of her twentieth-century biographers have invented conversation for her, without making clear to readers that they were doing so, which added to the myths. Even her own story of her life as published in her *Narrative,* first in 1850 and later in revisions, should be used cautiously. The first version was based on her recollections when she was already about fifty-three years old, and was supported by few written records. Moreover, because Truth was illiterate, her *Narrative* was written down by friends who interpreted her life to some degree in terms of their own interests and experience.

Perhaps some of the myths about Truth have served positive functions, up to a point. But they have also contributed, I believe, to distortions about American history, particularly about the history of blacks and women. Surely anyone who chose for herself the name of Truth, with— she believed—the help of God, would understand any effort to push the myths aside to discover the truth about her life.

I believe this book to be the first biography of Truth ever published that has been seriously concerned to discover the best available sources about her, to stay close to those sources, and to state what they are. Because the sources remain limited, portions of her story necessarily remain elusive. Recognizing that limitation, I have tried to tell the story of her life as directly as the most original and reliable available sources permit. Writing for the general reader, I have tried to avoid academic jargon. Writing for the long-term, I have tried to avoid currently chic or political interpretation.

The hunt for original sources on Truth has led me on a six-year search scouring old records, including manuscripts and local newspapers. It has led me to prowl where Truth lived or worked or travelled as a speaker, as from New York to Washington, DC, from Northampton to Rochester and Akron, from Battle Creek to Chicago and Topeka. With the aid of librarians, archivists, and devotees of Truth, I have located documents that give us significant new knowledge, as about her puzzling relation to her children, why she never learned to read, the authenticity of famous quotations attributed to her (such as "Ar'n't I a woman?" and "Is God Dead?"), why she moved from Massachusetts to Michigan, her relation to President Lincoln, her moving freed slaves from the South to the North, her policy on racial separatism, her role as a singer, and her participation in spiritualism. I hope this book encourages reassessment of the enigmatic Sojourner Truth and her place in American history.

In reporting what Truth said, some recent writers, in the understandable effort to avoid the nineteenth-century tendency to report blacks as speaking in an exaggerated, stereotyped black dialect, have freely translated her words into more standard English. However, this may remove us still further from her own peculiar style of speech, which was an ingredient of her charm. Although the original sources may be inadequate in conveying her language, they are nevertheless the best we have. Therefore, although occasionally I have altered punctuation for readability, my policy has been to preserve as much as possible the words that Truth was originally reported as saying.

I have felt encouraged to write about Sojourner Truth because I live in Ulster County, in the mid-Hudson River Valley of New York State, where she was born and grew up as a slave. I know the same essential landscape that she knew, including the grandeur of the Hudson River to the east and the sweep of hills toward the Catskill Mountains to the west. In this region, the State University of New York, College at New Paltz —of which I have long been a part—has named its library, the Sojourner Truth Library, in her honor, and has long been collecting materials about her. There are people connected with the library and other nearby libraries, historical societies, and towns—such as New Paltz, Hurley, Esopus, and Kingston where she lived as a slave—who have been eager to discover more about her life. I wish to thank them for their help and encouragement, especially Corinne Nyquist and Jean Sauer (Sojourner Truth Library), Harriett Straus (New York Supreme Court Library, Kingston), Dorothy Dumond (Town Historian, Esopus), and Kenneth E. Hasbrouck (Huguenot Historical Society, New Paltz). I wish to thank my colleagues for hints and criticism, particularly Albert J. Williams-Myers, Donald Roper, Margaret Wade, and Evelyn Acomb Walker. I wish to thank correspondents, archivists, and librarians everywhere for preserving materials about her and making suggestions, particularly Mary Wolfskill (Library of Congress), Marlene Steele (Willard Library, Battle Creek, MI), Ruth E. Wilbur (Northampton, MA, Historical Society), Betty Gubert, Nashormeh Lindo, and Ernest Kaiser (Schomburg Center, New York Public Library). I also wish to thank many others for information or stimulation, and regret I can name only a few, including William Gibbons (New York), Kathryn Weiss (Gardiner, NY), Wendell Tripp (Editor, *New York History*), William Gerber (Washington, DC), Nell Painter (Princeton University), Nancy Hewitt (University of South Florida), Richard Chartier (Cold Spring, NY), John Daniels (Cobleskill, NY), Jean Ray Laury (Clovis, CA). For checking my English, I wish to thank John Noffsinger (Norfolk, VA); for computer trouble-shooting, Karen Vassal (Gardiner, NY); for seasoned advice, editor Niko Pfund (New York University Press); for pointing the way, many who have studied and written about Truth before; for their sustained support, all my family, and particularly my wife Norma.

Our daughter, Susan Mabee Newhouse (Baltimore, MD), psychotherapist, has worked with me so closely on this book that her name has been placed on the title page as an associate author. She has suggested countless revisions in organization, expression, and interpretation which have made this book more readable and wise than it otherwise would have been.

New Paltz, NY   CARLETON MABEE

Chronology of Truth's Life

1797?–1829: Lived in Ulster County, NY

1797?	Born a slave of Johannes Hardenbergh, in Swartekill neighborhood, town of Hurley, NY
1799–1806?	Slave of Charles Hardenbergh, Swartekill, town of Hurley
1806?–8?	Slave of John Neely, town of Kingston, NY
1808?–10	Slave of Martinus Schryver, [Port Ewen] town of Kingston
1810–26	Slave of John Dumont, [West Park] town of New Paltz, NY
1826, Fall	Walked away from Dumont
1826–27	Legally slave of Isaac Van Wagenen, Wagondale [Bloomington], town of Hurley
1827, July 4	Legally freed, with all the remaining slaves in New York State
1827–28	Took legal action in Kingston, NY, to recover her son from slavery in Alabama
1827–28?	Converted to Christ; joined the Methodist Church, Kingston
1828?–29	Lived in Kingston, working as a domestic

1829–43: Lived in or Near New York, NY

1829	Moved to New York City; worked as a domestic

1832–34	In Matthias's utopian community, the Kingdom, in New York City and Sing Sing, NY
1843, June 1	Left New York City to became a wandering evangelist in Long Island, Connecticut, and Massachusetts

1844–57: Lived in Northampton, MA

1844–46	In the utopian Northampton Association, Northampton, MA
1850, Apr. 15	Bought her first house, Northampton
1850	Her *Narrative* first published, with help of William L. Garrison
1850, Fall	Her first documented speaking as a reformer: spoke for women's rights and against slavery, in Massachusetts and Rhode Island
1851, Feb.–May	Spoke against slavery across upstate New York
1851, May 28–29	Spoke at Akron, OH, Women's Rights Convention, saying women should have a chance to set the world "right side up"
1851–52	Itinerant antislavery speaker in Ohio
1852, Aug. 22	At an antislavery meeting in Salem, OH, confronted Frederick Douglass, asking, "Is God gone?"
1853	Visited Harriet Beecher Stowe, Andover, MA
1853–55	Spoke in New England, Pennsylvania, and New York
1854, Nov. 1	Paid off mortgage on her Northampton house
1856–57	Spoke in Midwest: Ohio, Michigan, Indiana

1857–83: Lived in or Near Battle Creek, MI

1857, July 28	Bought a house lot in Harmonia, a Spiritualist community, town of Bedford, near Battle Creek, MI
1858, Oct.	Spoke against slavery in Silver Lake, IN; when pro-slavery enemies accused her of being a man

	in disguise, she bared her breasts to the audience
1861, May–June	Spoke against slavery and for the Union in Steuben County, IN; threatened with violence and arrested
1863, Apr.	Harriet Beecher Stowe published an article on her, in the *Atlantic Monthly*
1863, Nov.	Carried donations of food from Battle Creek to black soldiers at Camp Ward, Detroit, for their Thanksgiving dinner
1864–67	In Washington, DC, counselling, teaching, resettling freed slaves
1864, Oct. 29.	Visited President Lincoln at the White House
1865, Mar.–Sept.	Rode in Washington streetcars, pressing to desegregate them
1867, Mar.–July	Moved freed slaves from the South to Rochester, NY
1867, May 9	Spoke at an equal rights convention in New York, for suffrage for both blacks and women
1867, Aug.–Nov.	Bought a barn in Battle Creek proper; began converting it into a house
1868, Aug.–Dec.	Spoke in New York State; quit smoking
1869–70, Sept.–Jan.	Spoke in Rochester; New York City; Philadelphia; Vineland, NJ
1870, Mar. 31	Visited President Grant at the White House
1870	Began to speak conspicuously against alcohol, tobacco, and fashionable dress
1870–74	Campaigned for western land for freed slaves, from Massachusetts to Kansas
1872, Fall	Spoke for the reelection of President Grant; tried to vote in Battle Creek, but was refused
1874, Mar.–July	Spoke in Baltimore, Washington, Pennsylvania, New Jersey, especially for western land for freed slaves
1875	Expanded version of her *Narrative* published; ill
1877–78	Spoke in Michigan, especially for temperance
1878–79, July–May	Spoke in New York State

1879, Fall	In Kansas working with the black refugees arriving from the South
1880–81	Spoke in Michigan, Indiana, Illinois, especially for temperance and against capital punishment
1883, Nov. 26	Died at her home in Battle Creek

SOJOURNER TRUTH

1

Growing Up a Slave

"I thought it was mean to run away, but I could walk away."

Isabella, or Sojourner Truth as she was later called, was born a slave in Ulster County, New York, near the Hudson River. Most Americans have long since forgotten that there ever was any slavery along the Hudson River. But Isabella was born at a time when slavery already had a long history in the Hudson region, reaching back to its early Dutch settlers.

Isabella's parents were slaves of the Dutch-speaking Hardenbergh family. The only language Isabella's parents spoke was Dutch, and it was the only language Isabella learned as a small child.

She was born in a hilly neighborhood then called by the Dutch name Swartekill (now just north of Rifton), part of the town of Hurley.[1] It was within sight of the Catskill Mountains, near where two small rivers, the Swartekill and Wallkill, converge into the larger Rondout Creek, about six miles before it in turn flows into the mighty Hudson.

Johannes Hardenbergh, the owner of the infant Isabella, had been a member of the New York colonial assembly and a colonel in the Revolutionary War. He operated a grist mill, and was a large landowner, his claims reaching from Swartekill south for several miles along the Wallkill River. Although most Ulster County households held no slaves, in 1790 the Hardenberghs, being wealthier than most families, held seven slaves.[2]

Both of Isabella's parents, Betsey and James, were probably of all-black African ancestry. But early in Isabella's career as a public speaker, a legend sprang up that there was a Mohawk Indian among her ancestors.

Perhaps the legend emerged to explain how straight Isabella stood, and how tall—she grew to be nearly six feet tall. Or perhaps it emerged because some whites felt a need to explain Isabella's intelligence by attributing it to Mohawk ancestry. But there is no substance to support this legend. Isabella, as her friend Lucy Stone was to say, was "as black as night." Isabella was to say of herself: "I am the pure African. You can all see that plain enough."[3]

Isabella did not know when she was born, and because records of slave births were not then kept, it is difficult to be sure. It was often claimed that she was born about 1776 or 1777. This claim was based in part on her early memory of a "dark day" when the sun seemed mysteriously shrouded (thought to be May 19, 1780).[4] However, there was probably more than one "dark day," and her memories of her childhood, like those of most people, may well have been hazy. Especially from the claim in the first edition of her *Narrative* that she was probably born between 1797 and 1800, and from a signed statement in 1834 by one of her former slavemasters saying that she seemed to be between twelve and fourteen years of age when he bought her in 1810, it is reasonably certain that she was born about 1797.[5]

When Isabella was still an infant in 1799, her master Colonel Hardenbergh died, and she and her parents became the slaves of the colonel's son Charles Hardenbergh, who lived nearby in the same Swartekill neighborhood. From soon afterward, Charles Hardenbergh was reported to have four or five slaves.[6] Charles Hardenbergh's house served both as his dwelling and a hotel, but he housed his slaves in its damp cellar, all in one room. Here they slept, according to Isabella's recollection, on straw laid on loose floor boards, which in turn rested on an earthen floor. The floor was often wet, and water could be heard sloshing under the floor boards.

Charles Hardenbergh seemed to carry on a modest farm and hotel enterprise. It was largely self-sufficient, like that of many of his neighbors, so that his slaves doubtless engaged in a considerable variety of tasks. Among his possessions, according to an inventory made in 1808 after his death, were three horses, eight hogs, four cows, thirteen sheep, five geese, eight fowls, a windmill, "cyder mill & press," spinning wheel, weaver's loom, pigeon net, eel-pot (for catching eels), log chains, a trivet (a three-legged iron stand for holding pots over an open fire), grindstone, scythes, a "whiting" (whitewash) pot, "cooper's compresses" (for making wooden barrels), tar barrel, vinegar barrel, fifteen other barrels, a wagon, and two sleighs, one for work and one for pleasure.[7]

Isabella's mother probably had ten or twelve children, Isabella being the youngest child save one, but most of the other children had been sold away before Isabella could remember. Isabella recalled how her parents, in "their dark cellar lighted by a blazing pine-knot," could "sit for hours . . . recounting every endearing, as well as harrowing circumstance that taxed memory could supply, from the histories of those dear departed ones, of whom they had been robbed."[8]

Her mother, Isabella remembered afterward, taught her to be honest, obey her master, and say the Lord's Prayer. On summer evenings her mother would sit outdoors and tell her that God "lives in the sky," and that "when you are beaten . . . or fall into any trouble, you must ask help of Him, and He will always hear and help you."[9] It is possible that her mother, or other slaves around her, also taught her something of African religious tradition, such as belief in communication between humans and spirits. For slaves brought religious traditions from Africa, and did not necessarily perceive these traditions as conflicting with the Christianity they learned in America. Nevertheless, we have no evidence of Isabella's learning any African religious tradition. She is not known to have spoken about it.

When Isabella was "near nine years old," according to her recollection, her slavemaster Charles Hardenbergh died. At that time the remaining Hardenberghs decided to free Isabella's father James, as he was too old to work any more. They also decided to free her mother Betsey, even though she was younger, to allow her to look after James, and to allow them both, for the time being, to continue living in the dark cellar. But they decided to auction off Isabella and her younger brother, along with Charles Hardenbergh's farm animals. At the auction Isabella was sold away from her parents and her brother. She was sold, she believed, with a lot of sheep.[10]

Isabella seldom saw her parents after that. She knew her mother died first. Her father, by this time blind and unable to care for himself, had been abandoned by the Hardenberghs and everyone else, to live alone in a shanty in the woods. Finally one winter—according to a haunting story that Isabella told—he died, covered with vermin, too feeble to keep a fire going, frozen by the cold.[11]

At the auction, Isabella herself was sold for $100, she recalled. She was sold to John Neely, who operated a store about a mile and a half from the village of Kingston, in the town of Kingston, on Rondout Creek. For his store, Neely imported goods from Europe and the West Indies. The goods came to him by sail up the Hudson River and then up the Rondout Creek to his landing. He sold them for cash, lumber, or almost anything else.

While Isabella spoke only Dutch, the Neelys spoke only English— Dutch was well on its way out in the mid-Hudson region by this time. When the Neelys gave her orders she did not understand, and therefore could not carry out, John Neely whipped her. He cut her so severely that she was scarred for the rest of her life.[12]

Long afterward during the Civil War, as one of her abolitionist friends told it, when Isabella—by then known as Sojourner Truth—was speaking against slavery at Kalamazoo College in Michigan, some of the students were hissing her, and thumping on their seats. She said to them, " 'Well, children, when you go to heaven and God asks you what made you hate the colored people, have you got your answer ready?' After a pause she continued in a deep voice like rolling thunder: 'When I go before the throne of God and God says, Sojourner, what made you hate the white people? I have got my answer ready.' She undid the collar of her dress and bared her arms to the shoulders, showing them covered with a perfect network of scars made by the slave master's lash. The effect was overwhelming."[13]

After staying probably only a year or two with the Neelys, she was sold to Martinus Schryver, a fisherman and tavern keeper who lived in the town of Kingston not far from the Neelys, but closer to the Hudson River, in what is now Port Ewen. The Schryvers were crude—she learned from them how to swear—but they were usually decent to her. For them, Isabella did hoeing, carried fish, and ran errands. She had a good deal of freedom to roam outdoors. Occasionally, watching the many white-sailed sloops on the Hudson, she was startled to see among them a newfangled steamboat throwing up black smoke.[14]

Once when Isabella was about ten, a "grand ball" was held at Schryver's tavern, and it so entranced her that she recalled it years afterward. The women wore "white caps" that were "high-crowned," Isabella recalled, and dresses that were "starched and ironed" so well that she could see her face in them. As the dancers pranced about the tavern to the music, they shouted out a popular song, "Washington's Ball," which celebrated George Washington for having planted the tree of liberty. From having heard this song at the ball, Isabella was able to sing it for the rest of her life.[15]

Isabella clung to the belief in God that her mother had given her, and developed the habit of talking to God, pouring out her grief to Him. She believed that God would not hear her unless she spoke to Him aloud, and that the louder she spoke the more likely He was to hear her. Sometimes she bargained with God. She would say, as she recalled later, "Now God, ef I was you, an' you was me, and you wanted any help I'd help ye; why done you help me?" In the long run she felt God did help her, and when He did, she would promise to be good, but found she could not always keep her promises.[16]

In 1810, at about the age of thirteen, she was sold to John Dumont, who like all the rest of her masters lived in Ulster County. Dumont operated a modest farm overlooking the Hudson River in West Park, about ten miles south of Kingston, in what was then part of the town of New Paltz. Dumont had only a few slaves, sometimes reported as four. The Dumonts, of French Huguenot extraction, spoke English. When Isabella became their slave, according to the Dumonts' recollection later, she still seemed to be learning English "with much difficulty."[17]

However, Mr. Dumont found Isabella unusually strong and energetic in plowing, hoeing, and reaping, and he praised her generously. She responded by working harder. He came to say that she could do as much work as half-a-dozen common farm hands. Not surprisingly, other slaves taunted her with being a "white folks' nigger."[18]

According to her recollections in her *Narrative,* Isabella was confused about how she felt being a slave. By the standards of the time, Dumont was humane. The most severe whipping Dumont ever gave her, Isabella recalled, was when she had tormented a cat. Although sometimes she considered slavery cruel and prayed to God to kill all whites, she recalled, at other times she believed slavery right, adored Dumont, and confused him with God.[19]

While she was a slave of Dumont, Isabella developed an attachment for Robert, a slave on a neighboring farm. But Robert's master forbade him to see Isabella, saying he was going to marry Robert to a slave on his own farm. Despite this prohibition, as Isabella reported it, Robert continued to visit Isabella, but "very stealthily."

Isabella's *Narrative* described Robert's master as a neighbor, an Englishman called "Catlin," which is probably a misinterpretation of Isabella's pronunciation for "Catton," Charles Catton, a neighboring farmer. Catton had been a flourishing artist in England, well patronized by the upper class, particularly a painter of animals. But after having accumulated some wealth, Catton emigrated to America, bought a farm overlooking the Hudson at New Paltz, and devoted himself to farming, with a son and several slaves. Catton was afflicted with gout, which may have contributed to his being irascible.[20]

One Saturday afternoon when Isabella was ill, Robert set out to see her and the Cattons heard of it. The Cattons, father and son, followed Robert to the Dumonts, and in a great rage seized him. While Isabella watched from an upstairs window, as reported in her *Narrative,* the Cattons "fell upon him like tigers, beating him with the heavy ends of their canes, bruising and mangling his head and face in the most awful manner, and causing the blood, which streamed from his wounds, to cover him like a slaughtered beast." Mr. Dumont, seeing what was happening, interfered, saying they could not spill human blood on his premises. He would have "no niggers killed" here.

The Cattons then tied Robert's hands behind him with a rope. They did it so tightly that Dumont insisted on loosening the rope, "declaring that no brute should be tied in that manner where he was." When the Cattons led Robert away, Dumont followed them for a time, as Robert's protector. On Dumont's return to his own house, he told Isabella that he thought the Cattons would not continue to strike Robert as their anger had cooled.

However, the Cattons, by beating Robert and by whatever else they did to him afterward, succeeded in breaking his spirit, and he stopped visiting Isabella. Robert took a wife, as the Cattons ordered, from among their slaves, but did not live many years thereafter.[21]

Isabella's *Narrative* reported that she eventually married Tom, a slave from her own farm, who was considerably older than herself and had been married twice before. According to her recollection, Isabella and Tom were married "after the fashion of slavery, one of the slaves performing the ceremony for them," and over some years Isabella "found herself" to be "the mother of five children." These children were, according to a variety of sources, Diana (born about 1816), Peter (born about 1820), Elizabeth (born about 1825), Sophia (born about 1826), and one more who did not live to grow up.[22] But the *Narrative,* sanitized as it was, does not specify who was the father of each of them, leading to the assumption that Tom was the father of all. There is reason to believe, however, that the father of her first child was Robert.

In the mid-1850s, long after Isabella had been freed from slavery, she herself twice said publicly that she had had two "husbands," evidently meaning Robert and Tom. Much later, when Isabella's first child Diana died as an aged woman, Diana's obituary, which was evidently based on family tradition, said that Diana was Isabella's child by the slave of a neighboring Englishman, while her other children were the children of another slave.[23]

When Isabella married Tom, probably in 1816, the law of New York State, like that of other slave states, did not recognize marriage among slaves as legal. Slave masters could force slaves to "marry." They could also separate a slave woman from her "husband" by selling one of them away. From 1817, as New York State law prepared to bring slavery in the state to a gradual end (New York State was one of the last Northern states to abolish slavery), it recognized that slave marriages could be legal if properly "contracted," as they probably seldom were.[24]

Isabella and Tom perhaps for a time got along fairly well with each other. Isabella reported in the *Narrative* that she and Tom dreamed of the time when they would be freed from slavery and could have "a little home of their own." But their happiness with each other seemed not to have lasted. A son of Mr. Dumont recalled much later that Isabella and Tom had "lived unhappy together." Dumont's daughter Gertrude, who was friendly to Isabella, recalled in her old age that Isabella and Tom argued about whether they were really married: Isabella claimed that they had been, but, Gertrude said, "Tom's version of the affair was that they had merely been out on a frolic together and had agreed to live together as man and wife."[25]

According to Isabella's recollection, while she was the slave of Dumont, she was sufficiently accepting of slavery that she was proud she had brought five children into the world for Dumont. She "rejoiced in being permitted to be the instrument of increasing the property" of her master.[26]

When Isabella went into the field to work, she sometimes took some of her children with her. She would put an infant in a basket, tie the basket by a rope to the branch of a tree, and set an older child to swinging it.

Many slaves reported that to survive they were forced to deceive, but

Isabella insisted on following her mother's urging to be honest. If her children were hungry and she had no food to give them, she would not steal it from her master for them nor let them steal it for themselves. Instead she would whip her children to teach them not to steal. Later Isabella recalled that her refusal to steal helped to form in her an honest character that served her well all her life.

Mr. and Mrs. Dumont had different attitudes toward Isabella. Mrs. Dumont was often displeased with Isabella's work, saying her kitchen work was shoddy. However, if Mr. Dumont came in the house and found one of Isabella's infants crying because Isabella was doing something for Mrs. Dumont, Mr. Dumont would scold his wife, according to Isabella's recollection, for not letting Isabella take care of her own child. "I will not hear this crying," he would say. "I can't bear it, and I will not hear any child cry so. Here, Bell, take care of this child, if no more work is done for a week."[27]

The explanation that the *Narrative* gave for the marked difference in attitude toward Isabella by Mr. and Mrs. Dumont was that Mr. Dumont, who had been used to slaves, found Isabella valuable as an unusually hard-working and honest slave, while Mrs. Dumont, who had not been used to slaves, found her and all slaves annoying. Their contrasting attitudes toward Isabella have induced some writers to suggest that Dumont was Isabella's lover, or that he raped her, and that he was the father of at least some of her children.[28]

One passage in her *Narrative* is particularly relevant to the question about whether any of Isabella's children could be Dumont's. After speaking of the contrasting attitudes of Mr. and Mrs. Dumont toward Isabella, the passage—clearly in the voice of Olive Gilbert, who wrote the *Narrative* for Isabella—reads: "From this source arose a long series of trials in the life of our heroine, which we must pass over in silence; some from motives of delicacy, and others, because the relation of them might inflict undeserved pain on some now living, whom Isabel remembers only with esteem and love."[29]

"Motives of delicacy" suggests that Isabella—in keeping with the customary inhibitions of the time—might wish to withhold information about her sexual life, whatever it was. Furthermore, could "some now living" mean Isabella was especially trying to protect her own children, or Dumont himself, or Dumont's wife and children? (He was known to have had nine children.) When the *Narrative* was written in 1850, Isabella seemed to have a good relation to Dumont. At this time her policy was to forgive slaveowners for the cruelty they had done to her and other slaves; in fact, by this time Dumont had come to believe, as he had confessed to her, that slavery was wrong. She commented: "What a confession for a master to make to a slave! A slaveholding master turned to a brother! Poor old man, may the Lord bless him."[30] Would her forgiving him for holding her as a slave be a reason for trying to protect him or his children from the knowledge that he was the father of any of her children?

Another similar passage in the *Narrative* explained that Isabella wished to omit some "hard things" that happened to her while a slave, things that she says because of their nature "are not all for the public ear." In this passage, however, Isabella said the persons from whom she had suffered the "hard things" had already died.[31] Since Dumont at the time was not yet dead, she apparently had not suffered these "hard things" from him. Perhaps she meant she had suffered them especially from what Charles Catton, who by this time was dead, had done to Robert.

There seems to have been no claim by Isabella or her children that any of her children were Dumont's, even later when such a claim might no longer have caused the hurt it could have earlier. Furthermore, there are no available reports that any of Isabella's children appeared light-skinned or Caucasian-featured. Also in the story of Dumont's effort to protect Robert from the Cattons' fury, there is no sign that Dumont was a lover of Isabella who might then be jealous of Robert or want him out of the way. Moreover, in her years as an antislavery speaker, Isabella did not focus on slavery as giving masters sexual power over their slaves, as she might have done if this were an aspect of slavery that had particularly victimized her. Altogether, while there is no evidence that there were any sexual relations between Dumont and Isabella, nevertheless the emotional ties between them seem unusually close for a master and slave, and a sexual relationship between them cannot be ruled out.

During all the time she was a slave, Isabella recalled, none of her slave masters taught her to read, or even allowed her "to hear the Bible or any other books read." It may be that books did not play a large role in the life of some of her masters. The inventory of Charles Hardenbergh's possessions after he died indicated that he had books valued at only $2, while he had guns valued at $6, and a silver watch valued at $12.50. As late as 1809 at least one of the Hardenbergh family wives could not sign her own name.[32]

Although some of Isabella's early owners seemed narrow or cruel, the Dumont family, the family that owned her longest, seemed less so. When Isabella was doing domestic work for them, as she often did, it is hard to believe that she would not be exposed in some way to school books, newspapers, the Bible, almanacs, or the like. Long afterward two of the Dumont children—who were only a little younger than Isabella—recalled that "it seemed almost impossible to teach her anything."[33] This suggests that by this time it was not only the immediate constraints of slavery on her that were preventing her from learning to read but also factors within Isabella herself.

In New York State from early colonial times, there had been a thread of concern to Christianize the slaves, which sometimes included teaching them to read the Bible. In the early 1800s, when the push to end slavery in the state was already well advanced, some whites were becoming convinced that blacks, because they were to become free, would look after themselves more responsibly if they were Christianized and taught to read. Churches in the region where Isabella lived sometimes admitted blacks, including slaves, to membership.

It is true that during slavery in New York State up to 1827 when it was abolished, most blacks, like Isabella, were illiterate. But educating slaves in New York State was never prohibited, as it was in many Southern states. And in 1810, about when Isabella was sold to Dumont, the state, as part of its plan to abolish slavery by gradual steps, adopted a law providing that slave masters must have their slave children taught to read the scriptures.

From soon afterward, a considerable number of schools in the state were open to slaves and other blacks. About this time, before public schools were yet common in the state, there was a strong movement for the establishment of Sunday schools, which were often intended to teach not only religion but also reading and writing to those who had little opportunity to learn them otherwise. These Sunday schools, sometimes church-affiliated, often welcomed slaves and other blacks; and blacks, including adults, attended them in numbers greater than their proportion in the population. There were separate Sunday schools for blacks in Ulster County, one in Kingston in at least 1811 and 1817, as well as another in Stone Ridge by 1818. There were probably other Sunday schools in the county open to blacks, and certainly other kinds of schools as well. Also there were Quakers in the area. The Esopus Friends Meeting House in Poppletown was only about four miles from where Isabella lived with the Dumonts, and one Quaker family whom she knew operated a school.[34] Why didn't Isabella, aggressive and capable as she was, seek out a school, or at least someone—perhaps a friendly Quaker—who would teach her?

Like Isabella herself, Isabella's three daughters—Diana, Elizabeth, and Sophia—never learned to read and write.[35] While Diana was still living with her mother at the Dumonts', as Diana recalled afterward, Diana "was sent to school for just one week, but had no idea what the school was for, or why she was sent there. The school teacher never spoke to her while she was at school."[36] Diana's recollection suggests that the Dumonts' sending Diana to school may have been merely their perfunctory response to the law requiring masters to have their slave children taught to read. Diana's story also suggests, however, that the Dumonts would not have directly prevented their slaves, including Isabella and her daughters, from attaining a basic education if they had pursued it actively.

Compare Isabella with another energetic slave child, Frederick Douglass. Douglass grew up as a slave in Maryland where there was a much higher proportion of blacks in the population (36 percent in 1820) than in New York State (3 percent), and thus more reason for whites to be anxious to keep slaves under control by not educating them. Douglass's master and mistress, after some wavering, tried to prevent him from learning to read and write. But Douglass learned anyway. One way he did so was by cajoling the white children he met on the streets of Baltimore, where he lived at the time, to teach him—he gave them bits of food they wanted, or made a game out of who could best write something on the pavement.

If Douglass could learn to read and write in Maryland, why couldn't Isabella do so, at about the same time, in more liberal New York State, even if her master did not encourage it? Douglass had the advantage of living much of the time in a city, where he was considerably free to mix with white children in the street, and do what his master did not know about, while Isabella, living in a rural area, may have had less freedom of that kind. She recalled later, in contrast to other of her recollections, that "as a slave she had never been allowed to go anywhere."[37]

Probably more important, Douglass, for whatever reason, had a burning drive to learn. For him learning was associated with his desire to be free. He insisted on learning to write, for one reason, so that he would be able to write a pass for himself, a pass such as slaves were obliged to carry, which he would need for his plan to escape from slavery. Not only did Isabella not associate learning with freedom as Douglass did, but in fact, during much of the approximately sixteen years that she lived with the Dumonts—if her *Narrative* can be believed—she did not even wish to be free.[38] She thought she was a "brute," she recalled afterward. She heard people say that blacks "were a species of monkeys or baboons; and as I had never seen any of those animals, I didn't know but what they were right."[39] Also, there is no available evidence that while she was a slave she herself desired to learn to read or write, or to have her children do so. She may have been, like most slaves, so weighed down by the experiences of slavery, so conditioned to the usual expectation that slaves would not learn to read or write, so lost in ignorance (she recalled afterward that slaves were so ignorant that their thoughts were "no longer than her finger"),[40] so lacking in role models of slaves who had attained any meaningful education, that she had no significant desire to learn.

New York State, following a policy first adopted in 1799, abolished slavery by gradual·steps. The proportion of slaves in the population of Ulster County went down from 9 percent in 1800 to 5 percent in 1820. Isabella knew that all the remaining slaves in the state were to be freed on July 4, 1827.

However, even though Isabella knew this, in the fall of 1826, only about nine months before the law was to free her anyway, she decided to escape from Dumont. She decided this, she said, because Dumont had promised her and her husband Tom that he would give them their freedom on July 4, 1826, a year earlier than when all the remaining slaves in the state were to be freed. Dumont had also promised that he would give them a log cabin as a home of their own. But when the time came in 1826, he refused to do so, explaining that because Isabella had recently hurt one hand, he had lost considerable work from her, and he believed she still owed it to him. (Gertrude Dumont recalled that one of Isabella's fingers had been cut off by some injury, and that Isabella always seemed confident that it would grow out again.)[41] Isabella saw this as unjust, and determined to escape from Dumont. However, amazingly conscientious as she was, she determined to do extra work for him first, to satisfy herself that she was doing right by him. So she spun about one hundred pounds of wool for him, and then, in the fall of 1826, one night shortly before dawn, she walked off from the Dumonts, carrying her infant Sophia.

Suggesting how limited her thinking was at this time, she explained years later, "I thought it was mean to run away, but I could walk away." Or another time still later: "I did not run off, for I thought that wicked, but I walked off, believing that to be all right."[42]

While it was still dark, Isabella walked out of the neighborhood where she was known, and then after it was light she walked on, several miles more, going perhaps six or seven miles altogether. She knew, as she recalled later, that Dumont would come after her, and she wanted to make it easy for him to find her. At least at first, her escape was intended not so much for her to hide from Dumont or to protest against slavery, as to protest Dumont's injustice in not keeping his promise.

Believing God was directing her, she walked first to the house of the young Levi Roe, a Quaker whom she expected to be friendly to her. She discovered, however, that he was ill, on his death bed, and unable to keep her. Roe directed her, however, to Isaac and Maria Van Wagenen, who lived in Wahkendall (Wagondale), now called Bloomington.[43]

The Van Wagenens, who had known her from infancy, took her in. Though not Quakers as they have often been called,[44] the Van Wagenens did not believe in slavery. They told Isabella that she could work for them voluntarily, as if she were a free person, which she decided to do. Mr. Van Wagenen "was a good man," Isabella recalled long afterward, "and treated me kindly."

Dumont soon found her at the Van Wagenens' and wanted to take her back into slavery. Having had a taste of freedom, however, she refused to go back with him. As she recalled it afterward, Dumont threatened that if she did not come back with him, he would see her go to jail. She said, "I can do that, but I won't go back."[45]

To prevent Dumont from forcing her to go back with him or to jail, the Van Wagenens offered to buy Isabella from Dumont on the spot, for $20, plus $5 more for the baby Sophia. Whatever his reasons, Dumont consented. Isabella continued to work for the Van Wagenens for about a year.[46]

It is natural to ask why Isabella, in escaping, did not take all of her family with her—not only her baby Sophia, but also her husband Tom and all her children. Peter, about five years old, had recently been lent or sold by her master Dumont to a neighbor, Dr. Gedney, without as far as is known any protest by Isabella, but at least Peter was probably still not far away.[47] Her other children were still young, too, Diana about ten, and Elizabeth only about one.

According to her recollections in her *Narrative,* she had apparently consulted with her husband Tom about her intended escape, but he preferred staying at Dumont's to taking the risk of escaping (when younger he had run away to New York City, been caught and returned to Dumont.) In any event, it is doubtful that there was much affection left between Tom and Isabella. As for the children she left behind, she felt Tom could keep an eye on them, she reported; and if she had taken them all with her, she knew she would scarcely be able to look after them herself. Also, while according to law, she and Tom were to be completely free in 1827, her children, while they were already technically free, would still be "bound" like apprentices to serve their masters for many years— Diana, because she was probably born before the law of 1817 was adopted, until she was twenty-five years old, the other children, because they were probably born after the 1817 law was adopted, until they were twenty-one. So her walking off with all her children would have compounded the illegality of her walking off with only Sophia, as well causing a much greater economic loss to the Dumonts—as Isabella might have been at some level aware.[48]

Moreover, as her *Narrative* explained, Isabella "had known the joys of motherhood" only briefly, "for she had been cruelly separated from her babes, and her mistress' children given to occupy the place which nature designed for her own." As a slave Isabella could give only limited care to her children, forced as she often was to work in the kitchen or fields, or to look after the Dumonts' many children, even to breast feed them. The Dumonts had several children of about the same age as her own children, and Isabella herself recalled that as a slave she had "suckled many a white babe."[49]

Afterward Isabella made much of the injury she felt slavery had done to her, not only to herself directly, but also indirectly through her relationship with her children. In one speech, she said that whites had "robbed me, took all my best days from me, took my chill'en from me." In another speech, she said in poignant words, that as a slave she had never owned any of her own children. "I . . . never could take any one of dem up and say, 'my child' . . . unless it was when no one could see me. . . . I did not know how dear to me was my posterity, I was so beclouded and crushed." If I had known it would have been "more than de mine could bear. . . . I'se been robbed of all my affection for my husband and for my children."[50]

2

Slave Mother

"I felt so tall within."

On July 4, 1827, all the remaining slaves in New York State were freed. This included Tom and Isabella, but it did not include Isabella's children. According to the law gradually freeing the slaves in the state, the children were already free, but they remained bound servants, required to continue serving their masters until they were in their twenties.

On this July 4th—chosen by the state as the day to free the slaves because the day symbolized American freedom—unusual numbers of Ulster County blacks found their way to Kingston, the county seat, to celebrate. We do not know whether Isabella or any members of her family were among them. According to a Kingston newspaper at the time, the black women wore "gay colors," vying with each other to look their best; and the blacks, both men and women, "conducted themselves, generally, with propriety." The newspaper itself indicated neither joy nor sorrow that the blacks were freed.

On this same day, Ulster County whites celebrated American Independence Day as usual, firing canon, ringing bells, and shooting off fireworks. They also held a big dinner at a Kingston hotel at which they drank many toasts, as to George Washington, women, and American liberty, but none particularly to blacks and their new liberty.[1]

A few months later, Isabella heard that her five-year-old son Peter had been sent into slavery in the South, and she was furious. Isabella understood that after the Dumonts had sold Peter to the neighboring Gedney family, the Gedneys in turn had sold him to another one of their family, who had then taken him to Alabama as his slave. She heard from her friends that it was illegal to have sold or otherwise sent Peter out of the state.

The law gradually freeing the slaves in New York State had made a point of prohibiting any blacks being sold or otherwise sent out of the state to circumvent their being freed within the state at the appropriate time. This provision of the law applied both to slaves and slave children, like Peter, who because of their age had become bound servants.[2]

Once Isabella understood that her son Peter had been sold out of the state illegally, she undertook strenuous action to recover him. First she walked from the Van Wagenens', where she was still working at the time, to the Dumonts'. As Isabella recalled it in her *Narrative,* she poured out her fury to Mrs. Dumont that the Dumonts had allowed Peter to be taken to Alabama. Mrs. Dumont replied, "A fine fuss to make about a little nigger! . . . A pity 'tis, the niggers are not all in Guinea!"

Isabella insisted, "I'll have my child again."

"How can you get him?" asked Mrs. Dumont. "And what have you to support him with, if you could? Have you any money?"

"No," replied Isabella. "I have no money, but God has enough." "I felt so tall within," she recalled afterward; "I felt as if the power of a nation was with me!"

Isabella also went to see the Gedney family, one of whom, Solomon Gedney, had sold Peter, she understood, to the relative who had taken him to Alabama. When Isabella vented her fury to Solomon Gedney's mother, the mother just laughed, it seemed to Isabella, in a manner that was "almost demoniacal."

Isabella also went to the nearby Quakers, in the Poppletown neighborhood, to get help in getting back her son. A Quaker family heard her story, and gave her a room for the night, with, as she remembered it, a "clean, white, beautiful bed." She was used to sleeping on the floor, so at first she thought that she would sleep underneath the bed, she recalled, laughing at the recollection of her timid, inexperienced self. Finally deciding that it would offend her hosts if she slept under the bed, she slept on it after all. In the morning her hosts arranged to have her driven to Kingston, with directions to go to the Ulster County Court House and enter a complaint to the grand jury.

On arriving in Kingston, she found the court house. Deciding that the first imposing man she met there was "grand" enough to be the grand jury, she began to tell him her complaint. He directed her upstairs to the grand jury room, and eventually she was able to present her story to the grand jury.[3]

It was astonishing that a poor black woman just out of slavery, and especially one who, as she herself later said, had been brought up "as ignorant as a horse," would take any case to court.[4] But she pushed it forward with the same ferocious energy with which she had worked in the fields for her slavemaster Dumont.

In the effort to recover her son, Isabella for a time travelled the five miles or so back and forth between her home at the Van Wagenens and Kingston, often barefoot, walking or trotting with a gait that was distinctly her own. She alternated, according to her later recollections, between confidence that God would help her bring her son back and fear that in her ignorance and poverty she could accomplish nothing. She kept waiting impatiently, month after month, as various legal steps were taken. When requested to wait, she did not even understand time—she had no idea how long an hour was, or a week. Eventually she decided that to be near the court house she should live in Kingston, a village of about 175 houses. By the summer of 1828 she found work there as a domestic for A. Bruyn Hasbrouck, a lawyer who had just served a term in Congress. Hasbrouck later testified that Isabella was "an industrious, and honest woman, with regular habits of great fidelity."[5] Hasbrouck and his law partner Charles H. Ruggles were among those who, apparently without fee, helped Isabella in her effort to regain her son.

Meantime, Solomon Gedney, doubtless fearing the considerable penalty the law could impose on him, brought Peter back from Alabama. But Gedney still avoided producing Peter in court, as he was supposed to do. Isabella kept pestering various lawyers to help her force Gedney to produce Peter in court until she worried that the lawyers were becoming tired of her. At length she found still another lawyer, Herman M. Romeyn, who asked no pay for himself, but asked $5 to hire someone to bring both Solomon Gedney and Peter in person to court. Though she recalled that she had never until this time had a dollar in her life, she managed to walk to Poppletown, about ten miles, probably barefoot, where she raised more than $5 from her Quaker friends. Instead of keeping the amount over $5 for herself to buy shoes as some of her friends suggested, she gave it all to lawyer Romeyn, explaining, "Oh, I do not want money or clothes now, I only want my son; and if five dollars will get him, more will *surely* get him."

Finally by late 1828, Gedney, prodded by lawyer Romeyn, brought Peter to court in Kingston. In court, when Isabella saw Peter, she was shocked to see that he was badly scarred on his forehead and cheek. When Isabella identified him as her son, Peter denied it, cringing from her as from a "monster." Isabella believed that his Gedney masters had trained Peter to deny it, and also trained him to explain his scars by saying they came from accidents rather than beatings. The judge, however, decided that he was Isabella's son, and turned him over to her, declaring him, because he had been wrongly sold out of the state, to be entirely free, as the law required. After that, it still took some time for lawyer Romeyn, the clerks, and Isabella to persuade the boy that she was really his mother who wanted to care for him.

Taking Peter home with her, Isabella soon discovered that he had been scarred "from the crown of his head to the sole of his foot," and that his back had welts as big as her fingers. "Oh, Lord Jesus, look!" Isabella exclaimed, as she recalled. "See my poor child! Oh, Lord, render unto them double for all this!" In Alabama, as Isabella gradually learned from Peter, his master Fowler had whipped Peter often. Sometimes Fowler had done so severely, and Peter, bleeding, would crawl in his misery under a porch, where Mrs. Fowler would discover him. Taking pity on him, when others were asleep she would "grease" his wounds.

Months later, Isabella heard that master Fowler had been cruel not only to Peter but also to his own wife—he had beaten her to death. Isabella immediately decided that God had punished the Fowlers "double" in answer to her prayer. But she did not therefore rejoice. Instead she told God that He had punished the Fowlers "too much." She said, "I did not mean quite so much, God!"[6]

This account of how Isabella recovered her son is based primarily on her *Narrative,* which depended on what Isabella recalled years later, as written down by an antislavery friend. Did the naive, illiterate Isabella understand what had happened well enough so that she could explain it, with reasonable accuracy, years later to her friend? Did the friend record it without significantly distorting the account for the benefit of antislavery readers? Not even the essence of the story—that someone sent Isabella's son into slavery in Alabama, that she went to court to recover him, and that she succeeded in recovering him—has been directly corroborated by court records or reports in newspapers of the time.[7]

However, some indirect corroboration of Isabella's story is provided by a New York City editor, Gilbert Vale, who came to know her well in the mid-1830s, and who became convinced that she was unusually honest. At that time Vale reported that she had recovered her son in two sentences thus: "One of these children [Peter] was sold illegally into southern slavery, by one Solomon Gedner [Gedney], and her exertions to get him back, which were crowned with success, mark the energy of her character. In this she was greatly assisted by Judge Ruggles, . . . Squire Chip, Lawyer Romain [Romeyn], Lawyer Hasbrouck, and others." All four of these persons named by Vale as assisting her, even if their names are spelled differently, are also named in her *Narrative* as assisting her, and can be identified in local sources.[8]

On the other hand, long afterward her master's daughter Gertrude Dumont believed, as reported by a Kingston journalist, that Isabella had been influenced by her abolitionist friends to give an "imaginary" picture of how the Dumonts had treated her, and that "none" of her children was "ever sold from her." Perhaps Gertrude, quibbling defensively, meant Peter was lent or rented out to the Gedneys rather than "sold." For Gertrude admitted, in what provides considerable support for Isabella's story of the recovery of her son, that the Dumonts allowed Peter to live for a time with the Gedneys, and "finally [Peter] went away to Alabama, which greatly troubled his mother when she heard of it, and she managed to get him back after a time."[9]

In her later life, Isabella was several times reported as saying that more than one of her children—and sometimes all—had been sold away from her.[10] Some twentieth-century writers have accepted such claims. We know, however, that at least two of her daughters, Diana and Elizabeth, were still living with the Dumonts long after Isabella and all the slaves in the state had been freed, and there is no corroborating evidence that any of her children other than Peter had been sold away from her.

As for Peter, his separation from his parents at the age of five, and the harsh treatment he had endured from his later masters left him with emotional as well as physical scars. As we shall see, he became a distress to his mother.

But Isabella's experience with Peter, cruel as it was, did not embitter her. In fact, Isabella was so forgiving that soon after the trial was over, when Solomon Gedney's uncle, Fred Waring, asked her to work for him, she decided to do so, even though Waring had declared, in connection with the trial, that Isabella was the "worst of devils." When her former master Dumont advised her not to work for Waring, she replied she was "glad to have people forget their anger towards her."[11]

Indeed, Isabella's recovery of Peter reinforced her optimism. It gave her experience of white assistance, not only from the Van Wagenens but also from the lawyers, jury, judge, Poppletown Quakers, and various people who had employed her as a domestic in Kingston. It gave her confidence that the courts were just. It also reinforced her faith that God was looking out for her. She believed, she said, that fundamentally it was God who had recovered her son.[12]

According to Isabella, while she was a slave some of her masters went to church.[13] Both the Hardenberghs and Dumonts were affiliated with the Dutch Reformed church, the traditional church of the Dutch settlers, and both families had at least some of their own children baptized. But as would be expected, there is no available record that they had Isabella or her children baptized.[14] Also, however, as would be less likely to be expected, Isabella recalled that they never took her to church, and so she never went. She also said, surprisingly, that during all the time she was a slave, which was until she was about thirty years old, she never heard the gospel preached or the Bible read.[15]

When she was living with the Van Wagenens, shortly before New York State legally freed her, Isabella Van Wagenen, as she was now called, became so comfortable, she said afterward, that she nearly forgot about God. To her, God had been someone she turned to for help in trouble, and because she had no trouble, why remember God? But she found herself bored with her placid life with the Van Wagenens. Early in 1827 as the big slave holiday of Pinkster (Pentecost) approached, she felt ready to give up her freedom at the Van Wagenens', and return to the Dumonts' where she could sing, drink, smoke, and dance with her slave friends. But then suddenly "God revealed himself to her," as her 1850 Narrative reported it, "with all the suddenness of a flash of lightning." As she reported it in the 1870s, she cried out:

"Oh, God! How big you be!" . . . and being overwhelmed with the greatness of
the Divine presence . . . falling upon her hands and knees, tried to crawl away
from the Almighty, but could find no place to hide from his presence.[16]

Then she felt her own wickedness, and the need for someone who
could speak to God for her, to ask Him to spare her. In what she later
considered to be her conversion to Christ, a space seemed to open between her and God, and in the space she suddenly saw, for the first time
in her life, Jesus. As she recalled it once long afterward: "I felt Him come
between God and me as sensibly as I ever felt an umbrella raised over my
head." Or at another time: "My voice sounded different, and then came a
great thought, like a hiccough. I seen him! I saw the hair on his head,
and I saw his cheek; and I saw him smile, and I have seen the same smile
on people since." After this experience, according to the recollection of
one of the Van Wagenen family, Isabella was "going around through the
kitchen preaching as she went," and he added, as if he felt she was a
nuisance, she "kept preaching all day."[17]

As she explained it afterward, her conversion not only saved her
personally, but also drastically changed how she related to other people.
As she declared once, "I was civilized not by the people, but by Jesus."
As she also put it, "When I got religion, I found some work to do to
benefit somebody." She also said, she used to urge God to kill "all"
whites, and not to "leave enough for seed." But when "de lobe [love]
come in me . . . I said, 'Yea, God, I'll lobe ev'ybuddy an de w'ite pepul
too.' "[18]

It is difficult to believe that Isabella's conversion could have conformed
so closely to the accepted form of Christian evangelical conversion in her
time, if indeed it came before she had been exposed in some manner to
evangelical experience. Nevertheless, as she recalled it, it was only after
her conversion and perhaps only a few months after her emancipation,
that Isabella first attended a church meeting. According to Isabella, it was
a Methodist meeting held in a private house. Knowing that it was not the
custom for blacks to enter white meetings unless they sat in a separate
"Negro pew," Isabella feared to enter, and so stood outside, peering in at
an open window. The preacher, Mr. "Ferriss," a circuit rider, as she
recalled it, "lined" the words of the hymn, "There is a holy city, a world
of light above," describing the immortal life that awaited the faithful; as
he sang it line by line, perhaps thumping the rhythm on the floor, the

congregation sang it after him. From thus hearing the hymn repeated, Isabella learned it, and sang it often during the rest of her life.[19]

Continuing to attend such Methodist meetings, Isabella learned to accept the advice she heard from her Methodist friends, to tell all her troubles to Jesus. At one meeting, when she said a devil was after her, apparently meaning it quite literally, a Methodist brother advised her that if she called on Jesus, the devil would leave. Recalling this once, she said, in her droll style, "An' I tole him I knowed dat all de time, but I didn't happen to think of it afore."[20]

While living in Kingston, she joined a church for the first time; it was a Methodist church.[21] In Ulster County at this time, Methodists were a new, populist denomination, disdained by the more formal, more elitist Dutch Reformed who tended to dominate the area. The Kingston Methodists, like many Methodists elsewhere, welcomed blacks, if ambivalently, and had established a Sunday School for them as early as 1811. By the mid-1820s Methodists had built their first church in Kingston, a primitive building of rough hewn timber.[22] Methodists emphasized direct, personal experience of God; they witnessed and preached extempore, in the vernacular, and liked to sing, all of which suited Isabella. One of the Dumont family recalled Isabella in this period as having become a "roaring" Methodist. Isabella herself recalled that when she could, she prayed with her children and took them to church with her.[23]

In accord with the evangelical expectations of the time, Isabella's conversion—and her subsequent struggle to respond to God's voice within her—led her, as similar experiences led others, toward a conviction that she could be an instrument of God. They led her, regardless of her race, class, gender, or education, toward feeling empowered to "perfect" herself and the world.

Isabella was going through profound alterations in her life. By walking away from her slavemaster, being legally freed, going to court to recover her son, being converted, and attending church for the first time, she was opening herself to new ways of looking at herself and the world.

By 1829 when Isabella was about thirty-two years old, she decided to move out of Ulster County, down the Hudson River to New York City. Still considerably mired in ignorance, she wanted to widen her experience of life. She went with a Miss Gear, a white teacher who was interested in Christian evangelism.[24]

This time Isabella took Peter with her. She could also have taken her

youngest child, Sophia, then about three. Although legally Sophia probably owed years of service to the Van Wagenens, because they were
antislavery they were not likely to ask for such service. However, because
Isabella intended to work as a house servant in New York, she would be
expected to live-in with her employers, and her being accompanied by a
small child of her own might be a hindrance. In fact, in an ironical twist,
Isabella left Sophia, if not at first, at least eventually with the Dumonts;
the Dumonts recalled later that Isabella left Sophia to live with them for
many years.[25] Her leaving Sophia with her former master suggests the
sardonic power of the slave system, even after it had been legally destroyed, to perpetuate itself in the behavior of both whites and blacks.

Isabella also left behind at the Dumonts' her two older daughters,
Diana, about thirteen, and Elizabeth, about four, both of whom still
legally owed many years of service to the Dumonts. In addition, Isabella
left behind her husband Tom. His having been freed from slavery was
not much of a boon to him, as he was old and ill. He remained in the mid-
Hudson area but was scarcely able to earn a living, and eventually died in
a poor house.[26]

Isabella was choosing to go far enough away from her husband and
most of her children, about 100 miles, so that she would seldom be able
to see them. Still, if she had not dared to strike out boldly for new
experience, away from most of her family, would she ever have become
Sojourner Truth?

3

Monstrous Kingdom

"I will crush them with the truth."

In New York City, with the help of Miss Gear, Isabella Van Wagenen found work as a domestic in white households. Keeping a certain self-respect, she refused to allow herself, she said, to "bow to the filth of the city." [1] Nevertheless, she was uncertain of herself, still trying to discover who she was, what she believed, and what she could do.

She joined Methodist churches, at first the John Street Church, the mother church of American Methodism. It was a predominantly white church that had included blacks from its beginning; she joined it by bringing a letter from the Methodist church in Kingston. Later she joined a black church instead, the Zion Church in Church Street, which had split off from the John Street Church in a protest against its discrimination—white Methodists refused to ordain blacks as ministers. This church was becoming, through a series of gradual steps, the mother church of the African Methodist Episcopal Zion connection. [2]

It was clear that after she was freed, in both Ulster County and New York City, Isabella was circulating among people who could open the way for her to pursue an education—Quakers, Methodists, benevolent whites, activist blacks—if she asked them. Isabella recalled afterward that in New York City at this time, "despised" as she was as an "ignorant" black who could not even "speak English very well," she was determined to "go among the white people and learn all she could." [3]

What Isabella meant by going among whites to "learn all she could" seems especially to have been learning to become an evangelist, one of the few leadership roles outside the home that was open to women, both black and white. At this time Methodists, like nearly all denominations, did not ordain women as ministers, but they welcomed women, with supervision, as group leaders, evangelists, and activists in moral reform. Isabella vigorously prayed, preached, and sang, often in association with whites, in church meetings, at camp meetings, at meetings to evangelize prostitutes.

New York City in this period, just after the last slaves in the state had been freed from slavery, was an exciting place for ambitious blacks. New York blacks were not only organizing their own churches but also their own self-help societies. They started the city's first black newspaper. They worked with whites in abolitionist societies and in the Underground Railroad. They supported existing schools for blacks and helped to organize more such schools, public and private. They pushed for more black teachers for the black schools in the state. By the 1840s probably most of the teachers were blacks, and about half of them were women, women who were setting new standards for other black women to emulate.[4] Though exposed to this new black activism, as through her black church, Isabella is not known to have responded directly to it. She is not known to have attended any black schools, or participated in any abolitionist or self-help societies.

During this period Isabella was handicapped by not knowing how to read and write. She could not read the Bible even though she believed that knowing the Bible was important. She could not guide her son Peter in his schoolwork: He was supposed to be attending a navigation school, but she did not know for a long time that he was only pretending to attend. She had a bank account, but could not read the bank records.

The only available evidence for anywhere near this period that associates her with an attempt to learn to read is the following: According to a newspaper report of a speech she gave in her old age, she recalled that, "when liberated, and an attempt was made to educate her . . . she could never get beyond her a, b, abs [sic.]."[5] It may be significant that her recollection is expressed as someone else trying to teach her, not as her initiating an attempt to learn.

Although Isabella remained illiterate, she became "zealous" among Methodists, her style being to preach and pray long and loud. According

his Kingdom cult. After a scandal had exposed the Kingdom, the New York *Sun* was to say the story of the Kingdom was "almost too monstrous" to be believed.[10]

When Isabella met Matthias, he was in his forties, and wore profuse shoulder-length hair and a long beard. He said that any man who did not wear a beard was a devil. Matthias was born as Robert Matthews, of Scottish ancestry, in Washington County, New York. He called himself, as variously reported, a Jewish teacher, or a prophet of the Lord, or the Spirit of Jesus, or "Matthias, the twelfth and last of the Apostles." Some of his followers, including Pierson and Isabella, seem to have considered him to be God, but whether he himself directly so claimed was disputed. He made it clear, however, that he believed he had power to heal the sick, to forgive sins, and to punish the wicked. He rejected fasting, but abstained from wine and pork, and inclined toward vegetarianism. Believing in reincarnation, he said that when good people die, their spirits enter the bodies of the living. He sometimes preached in the streets, boisterously, and before coming to New York City he had sometimes invaded churches, interrupting clergymen, and had been jailed.

Matthias had a wife and children who lived in Albany, New York. His wife, who believed him honest, nevertheless opposed his calling himself a Jew, rejected his beliefs, and declined to accompany him in his travels to convert the world. For long periods he had virtually abandoned her and their children.

A little of what we know about Matthias and Isabella's relation to him comes from Isabella's recollection, as recorded in her *Narrative*. More of it comes from newspapers, and from the books and pamphlets that fed the public curiosity about Matthias, particularly two books written by two very different New York newspaper editors.

One of these editors was the conservative William L. Stone, of the *Commercial Advertiser,* a popular New York newspaper. He was born the son of a minister in New Paltz, where Isabella had lived as a slave. Inclined to establishment-approved opinions, he opposed the extension of the suffrage, ridiculed women's rights advocate Frances Wright, and favored the colonization of American blacks in Africa. In his book about Matthias, published in 1835, Stone called for Christian charity toward those who had been deluded by Matthias, but declared extravagantly that there was not "the slightest admixture of truth" in Matthias's teaching, that Matthias himself was insane, and that Isabella was "probably . . . among the most wicked of the wicked." [11]

The other editor was Gilbert Vale, a recent immigrant from England. Vale had been educated for the Anglican ministry but had since become a religious skeptic, and an advocate of such liberal reforms as labor's right to organize. Vale made his living as a teacher of the science of navigation, but he also was the editor of the *Citizen of the World,* an obscure reformist newspaper. Vale admired Tom Paine and Frances Wright. He was suspicious of revelation, and was a fanatic for facts. He was hard-headed— Walt Whitman called him a "hard nut" with no poetry in his soul. Vale was drawn into writing a book about Matthias, he explained, partly because he wanted to make clear what dangers even sincere people get into when they "ascribe their feelings to divine influence," and also because he became convinced that Stone was wrong to call Isabella "among the most wicked of the wicked." [12]

According to editor Stone, after Isabella began to work for Matthias as a domestic, Matthias was suspected of being licentious because he was seen to have female visitors. Also according to Stone, sometimes Matthias would preach to the crowd that gathered at his front door, but "whenever he became irritated with Isabella . . . in regard to household or other matters, he would remain at home, and preach to her the whole day." According to rival editor Vale, Stone thus conveyed the possibility— without saying it directly—that at this time Matthias had sexual relations with Isabella, but editor Vale, defending Isabella, wrote that he saw no reason to believe so, explaining that Isabella is "neither very young or beautiful." [13]

When the family of one of Matthias's followers brought a charge against him for lunacy, the police came to Matthias's house to arrest him and were rough with him. They stripped him, took his money, and cut off his beard. As Vale recounted it, Matthias submitted philosophically to this treatment. But Isabella, "who is a powerful and energetic woman, offered some resistance to the violence to Matthias," and was struck by one of the family that had brought the charges against Matthias. She kept being put out of the house, but kept coming back in. A crowd gathered outside the house to cheer on the arrest and the roughing up of Matthias. The crowd included some Christian clergymen, and some in the crowd called out that Matthias was an impostor. But according to Vale, this claim was lost on Isabella "from the fact of these persons sanctioning the tormenting, as she expresses it, of Matthias. She could see nothing humane in this treatment, or anything to recommend the religion which suggested it," and so she was drawn closer to Matthias. The police took Matthias to Bellevue prison, to the section for the insane, but Pierson, supported by Isabella, arranged to secure a writ of habeas corpus to release him.[14]

While Pierson had led his followers to work with the poor, Matthias, according to the New York *Sun,* "never evinced any ambition to become the apostle of the poor."[15] Among Matthias's followers were Benjamin H. Folger and his wife. Folger was a wealthy, respected New York hardware merchant, who had long been a friend of Pierson's and recently had joined Pierson's fellowship of believers. The Folgers owned a summer house and farm about thirty miles up the Hudson River, near Sing Sing.

In August, 1833, Matthias visited the Folgers' Sing Sing house and then stayed on. It was particularly in this house that Matthias gradually gathered his little religious community, the Kingdom, including Pierson and the Folgers. There came to be fifteen or twenty members in the Kingdom, all of whom were expected to hold their possessions in common, which meant that the wealthy Folger and Pierson put in considerable money. The Kingdom also at times occupied the Folger and Pierson houses in New York, on Third and Fourth Streets, the members at various times passing back and forth between Sing Sing and New York by carriage or steamboat. On Matthias's invitation, Isabella joined the Kingdom in Sing Sing as a housekeeper, taking her furniture and her savings with her, and merging them in the property of the Kingdom.

Isabella continued to distance herself from her children. There is no indication that she brought any of them with her to the Sing Sing Kingdom, even though there were other children there. Pierson brought his youngest daughter, Elizabeth, aged about twelve; the Folgers brought two children, aged about five and ten; later Matthias brought four of his children there too; and Catherine Galloway, another member of the Kingdom who was invited to help with housekeeping, brought a child as well. Because Isabella did not bring any of her children with her, she might have bound to service her son Peter, who was now about twelve, as poor children, whether white or black, often were bound at the time. (Earlier Isabella had placed Peter near Kingston as a canal lock tender, on the recently opened canal that connected the Hudson and Delaware Rivers;

later she placed him as a coachman in New York.) Sophia, who was only about seven, Isabella probably continued to leave with the Dumonts.

At the Kingdom, as Vale reported it, Isabella "had no wages, put in some goods, and had all things in common [with the rest of the community]; her regular employment was, however, in the kitchen." The Folgers later said that Matthias was easy on Isabella as an ex-slave, because his policy "was to requite those who had been oppressed with extra blessings." It is not evident, however, that Isabella had any special exemption from work. In fact, as usual it seems as if she did more than her share of work. Besides cooking, Isabella helped care for the sick—when Mr. Pierson was sick, Mrs. Folger recalled, she would often "call the coloured woman to change his position, as she was a strong and able person, and was always willing to do it."[16] Isabella also worked sometimes on the farm, as by helping to bring in the hay. The Folgers already had one black hand working for them, but Isabella was apparently the only black who was regarded as a member of the Kingdom. All the members did some physical labor—even Pierson did some light work on the farm and Matthias in the garden—and all ate at the same table.

In his Kingdom, Matthias preached and prayed, but scarcely allowed any one else to do so, and certainly not women; the correct role of women, he believed, was to be obedient and stay home. Although Isabella herself had been accustomed to preaching and praying in public, she seemed to find Matthias's frank insistence on the subordination of women acceptable. According to Vale, Isabella liked "Matthias' apparent candour and openness, which has fascinated her; she does not conceive of such openness with a base design."[17]

Matthias insisted on being the head of the Kingdom household. He expected to be called "Father." Under his firm authority, the house was clean and orderly. At meals he presided, with decorum, and served all the food. All the members drank water, not alcohol, but Matthias drank from a silver goblet, while the rest drank from ordinary glass tumblers. Except for Matthias's fine clothes and carriage, their life was generally plain, so their expenses were not great. Matthias gave orders to everyone, even Pierson, as if they were servants. He whipped his own children, including his daughter who had just been married. He whipped Isabella once too, as the Folgers explained, when Isabella was sick, and Matthias gave his permission for her to rest. She was resting in the kitchen sitting by the fire, when Matthias came in, "found one of his sons in some mischief, which he corrected him for, and the coloured woman undertook to intercede, which was offensive to Matthias, as it was a female intercessor, possessed of a sick devil withal—upon which he quickly lashed her with his cowhide, saying, 'Shall a sick devil undertake to dictate to me?' "[18] Much as when Isabella had been a slave, she had not fundamentally rebelled against slavery as wrong, so in the Kingdom, she did not fundamentally rebel against Matthias's authoritarianism. Also much as she had once seemed to regard Dumont as God, now she accepted Matthias as God, or at least as specially ordained by God, and was devoted to him— and her devotion persisted.

It gradually became apparent that Matthias, once he secured enough money from his followers to permit it, had a taste for swaggering. When in New York, he would drive on Broadway, elegantly dressed, in a fine carriage. Or he would walk on the Battery, his usual style being to walk slowly, with dignity. His hair now was neatly parted in the middle, and worn long with ringlets hanging over his shoulders. With money especially from his wealthy supporters Folger and Pierson, Matthias might appear with a green frock coat heavily embroidered with gold, a linen shirt with wristbands fringed with lace, a crimson silk sash around his waist, well-polished Wellington boots, and a gold watch. Said editor Stone, "His appearance was striking and calculated to attract notice."[19]

From the first, one of the ceremonial practices of the community had been for the members, in accordance with biblical tradition, to wash and kiss each other's feet, as an act of humility. One commentator later made sport of this practice: Focusing on Isabella, he reported that after a discussion of humility, "One brother, who believed in doing and not talking, proceeded in humility to kiss the foot of the colored cook."[20]

However, the community's ceremonial washing went beyond foot washing. According to a rumor, when they were all nude, Matthias washed the bodies of all of them, male and female, explaining that this was for the purpose of washing unclean spirits away. This was done, so the New York *Sun* claimed, when they were all together, including Isabella, standing naked around a stove. According to Vale, they did practice a ceremony of washing for purification in the nude, and Matthias did preach that all shame was a sin and that the most pure persons would have the least shame, but the women washed only the women, and the men washed only the men.[21]

Isabella noticed that Folger's wife, Ann Folger, a cultivated woman of

soft manners, appeared particularly desirous of pleasing Matthias, and
flattered him. Isabella herself was quite different from Mrs. Folger: She
was not coquettish. According to Vale, Isabella "has shrewd, common
sense, energetic manners, and apparently despises artifice" such as she
saw in Mrs. Folger.[22]

One of the doctrines Matthias taught his followers was that ministers
were devils, and therefore marriages performed by them were not binding. Marriages, Matthias taught, should be performed by him, to bind
together "match spirits," that is, persons whom God recognizes as be-
longing together. Eventually, in accordance with Matthias's doctrine,
Mrs. Folger became convinced that her spirit was matched to Matthias's.
She and Matthias proposed openly within the community that they should
be united. Mrs. Folger tried to persuade Mr. Folger to give her up, so
that she could follow the will of God to become Matthias's lover.

To Vale it seemed a "monstrous proposition" that "a virtuous, respected, and amiable married female" like Ann Folger would openly
"undertake to induce her husband to give her up" to someone "claiming
to be very holy, and endowed with the Spirit of God."[23]

To persuade Mr. Folger to consent to losing his wife, Matthias promised Folger that he could have as his "match spirit" Matthias's daughter,
aged eighteen, even though she had recently married someone else. While
Matthias was trying to work out this arrangement, Isabella thought Mr.
Folger "looked like a dog with his tail singed," and pitied him.[24]

According to Matthias's daughter, Matthias whipped her to persuade
her to consent to become Folger's lover. But Vale's view was that the
daughter was so enamored of Mr. Folger's polished manners and kind
treatment of her, so different from her husband's crude, low-class style,
that she did not need to be whipped for this reason, but was really
whipped primarily for impertinence to her father. Whatever the reasons,
eventually Matthias's daughter consented to be swapped, and the whole
community, including Isabella, consented to the double wife-swapping;
to accomplish it, appropriate solemn "marriages" were held, within the
community, under Matthias's direction.

Before long, however, the husband of Matthias's daughter discovered
where she was, and after considerable difficulty was able to take her away,
depriving Mr. Folger of his lover. Mr. Folger then took another of the
Kingdom members as his "match spirit": Catherine Galloway, a homely,
uneducated, unpolished servant. Isabella, who, according to Vale, had a

profound sense of her own integrity but also of her ignorance and low class, considered Catherine was "only fit to be in the kitchen with her," and felt Folger was taking Catherine as "a hack."[25] Folger, dissatisfied with this switch, gradually lost his faith in Matthias, became convinced that Matthias was an impostor, and began to prod Matthias to give him back his own wife.

In reply Matthias shouted at Folger and cursed him for no longer having faith in his prophetic powers. Folger then threatened Matthias with brooms, a poker, and knives. They fell into periodic fighting, and once when they fought Isabella seized Folger by the arms and held him against a door till he calmed down.

Isabella herself, although she did not oppose the community policy of mating members with "match spirits," did not take anyone as her "match spirit." Isabella explained later, as Vale reported it, that this happened because of "circumstances, as much as anything."[26]

Meanwhile, Pierson, who had begun to have seizures before coming to Sing Sing, was developing more serious seizures. By the summer of 1834, he had become so weak that he often stayed in bed. The community did not call for a doctor, as that would have been against both Pierson's and Matthias's beliefs. In fact, Matthias believed that diseases were caused by the presence of devils, and that he had power to cast them out, so none of the members of the Kingdom would die. From time to time Isabella, Pierson's daughter Elizabeth, and Mrs. Folger sat up with Pierson, and Isabella and others bathed him. Once when he had been in a seizure and was unconscious, Isabella, in accordance with Matthias's beliefs, slapped Pierson on the neck and face, saying, "come out of your hellish sleep," trying, as Mrs. Folger, who was present, afterward explained, to drive the evil spirit out of Pierson.[27] But in a few days, on August 6, 1834, Pierson unexpectedly died.

Pierson's relatives and friends raised questions about his death. The people of the neighborhood raised questions too. They were already suspicious of the Kingdom, and Matthias had fanned their suspicions because he insisted on identifying as "devils" all those who refused to agree with his doctrines, which included nearly everyone in the neighborhood. Suspecting murder, the local coroner asked doctors to examine Pierson's body. A jury investigated, reveling in the opportunity to poke into the affairs of the notorious Kingdom. One of the jurors asked Isabella what she considered an impertinent question: What has become of Pierson's "evil spirit"? Isabella replied with what she considered an appropriately impertinent answer: It may have entered one of the jurors.[28]

Pierson's death and the suspicions arising from it led the Kingdom to fall apart. Westchester County seized the Sing Sing house, forcing all the Kingdom members out. Mrs. Folger decided to return to her husband, and the Folgers together moved back to their house in New York, on Third Street. Isabella and Matthias and his children moved in with the Folgers there, but the Folgers by this time were reluctant to have them.

In September, 1834, Folger, who was having business losses, explained to Matthias that he could not afford to support the Kingdom any more. This led to painful wrangling between the Folgers and Matthias. Then the Folgers, with the hope that it would help Isabella leave, paid Isabella $25 as wages, contrary to the Kingdom's policy that everyone served without wages. Isabella, still loyal to Matthias, turned over the $25 to him, making clear that she wanted to stay with him. But Matthias returned the money to Isabella. Also the Folgers, hoping to fend off Matthias, gave him $530, with the expectation, as Isabella understood it, that he would use it to carry out his dream of buying a farm in the West. By September 19, 1834, Matthias had left the Folger house and gone to Albany, preparing to go west.

At that time Isabella was expecting that she would soon go west with Matthias. Once again she was willing to move away from her children, including Peter and Sophia, young as they still were. On the same day that Matthias left the Folger house, Isabella also left, separately, taking her luggage with her. She parted from the Folgers on good terms, she thought.[29]

Isabella went north, visiting those of her children who were still at the Dumonts' in New Paltz, and then went on by Hudson River steamboat to Albany to join Matthias. She found Matthias at his wife's house. But while there, on about September 21, 1834, Isabella was astounded to learn that the police, on charges brought by the Folgers, were about to arrest Matthias for stealing the $530 that Isabella understood the Folgers had given him. Confused and upset, she returned to New York.

What the Folgers had done, once Matthias was out of the city, was to complain to the police that Matthias, by claiming he was divine and asking them for money, had obtained money from them under false pretenses. The Folgers at once circulated other charges, too, feeding the suspicions about the Kingdom that were already rife. The Folgers charged that Matthias, with Isabella's help, had murdered Pierson by serving him poisoned blackberries. The Folgers also charged that Matthias, with Isabella's help, had tried to murder them too by serving them poisoned coffee. According to Vale, the Folgers were trying to fix the blame for their own folly and humiliation on Matthias and Isabella, both persons it would be easy for the public to distrust.[30]

In response to the new charges, officials ordered that Pierson's body be disinterred and re-examined by doctors. Although the doctors did not find any clear evidence of poison in the body, they found some unknown but "deadly" substance in it. But Isabella did not panic or run away. She acted forthrightly. To protect herself she went to her former employers— in Ulster County as well as in New York City—to get written endorsements of her character, and succeeded in getting excellent ones. As it turned out, the district attorney charged Matthias with murder, but did not charge Isabella. Apparently the accusations against her seemed too flimsy. But Isabella believed that Matthias had not tried to murder anybody, and she wanted to assist him in vindicating himself. After Matthias had secured a lawyer, Henry M. Western, Isabella went to Western and told him the whole story of the Kingdom, as she understood it.

Western, a skillful lawyer, advised Isabella to prosecute the Folgers for slander against her as the only way to clear her name, and make her a credible witness in support of Matthias. She agreed to do so. As Vale reported it, Isabella exclaimed, "with much energy (for she is really very energetic and not very timid), 'I have got the truth, and I know it, and I will crush them with the truth.' " Vale came to agree that Isabella did have the truth; Vale even declared, "We have never detected her in a single exaggeration, nor has Mr. Western." However, as Vale explained, much of the public, finding it difficult to believe the testimony of any black, wanted the testimony of whites.[31]

Meanwhile, Isabella was working as a domestic for Perez S. Whiting, as she had before, at his house on Canal Street where he operated a shoe store. Whiting was among her many former employers who had attested to her honesty: "I do state unequivocally," Mr. Whiting had written, "that we never have had a servant that did all her work so faithfully, and one in whom we could place such implicit confidence—in fact, we did, and do still, believe her to be a woman of extraordinary moral purity."[32]

On October 16, 1834, New York City's Court of Sessions arraigned Matthias on the charge of stealing. According to the New York *Journal of Commerce,* when Matthias appeared in court—with "the eyes of several hundred spectators . . . intently fixed on him"—his manner "was more that of a dandy in a drawing-room than a prisoner about to be tried." He appeared dressed in a claret-colored frock coat, with lace ruffles at his wrists, a scarlet sash around his waist, and seven silver stars on each side of his breast.[33] Lawyer Western, defending Matthias, argued that he had never claimed that he was Jesus or God the Father, only saying that he was imbued with their spirit. Though the district attorney said he doubted whether the evidence justified an indictment, a jury did indict him. But the trial for stealing was postponed so that Matthias could be moved to Westchester County to be tried especially for murdering Pierson, and ultimately the charge of stealing was withdrawn.

In Westchester County, the murder trial was held in White Plains, in April, 1835. The presiding judge was state circuit judge Charles H. Ruggles, of Kingston, who before he became a judge, had helped Isabella recover her son from Alabama. Probably Judge Ruggles had a favorable impression of Isabella not only because of her effort to recover her son, but also because his law partner A. Bruyn Hasbrouck respected her as a servant in his house. As lawyer Western told the court, he had brought to court character references to help show that Isabella would be a reliable witness, and a recently written reference from Hasbrouck was one of them.

At the trial, lawyer Western frankly declared that "his principal witness" was "Isabella, a black woman," even though he very well knew that many whites would find any black witness hard to believe. Isabella, Western explained, "was in court and ready to give her evidence, but as her character for veracity had been impeached, he wished to support it by the testimony of some witnesses who had not yet got there."[34] To give Western more time, the court postponed the trial until the next day.

When the trial proceeded, Matthias pronounced a curse of God on the jury, for which he was examined for insanity, but declared sane. Doctors testified that they had not clearly found any poison in Pierson's stomach. Lawyer Western argued that Pierson died of epilepsy. The prosecution could offer no substantial evidence that Pierson had been murdered, nor that Pierson, even if he had received adequate medical care, would not have died soon from epilepsy anyway. Judge Ruggles advised the jury that in the absence of adequate evidence, Matthias should be acquitted, and the jury promptly agreed.

Isabella believed that justice had triumphed in this case. But the character witnesses for Isabella had never been called to testify, as the trial had not gone that far; also Isabella herself had never been called to testify. Vale reported that she was "grievously disappointed."[35] It was partly because Isabella had never had a chance to tell her story that Vale asked her to tell it to him, and decided to write it up.

According to Vale, the district attorney, in sympathy with the public's feeling that Matthias was a rogue who should be convicted of something, immediately pressed against Matthias another charge, assaulting his daughter. Even though his daughter, the pretty young Mrs. Laisdell, asked the court to drop this charge, saying she had forgiven her father, her husband, Charles Laisdell, who was present, insisted that the case go forward. The daughter, called to testify, said that her father Matthias had whipped her with his cowhide across her arms and shoulders, one reason being that he intended to find another husband for her, which, she said, she refused to accept.

Instructing the jury, Judge Ruggles said that because this daughter was legally married, Matthias could not legally chastise her. The jury then convicted Matthias of assaulting his daughter, and Judge Ruggles sentenced him to three months in prison for this conviction, plus one more month for contempt of court for cursing the jury. In sentencing him, Judge Ruggles called Matthias a "barefaced impostor," who had tried to tell his daughter her marriage was void, "and endeavored to inculcate in her the same immoralities that he had already inculcated" in the other "inmates of the house."[36]

Newspapers splashed the juicy story of Matthias and his Kingdom over their pages, at least one paper in New York and one in Albany devoting a whole front page to a report of the murder trial.[37] The New York *Times* found it intriguing that among those at Sing Sing who, at Matthias's "command," had "submitted themselves to the deepest degradation" were such an educated and wealthy family as the Folgers. The Albany *Argus* called Matthias "the most notable impostor, at least, of modern times." The New York *Sun* circulated the rumor that in the community Matthias had had one wife for each day of the week, and that he reserved Isabella for Sundays.[38]

After coming out of prison, Matthias went west, without Isabella. It is not clear whether by that time Isabella any longer wanted to go with him.

In Ohio in November, 1835, Matthias visited Joseph Smith, the Mormon church founder, at the Mormon settlement in Kirtland. Matthias identified himself as Joshua, a Jewish teacher, and Smith, his curiosity aroused, invited him to stay with him several days. After listening to him at length, Smith figured out that he was in fact the notorious Matthias. Smith decided he was a murderer and his doctrines were of the devil, and asked him to leave.[39]

When Isabella's suit came to trial—the suit that she had brought against Benjamin Folger for slander—her employer, Perez Whiting, testified that Folger, after charging that Isabella had tried to help murder both Pierson and the Folgers, had admitted to Whiting that his charge was not true. Folger offered no defence. So Isabella won, but again without having the opportunity she wanted to testify in court. Isabella was awarded the large sum of $125, plus costs.[40]

This was, remarkably, the second time this illiterate black woman had taken a case to court (the first being her suit to recover her son Peter), and the second time she had won. These two victories, along with her belief that Matthias was justly acquitted of murder, may have left her with an exalted respect for the law.

After the trials were over, Vale talked at length with Isabella. In part from what she said, Vale decided that Matthias at least originally had been "sincere," but that in time his "cunning" predominated. As for Isabella herself, Vale reported that she no longer believed in the "supernatural character of Matthias." But she still regarded Matthias as "more rational" than any other teacher of religion.[41] She had remained faithful to Matthias, as far as is known, longer than any other member of his Kingdom.

Isabella had been the most faithful among those the New York *Times* called "the miserable fanatics who have been the willing dupes of this rascal." She had been part of a community that was cited by a churchwoman long afterward as an illustration of how easily religion without the constraints of the organized church can run to excess, and by an advocate of psychoanalysis as an illustration of how rapidly the "road from spiritual love to . . . final abandon to carnal appetites" can be travelled.[42]

In the breakup of the Kingdom, Isabella recovered some of her furniture, but lost all her savings. For her role in the Kingdom, she had been accused, on the basis of flimsy circumstantial evidence, of licentiousness and murder. Her honesty had been attacked by the Folgers, editor Stone, and many others. But lawyer Western had been willing to rely on her as his chief witness. Also her honesty had been directly attested to by many of her former employers, vindicated by a court, and even celebrated by Vale. In fact Vale, after talking with many witnesses, decided that "every material point of her evidence has been verified by other respectable witnesses."[43] That was something she could prize.

In the Kingdom, Isabella had been considerably accepted. When Ann Folger found that she could not sleep with either of her husbands, she would come to Isabella's bed, and tell her her woes. But there is no sign that Isabella's voice had been especially influential in the Kingdom. Although she had not been allowed to preach or otherwise freely express herself, as Vale had discovered she had quietly kept making independent judgments: "From our listening to this coloured female, questioning her frequently, and often recurring to very curious and doubtful subjects, we have discovered" that while she did not seem "very observant or intelligent in her looks," yet she is always "reflecting," and "she had her own or private opinion on every thing; and these opinions of her own we have frequently found very correct."[44] Also as Vale seemed to hint, her energy, competence, and sense of responsibility meant that she had contributed more than her share of work to the community and thus had won respect, and she was always aware that she could at any time return to supporting herself outside the community if she wished, as in fact, soon after she left the community, she did.

If Stone or Vale had seen in Isabella any involvement in the larger reform community, it is likely that one or the other, particularly Vale, would have said so—any connectedness to the movements for black self-help or to abolish slavery, for example. They reported no such involvement. Isabella was remote from any such movements at this time, too isolated from other blacks, too isolated from main currents of progressive thought, not enough inwardly emancipated as yet, for any such involvement. While progressive reform often bubbled out of the prevailing American faith in both evangelicism and the perfectibility of man, and while both Pierson and Matthias could be seen as at least on the foaming edge of this bubbling, still Isabella's willingness to play a submissive role in such an authoritarian, male-dominated community as the Kingdom makes it clear that she was not yet close to being a significant advocate of the liberation of blacks or women.

As she emerged from her experience of the Kingdom, she continued to believe that God cared for her, though she might be a bit shaky about who God was. She still esteemed herself as hard-working and honest. "Her moral principles are the same as formerly," Vale reported. "She is still faithful, attached to truth, industrious, and consequently independent; with a ready perception of right and wrong, and with an uprightness and energy of character not apparently very common among the class from which she originated."[45]

Isabella had been gullible to enter the Kingdom and cling to it so long. Her ignorance and naivete had doubtless contributed to her being gullible. So also had her experience of slavery, including her heavy dependence on her slave master for care for herself and her family. So also had her hunger for being part of an intimate familylike circle of mutual support. With high hopes, she had entered an idealistic community only to find herself caught in a mortifying delusion, and she resolved, according to her *Narrative,* "not to be thus deluded again."[46]

Perhaps trust in authoritarian figures was the kind of delusion she was most determined to avoid. For she never again allowed herself to be as submissively trusting in any authoritarian individual or group.

4

New Missions

"God, you drive."

After living fourteen years in or near New York City, Isabella Van Wagenen decided that New York was no longer the place for her. She felt it was "a wicked city," a "Sodom." In New York, she said, "the rich rob the poor, and the poor rob one another." She became convinced that she herself had been robbing the poor because she been miserly in trying to save her money, and because she had been taking jobs away from the poor by taking on extra jobs that she did not really need. She felt she herself had been "unfeeling, selfish and wicked."[1]

Furthermore she believed that "every thing she had undertaken in the city of New York had finally proved a failure." She had tried to preach, but felt that blacks at least, whom she especially wanted to reach, had rejected her. She had tried to help build the kingdom of God on earth through Matthias's community, but it had blown up in scandal, tainting her name. She had tried to save money enough to have a home of her own, but had failed. She had tried to raise her son Peter, when she had time to see him, to be honest and industrious like herself, but he had fallen into stealing, and been imprisoned several times. At first when he had appealed to her from prison for help, she had tried to help him. But when he continued to steal and be imprisoned, she declined to help him any further. Finally Peter had taken a job as a seaman (one of the few occupations easily open to black men), travelled the world, and disappeared—she hadn't heard from him for two years.[2]

In her unease with herself, she decided she must leave the city, but for some time she said nothing about it to anyone. She was afraid that if her children and friends knew about it, "they would make such an ado about it as would render it very unpleasant, if not distressing to all parties."[3] It was 1843 by this time, and she was about forty-six years old. Even Sophia was about seventeen now; she was probably still at the Dumonts' with her older sisters.

Isabella had decided to become a travelling evangelist. Although it was unusual for women to preach, there were several black women in the Northeast who had become travelling evangelists, including Rebecca Jackson (Philadelphia), Jarena Lee (Philadelphia), and Julia Foote (Boston and Binghamton, New York).[4] Before becoming travelling evangelists, these women, like Isabella, had gained experience as exhorters among Methodists. Also several of them, like Isabella had been widowed or otherwise separated from their husbands, thus freeing them from the constraints that husbands might put on such unconventional behavior. However, although Bishop Richard Allen of the African Methodist Episcopal Church at least helped Jarena Lee to find places to preach, Isabella was setting out to be a travelling evangelist, as far as we know, without connection to any church or any other group, without anyone to advise her, and without promise of support.

For any woman just to wander and speak as the way opened was unusual and even dangerous. But Isabella felt that God had called her to repudiate her unhappy, "wicked" life in New York, and that she had a mission, dangerous or not, to cleanse herself and speak for God.

On June 1, 1843, she prepared to leave, placing a few articles of clothing in a pillow case to carry with her. About an hour before she left she informed the Whitings, for whom she had long been working as a live-in domestic on Canal Street, that she was quitting. According to her *Narrative,* she told Mrs. Whiting that she was going to go east: "The Spirit calls me there, and I must go." She also told her that her name was no longer Isabella but "Sojourner." She did not say specifically where her new name came from or what it meant, but because she said God called on her to travel, "Sojourner" could be understood as an appropriate name. She left the city by taking a ferry to Brooklyn, and then walked east on Long Island. She had scarcely any money, but believed that the Lord would provide.[5]

Although her *Narrative* explained how she acquired her new first name of "Sojourner," it did not explain how she acquired her new second name of "Truth." But in 1853 she explained how she acquired both names to Harriet Beecher Stowe, as Stowe reported it later:

When I left the house of bondage, I left everything behind. I wa'n't goin' to keep nothin' of Egypt on me, an' so I went to the Lord an' asked Him to give me a new name. And the Lord gave me Sojourner, because I was to travel up an' down the land, showin' the people their sins, an' bein' a sign unto them. Afterwards I told the Lord I wanted another name, 'cause everybody else had two names; and the Lord gave me Truth, because I was to declare the truth to the people.[6]

If Truth really said, as reported by Stowe, that in leaving "the house of bondage" she did not want to leave anything of "Egypt" on her, she might have meant not only to repudiate the "bondage" of her unhappy life in New York City, as the *Narrative* indicates, but also in a larger sense to repudiate the "bondage" of all her past life, including slavery. Since "Egypt" as referred to in the Old Testament often served as a metaphor for slavery, Truth might have deliberately meant to repudiate slavery by putting behind her the name with which she had come out of slavery, especially the name Van Wagenen, the name of her last legal slavemaster, the name she had been going by during all her years in New York City.

However, in 1843 when according to her later recollections she acquired both of her new names, she was not yet, as far as we know, focusing on slavery as an issue. Even in 1850 her *Narrative* did not connect her choosing her new name to her wish to put slavery behind her, but only to her wish to put behind her own unhappy life in New York City. In 1853 when according to Stowe, Truth gave the previous account of how she acquired her new name, it might have been natural for Truth to have enlarged her explanation to include an antislavery aspect, such as this explanation can be interpreted to include, because by that time she had become an antislavery speaker. Or perhaps Stowe, a writer of fiction inclined to romanticize Truth, recognized the dramatic possibilities in interpreting Truth's choice of her new names as a rejection of slavery, and simply added a hint of this interpretation to Truth's story.

It may also be said that if by choosing a new name, Truth meant to repudiate slavery, repudiating the name Van Wagenen would not do this very clearly because the Van Wagenens, though legally her last slave owners, opposed slavery, and did not treat her like a slave. Moreover, if a significant reason Truth chose her new name was really to repudiate slavery, it seems odd that she waited sixteen years after she was freed from slavery to choose it.

Much later, in the years 1869 to 1879, Truth repeatedly told how she had acquired her new name, as reported in seven different newspaper accounts.[7] By this time Truth had many years experience of thinking of herself as an antislavery speaker; moreover, she had talked with many people who were familiar with Stowe's account of how she got her new name, so that Truth herself might have been influenced by Stowe's account.

While in several of these seven newspaper accounts she mentioned slavery, in none of them did Truth clearly say that she chose her new name as a deliberate protest against slavery. In the most detailed of the seven accounts, in which she said the story of her getting her new name had "never been truly given before," she at first associated her new name with her leaving New York because she felt she had been selfish, a "miser," taking work away from the poor, and with God therefore directing her "to go East." But then in an indirect allusion to slavery, she associated her new name with her having chosen God as her master: After she started walking east, and God gave her the name of Truth, she said she thanked Him for it: "Thank you God, that is a good name; Thou art my last master, and Thy name is Truth."[8]

In another of these accounts, she mentioned her having been sold five times as having caused her name to change each time, but without saying that her own choice of a new name was a repudiation of slavery:

She stated that during her term of servitude, she was sold and re-sold five different times, and was known by as many names, taking a cognomen each time from the most recent purchaser. But after slavery had ended, "It came to her, from de Lord, dat her name was to be Sojourner; an' also it came to her, whilst trabling thro' Long Island, on her way to de East, dat de oder part—de handle to her name—was Truth; an' a person who has got 'Truth' always present as I have," she remarked, "cannot be far astray."[9]

A historian, in his "Foreword" to a reprinting of Truth's *Narrative* in 1970, claimed that Truth's acquiring of her new name, as reported by Stowe, is an example of how a great many ex-slaves deliberately repudiated slavery—or even repudiated the whole "culture prison of the

West"—by dropping the names their slave masters had forced on them, choosing new names instead. Scholars, the historian wrote, have usually thought that ex-slaves chose such new names beginning only with the Civil War, but Truth's example, he continued, reminds us that ex-slaves had been adopting such new names much earlier. However, it would be easier to believe that Truth chose her new name—or allowed God to choose it for her—as a deliberate protest against slavery if we had persuasive evidence that she seriously worked against slavery before she left New York, or even in the next few months while she was a sojourner in Long Island, Connecticut, and Massachusetts. But we lack such evidence.

In 1879 she was quoted in a Chicago newspaper as saying that after she left New York and became a wanderer she talked "religion and abolition all the way" until she settled down in Northampton. But this claim, made so late in her life, has not been substantiated. Her recollections in her 1850 *Narrative* do not say that she left New York in order to preach for the abolition of slavery or for any other public reform cause, but rather to exhort the people "to embrace Jesus."[10]

Once in her wandering, according to her *Narrative,* she came across a temperance meeting, to which she contributed by helping to cook, concocting "dishes a la New York, greatly to the satisfaction of those she assisted."[11] Thus temperance appears to be a cause with which she was comfortable during her wandering—her experience with Methodists, and with Pierson and Matthias, would doubtless have prepared her to be comfortable with the temperance movement. But her *Narrative* does not say that while she was wandering she spoke at any temperance meetings, much less that she addressed or even attended any abolitionist meetings.

While wandering, she was likely to stay with whoever offered her food and lodging. She found it was usually the poor, not the rich, who made such offers. She did not seem particularly afraid to live this way. If she needed to earn money, she would stop to do domestic work for a while.

Like evangelicals generally, Truth believed the world was wicked; she often said that it would look much better if we could see it "right side up," an idea she would later link to her advocacy of human rights. She was already denouncing the folly of fashion, a theme she would develop later.[12]

In her wandering she attended evangelical meetings at which, as opportunity offered, she spoke, prayed, and sang. Also from time to time she got up religious meetings of her own, or friends she met along the way arranged them for her. She "found many true friends of Jesus," it seemed to her, "with whom she held communion of spirit."[13] However, when she attended meetings of the Second Adventists, as the followers of William Miller were sometimes called, she found herself somewhat uneasy. She found that they expected Christ to appear very soon and at once send fire to destroy the wicked, and she felt they were too excited and fearful. She tried to calm them. She believed that if people had faith—as she felt she did—they could withstand any punishing fire God might send. Although Truth was clearly an evangelical, she did not necessarily agree with all the evangelicals she met. She was continuing to do what Vale perceived her as doing while she was in the Kingdom, that is, making judgments for herself.

When winter came, she was ready to settle down for a while. She had been for some time in the region of Springfield, Massachusetts, and as a friend there afterward reported, she looked near there for "a quiet place, where a way-worn traveller might rest."[14]

Despite her having been hurt by her experience in Matthias's community, she was open to the idea of settling again in an intentional community. She heard of the Shaker community at Enfield, Connecticut—the Shakers emphasized personal experience of God and welcomed blacks as members—and thought of visiting there to see if they had an opening for her. She also considered the quite different Fruitlands, a farming community at Harvard, Massachusetts, led by Bronson Alcott, the progressive educator and transcendentalist. The 1840s was a time when many Americans were caught up in evangelical excitement and also many of them—sometimes the same persons—were caught up in planning utopian socialist communities, like Fruitlands. Emerson said that at this time there was "not a reading man but has a draft of a new community in his waistcoat pocket." But Truth's Adventist friends advised her that there was a relatively moderate intentional community that would suit her better in Northampton, Massachusetts. Called the Northampton Association, it was oriented to reformist causes.

Visiting the association probably early in 1844, at first she found it stark, and resolved to stay only one night. She found it was located on a 500-acre site, kept the usual horses, oxen, cows, swine, and poultry, and operated both grist and saw mills. But the association's activities centered in a four-story, red-brick factory building, which was used both to house many of the 130 participants in Spartan quarters, and also to manufacture silk thread—the association was unusual among utopian communities in being basically an industrial rather than a farming community. Although it was sinking into debt, Truth found that refined and educated persons were members of the community, and that they seemed content to live and work there in a "plain and simple manner," hoping to make their experiment work. She found that they had already accepted blacks as members. She also found that the association was not dependent, like the Millerites and Matthias's Kingdom, on one man as a leader, whom they were expected to trust for their interpretation of what God was saying, but rather had no creed, and practiced liberty of religion, thought, and speech. Although this community's effort to create a utopian life reflected the perfectionist spirit of many evangelicals, this community was more liberal than evangelical. She decided she liked this community after all and stayed.[15]

At the community everyone did some physical labor, much as at the Kingdom. Truth was soon in charge of the laundry, in the basement of the factory building, where there was vigorous scrubbing to be done. Unlike at the Kingdom, however, here everyone was paid, and all were paid alike, or nearly so, without distinction of sex or color, no matter what work they did. The participants worked at first twelve hours a day, later eleven hours. They ate together in a common dining room. They had their lights out at ten o'clock.

Why did Truth choose to live in intentional communities, as she did in Matthias's Kingdom, in this Northampton community, and later in still another one? Did she believe that intentional communities might offer a way of life that remedied what was wrong with the world? Was she searching for the experience of home and family of which slavery had deprived her? Did she still need the nurture of such a community to further her inward emancipation?

The Northampton Association, founded in 1842, was led among others by two advocates of the abolition of slavery, Samuel L. Hill, an ex-Quaker, and George Benson, who was William Lloyd Garrison's brother-in-law. Garrison, who edited an abolitionist weekly in Boston, was a frequent visitor. A member of the community was the black David Ruggles, who had worn himself out trying to protect fugitive slaves in New York City and was becoming blind. He found Northampton a refuge where he could experiment with water cures for his health, and in the process gradually sensitized his touch so that he could use it as a means of diagnosis; he became a recognized water-cure physician.

Frederick Douglass, one of the many fugitive slaves Ruggles had helped to pass through New York, came to the community to visit Ruggles. Douglass, already becoming well known as an antislavery orator, found the community's people to be "the most democratic" he had ever met, and found himself tending to accept utopian communities "as a remedy for all social ills."

Here Douglass met Truth for the first time. Douglass found her, he recalled, "industrious" and "much respected." "Her quaint speeches easily gave her an audience, and she was one of the most useful members of the community." [16]

The community had its own boarding school, directed by a former professor of literature at Harvard. Garrison sent a son there. Ruggles called it the best school he knew in the nation and urged blacks to send their children there. But Truth is not known to have made any effort to learn to read and write while at Northampton.

Among other people Truth met at the community were the young Giles B. Stebbins, who was studying to be a Unitarian clergyman. Stebbins found that the community changed him from being pro-slavery to antislavery. He became Truth's life-long friend.

As Truth recalled her experience in this community long afterward, "I was with them heart and soul for anything concerning human right, and my belief is in me yet and can't get out. . . . What good times we had." [17]

A few months after Truth joined the Northampton community, she attended a nearby camp meeting, held in open fields. The story of her speaking there, as she recounted it for her *Narrative,* suggests the commanding power as a speaker that she had developed by this time.

As often happened at camp meetings, young rowdies invaded this meeting to amuse themselves. They hooted to interrupt the services, and said they would burn the tents. The leaders of the meeting threatened the young men, but this only seemed to make them more boisterous. When they began to shake the tent she was in, Truth, catching the fear of the camp meeting leaders, hid behind a trunk, thinking to herself that if the young men rushed in, they might single her out, because she was the only black present, and kill her.

But then as she cowered, she wondered whether as "a servant of the living God," she should hide. "Have I not faith enough to go out and quell that mob, when I know it is written, 'One shall chase a thousand, and two put ten thousand to flight'?"

She came out from hiding, and invited a few of the camp meeting leaders to go outside with her to try to calm the rowdies. When the leaders refused, she went out by herself. She walked to a small rise of ground, and commenced to sing, fervidly, in her powerful voice. She sang one of her favorite hymns, on the resurrection of Christ, beginning, "It was early in the morning."

A few of the rioters gathered around her. In a pause in her singing, she asked them, "Why do you come about me with clubs and sticks? I am not doing harm to any one."

Some answered, "We aren't a going to hurt you, old woman; we came to hear you sing." Others asked her to sing some more. Still others asked her to speak. Believing that there were some among them who would be susceptible to what she wanted to say, she began to preach to them. From time to time they asked questions, and she answered. They were calming down.

As the number of youths listening to her grew, they asked her to stand on a nearby wagon so they could see her better. When she prepared to step up on the wagon, she asked them, if I step up on it, will you tip it over? Some replied that if anyone tried to, they would knock him down.

They helped her climb up on the wagon. She talked and sang to them for some time, and finally asked them whether, if she sang one more song, they would go away and leave the camp meeting in peace. Some of them said they would. She asked them to say it louder, and they said it louder. She sang one more song, and then they began to move off, some of their leaders disciplining those who were reluctant to join them, until all of them had left the camp grounds.[18]

Truth had developed skill in handling a rough crowd, a skill she was apparently as yet putting to use only in the cause of evangelism, without as far as we can document significantly mixing it with the cause of reform.

In 1846 the association as a utopian enterprise broke up, largely for want of adequate capital. But for several years afterward, Samuel L. Hill stayed on to operate the silk mill. Also George Benson stayed on to operate a cotton mill in what had been part of the community property. In doing so, Benson helped Ruggles build a water-cure resort near the community grounds, a resort Garrison patronized. Benson also employed one of the community's fugitive slaves to take charge of the mill's teams, and in his home nearby he employed Truth as a housekeeper, in the style of a guest.

Through the association and the people she had met there, and continued to see afterward, Truth was exposed to liberal religion, re-exposed to temperance, and awakened to a great variety of other reforms that the friends of Garrison were likely to support, including antislavery, women's rights, and nonviolence.

It was through the association that Truth met Olive Gilbert, of Brooklyn, Connecticut, who was to write the first version of the *Narrative* of Truth's life. Although Gilbert herself was not a participant in the Northampton Association, she was an abolitionist-feminist friend of Garrison. Hearing of Truth and her singing, Gilbert visited the association to meet Truth. Gilbert found Truth working diligently at the association, but felt her to be prematurely aged by the hard life she had led. Gilbert also found her to be naively convinced—quite mistakenly—that the association would look after her for the rest of her life.[19] It was soon after Gilbert met Truth that the association closed.

Not until several years later did Gilbert arrange to listen to Truth tell the story of her life, to write it down, and to put it together into a book, called the *Narrative of Sojourner Truth*. As first published in 1850, it was a small book, basically only 125 pages. Modestly, Gilbert kept her own name off the title page, and out of the book altogether. Someone, perhaps Garrison himself, also kept Garrison's name off the preface he had written for the book, where it might have had some influence in encouraging advocates of blacks' and women's rights to buy it.

Gilbert's writing in this book is earnest and sometimes, by later standards, gushing. The book contains contradictions and disturbing omissions, and is not well organized. But the book preserved for the future Truth's story of her early life, and helped to make her better known. Truth's plan in regard to this book from the first seemed to have been not to sell it as books were usually sold through book stores, but rather to sell it directly herself, by carrying copies with her when she went about speaking, as she occasionally continued to do. She sold it not, as has sometimes been claimed, to support the causes she favored, but to pay her expenses and support herself.[20]

In statements printed at the back of the book, several friends of hers commended the book to the public. One statement, dated March, 1850, was by three of her former Northampton community associates: George W. Benson, Samuel L. Hill, and A. W. Thayer. They testified to Truth's "uniform good character, her untiring industry, kind deportment, unwearied benevolence." Another statement was signed by Garrison—at least here Garrison's name appeared—testifying to this illiterate woman's "under standing" and "enlightenment."[21] While Gilbert, in her commentary, showed some inclination to make the book into an antislavery tract, the book focused on the story of Truth's life, and did not report that Truth had ever done any speaking for the abolition of slavery or any other human rights cause.

Garrison arranged for the private printing of the book in Boston. Much as Garrison was a father figure for Frederick Douglass in his rise to become a well-known advocate of blacks' and women's rights, so also Garrison was a father figure for Truth in her rise to become a well-known advocate of blacks' and women's rights.

At about the time her book was coming out, George Benson's business was going bankrupt, and he was losing the house where Truth lived and worked for him. In this situation, Truth, according to Gilbert in Truth's *Narrative,* dreamed again, as she had before, of securing "a little home of her own," but, said Gilbert, for such a home she was "dependent on the charities of the benevolent," probably meaning dependent especially on those who were willing to buy her book. At about this same time, Benson's earlier associate in leading the association, Samuel L. Hill, who made a point of encouraging families to own their own houses, built a house for Truth near where the association had been and near where he lived himself, in the town of Northampton, in a predominantly white neighborhood that came to be called Florence. On April 15, 1850, Hill sold it to Truth for $300 and gave her a mortgage for the whole amount. In the deed her name was given as "Isabella Vanwagner . . . sometimes called 'Sojourner Truth.'" She signed the mortgage with her "X."[22] It was the first house she had ever owned.

Undoubtedly Truth hoped that she would be able to pay off the mortgage by touring the country to speak and sell her books. Ironically, this touring kept her away from her house for long periods, even years at a time.

• • •

When did Truth first become a public speaker for reform? William L. Chaplin, who published an antislavery paper in Albany, New York, claimed in Truth's later years that she had "commenced her advocacy of the rights of her race during our war with Mexico," which would mean in 1846 or 1847.[23] Chaplin's claim seems plausible, but documentary evidence—citing where she spoke during the Mexican War, and what she said—is not available to support it.

Truth's first documented public speaking as a reformer was in 1850, and probably occurred as incidental to her promoting her book. In October she spoke at a national woman's rights convention held in Worcester, Massachusetts, a meeting that many of her friends also attended, including George Benson from Northampton, Frederick Douglass from Rochester, and Garrison from Boston. This was one of the earliest women's rights conventions ever held in the nation. It was held at a time when only a few women were beginning to awaken to such issues as their lack of freedom to vote or enter many occupations.

According to Horace Greeley's New York *Tribune,* Truth "gratified" the convention "highly," showing "that beneath her dark skin, and uncomely exterior there was a true, womanly heart." Illustrating her talent for coming to the meat of a subject tersely, Truth, speaking to the convention, used two epigrams. In one of them, perhaps building on her earlier conception that the world would look better if we could see it "right side up," Truth argued for a responsible role in the world for women, saying, "Woman set the world wrong by eating the forbidden fruit, and now she was going to set it right." In the other epigram, Truth not only showed her optimism but also hinted at her increasing religious liberalism, saying: "Goodness was from everlasting and would never die, while evil had a beginning and must come to an end." The venerable Quaker minister Lucretia Mott picked up this second epigram, and in her address that closed the convention warmly repeated it.[24]

At this time most of the public was hostile toward the campaigns for both women's rights and the abolition of slavery. The New York *Herald,* catering to this hostility, described the Worcester convention as a "motley mingling of abolitionists, socialists, and infidels, of all sexes and colors," which intended to "abolish" the Bible, "abolish" the U.S. Constitution, and establish an "amalgamation of sexes and colors." The *Herald* said that Lucretia Mott, though a Quaker, had the "hard iron expression" of a general. Exaggerating the role of the few blacks in the convention in order to ridicule the women's rights cause, the *Herald* said that Mott, the "raving" Garrison, and Douglass "in all his glory" "headed" the convention, while "Grabby [Horace] Greeley" and "Sojourner Truth, a lady of a very dark color," brought up "the rear." It called Truth "deluded," but "well posted up on the rights of woman." It reported sarcastically that, "with something of the ardor and the odor of her native Africa," Truth "contended for her right to vote, to hold office, to practice medicine and the law, and to wear the breeches with the best white man that walks upon God's earth."[25]

No available reports of the convention from the time indicate that Truth spoke directly against slavery. Several speakers at the convention did, however, compare the condition of women with the condition of slaves, as feminists often did, and the convention adopted a resolution declaring that among all women, slave women were "the most grossly wronged." It was claimed long afterward that the adoption of this resolution was a reflection of the presence of Truth, among others, at the convention, but direct evidence to support this claim is lacking.[26]

The next month, November, 1850, when Truth was about fifty-three years old, she gave her first antislavery speech that has been documented. She spoke, along with Douglass and others, at a state antislavery society meeting in Providence, Rhode Island. The meeting centered on a new federal law that pressed the North to return fugitive slaves to their masters in the South. Speaking about the new law, Truth said, as reported in an antislavery paper, that she "could not read the newspapers" and "did not know anything about politics," suggesting that she had already discovered that many listeners found her more fascinating if she played up her naivete. But she added enigmatically that the new fugitive slave law meant "the worst had come to worst," so now, in reaction, "the best must come to best."[27]

In December, 1850, she spoke again against slavery, this time at an antislavery meeting in Plymouth, Massachusetts. Not deterred by speaking on the same platform with Garrison and a visiting member of the British Parliament, George Thompson, according to a Boston newspaper she made some "capital hits" at Daniel Webster, whom abolitionists perceived as largely responsible for the North's acquiescing in the adoption of the odious new fugitive slave law. Also in December, Antoinette Brown, a recent theological graduate of Oberlin College who was defying the customary male domination of the church by trying to become a minister, heard that Truth was speaking near Andover, attending an antislavery fair in Boston, and selling "a good many" of her books.[28]

When Truth spoke against slavery in 1850, she was not, as has often been claimed, the first black woman to do so. The black Maria Stewart had spoken publicly against slavery in Boston as early as 1833, which was very early for any woman, black or white, to speak in public on any subject.[29] (Stewart, however, shortly became discouraged and gave up her speaking.) Though Truth had already done evangelistic speaking in the early 1830s, even in 1850 when Truth was speaking for black and women's rights, it still was not common for women to speak in public, especially to men as well as women, though it was distinctly more common than in the 1830s.

In early 1851, Garrison planned an antislavery speaking trip with Member of Parliament George Thompson, and invited Truth to accompany them, explaining to her that this would provide her a chance to sell her books. Many years later, when a testimonial subscription to Thompson was being collected, Truth recalled this invitation in a letter to Garrison:

My heart is glowing just now with the remembrance of his [George Thompson's] kindness to me in 1851. I had been publishing my *Narrative* and owed for the whole edition. A great debt for me! Every cent I could obtain went to pay it. You said to me "I am going with George Thompson on a lecturing tour. Come with us and you will have a good chance to dispose of your book." I replied that I had no money. You generously offered to bear my expenses, and it was arranged that I should meet you in Springfield.

On the appointed day I was there, but you were not at the Hotel. I enquired for Mr. Thompson & was shown into his room. He received & seated me with as much courtesy and cordiality as if I had been the highest lady in the land, informing me that you were too ill to leave home, but if I would go with himself and Mr.[G. W.] Putnam, it would be all the same. But, said I, I have no money, & Mr. Garrison offered to pay my passage. "I'll bear your expenses, Sojourner," said he. "Come with us!" And so I went.

He accompanied me to the cars and carried my bag. At the hotel tables he seated me beside himself & never seemed to know that I was poor and a black woman. At the meetings he recommended my books. "Sojourner Truth has a narrative of her life. 'Tis very interesting. Buy largely friends!" Good man! genuine gentleman! God bless George Thompson! the great hearted friend of my race.[30]

On this trip, in February and March 1851, Truth, Thompson, Putnam, and others made their way by train from Springfield west into New York State, speaking at a series of antislavery conventions. At times they were joined by Frederick Douglass. All along the way Truth sold her books.

At Union Village, Washington County, New York, Truth made a speech, it was reported, "in her peculiar manner." She said that while others "had been talking about the poor slave . . . she was going to talk about the poor slaveholder. She wanted to know what would become of him; she feared he would go down to perdition, unless he could be reformed." According to Putnam, writing to Garrison's *Liberator,* Truth "was most kindly received by the audience, who pressed around her to purchase her books, and who saw in her proof of the natural equality (to say the least) of the negro and the white. It is devoutly to be wished that all whites were her equals."[31]

By the time the travelling speakers reached Rochester, where they ended their trip, Putnam had become enthusiastic about Truth. Though she could neither read nor write, he reported, she

will often speak with an ability which surprises the educated and refined. She possesses a mind of rare power, and often, in the course of her short speeches, will throw out gems of thought. But the truly Christian spirit which pervades all she says, endears her to all who know her. Though she has suffered all the ills of slavery, she forgives all who have wronged her most freely. She said her home should be open to the man who had held her as a slave, and who had so much wronged her. She would feed him and take care of him if he was hungry and poor. "O friends," said she, "pity the poor slaveholder, and pray for him. It troubles me more than anything else, what will become of the poor slaveholder, in all his guilt and all his impenitence. God will take care of the poor trampled slave, but where will the slaveholder be when eternity begins?"[32]

As Truth was no doubt discovering, her repeated concern for slaveholders had a dramatic effect on her white listeners, especially as coming from a former slave. Also, as she knew, this concern was in keeping with the Garrisonian moral suasionist, nonviolent viewpoint.

While in Rochester, Truth stayed with Isaac and Amy Post, who were of Quaker background, and were advocates of both women's and blacks' rights.[33] Truth found she liked the Posts. She stayed with them two and a half months, which proved to be the beginning of a long friendship.

While Truth was in Rochester, a visiting Ohio abolitionist, Esther A. Lukens, wrote about her warmly in more than one letter to the *Anti-Slavery Bugle,* an Ohio Garrisonian weekly. According to Lukens, despite Truth's illiteracy, Truth was "springing upon the arena of this great conflict [a phrase that suggests that Truth had not been speaking against slavery very long] with an energy and overwhelming power that we might look for in vain among the most highly civilized and enlightened. Her heart is as soft and loving as a child's, her soul as strong and fixed as the everlasting rocks, and her moral sense has something like inspiration or divination."[34]

Near the end of May 1851, Truth left Rochester, going on alone to Ohio to attend a state woman's rights convention, and then to begin a speaking tour of her own.

In Ohio she sometimes drove about alone, in a buggy a friend had lent her. She recalled that whenever she came to a fork in a road, because she could not read the signs, she would lay down the lines, and say, "God, you drive," and she believed God would always lead her to a good place to hold a meeting.[35]

In August, still in Ohio, she wrote—that is, of course, someone else wrote down for her—to her mentor Garrison, in Boston, a letter that suggests her fierce determination:

Salem [Ohio], August 28, 1851

Dear Mr. Garrison:

Will you please inform me how much I am now indebted to Mr. Yerrington[36] for the printing [of the *Narrative*]. . . .

I wrote to you for a report of the number of books on hand but have as yet received no answer. I am anxious to know just what is the amount of my indebtedness—what my means for paying it.

I have sold but few books during the summer but now the way seems opened for me to do better at the conventions which are now being held. Will you please forward to me care of John Skinner, Ravenna [Ohio], 600 of the books.

My last box cost me $7.00. It was nearly half full of paper & shavings. Don't send so much [paper and shavings] next time. I don't like to pay transportation on it.

Since I gave the fifty dollars to you I have only made $30 which I sent to Mr. Hill [of Northampton]. . . .

I don't know but I shall stay in Ohio all winter. I have heard that Mr.[William F.] Parker & his family have moved to Cleveland, so that I shall have a good comfortable place to winter.

Don't fail to send these books without delay. I may get out of books before they arrive. Pack them tight. Send by the most speedy safe conveyance. Don't get any more books bound. I can't sell the bound volumes. [She prefers paper-covered ones.]

I am now in Salem. My health is pretty good. .... I saw Mrs. Boyle at the anniversary [of the Western Anti-Slavery Society]. Mr. Boyle is boarding at Mr. Benson's in Williamsburgh [George Benson had recently moved from Northampton to Williamsburgh, Long Island] while Mrs. Boyle is visiting her friends in Ohio.

Affectionately, your Friend,
Sojourner Truth [37]

In this letter Truth seems preoccupied with her survival. She does not mention to Garrison events or issues of common interest in the abolitionist movement. She refers to friends from the Northampton Association even five years after it disbanded: Hill, Benson, the Boyles, and Parker were all association friends. She feels close enough to her Massachusetts friends so that she feels justified in expecting Garrison to assist her with the details of her books and Parker, because he was moving to Cleveland, to provide her a comfortable place there for the winter.

5

Why Did She Never Learn to Read?

"I can't read a book, but I can read de people."

Isabella emerged from the miasma of slavery in New York State to become, as Sojourner Truth, a national figure in the movements to advance the rights of women and blacks. Amazingly, she accomplished this without ever learning to read or write. "I neber had no eddication," she once told an audience, seeming to mix apology with boast.[1]

Her illiteracy has long been well known, but the question of why such an able and purposeful woman remained illiterate has been considered only casually, if at all. The question is difficult to answer because the original sources available on Truth are thin. Also Truth herself, with her imprecise language, humor, and exaggeration, lent herself to the development of myths, including myths about why she remained illiterate.

The common explanation for her never learning to read and write, often casually given or merely implied, is that she was brought up a slave and thus was denied the opportunity to learn. It is a natural explanation especially because, as an antislavery speaker, she was often presented as having felt in her own person the wrongs that slavery could inflict, and these wrongs were commonly understood to include denying slaves an education.

Truth's friends often seemed to accept this explanation. The abolitionist Sallie Holley, while speaking with Truth in Ohio in 1851, wrote privately that she "shows what a great intellect slavery has crushed." The novelist Harriet Beecher Stowe, writing on Truth in 1863, mourned that Truth, like other noble blacks, had come out of bondage cramped and scarred, and Stowe longed to know what Truth would have been like if she had been allowed to "unfold" under the "kindly" influence of education.[2]

Truth herself directly claimed in a speech that slavery had "robbed" her of an education. In another speech she recalled, as we have seen, that her slavemasters had not even allowed her "to hear the Bible or any other books read." In an interview, Truth said that while she was a slave, "There was nobody to tell me anything." My slavemasters, she explained, "were very close and ignorant, and so, naturally, to this day I can neither read nor write."[3]

Surely Truth experienced much in slavery to scar not only her body but also her mind and emotions. She was sold away from her parents; she was kept dependent, ignorant, and preoccupied with physical labor; and she was cruelly whipped as a Dutch-speaking child for not understanding English. She may have developed a psychological block regarding language that made it difficult for her to learn to read and write. At the least, her masters did not encourage her to learn to read and write, and she lacked adequate black role models for learning.

In addition, she reacted to her early experiences by developing personality traits that could have interfered with her learning. She struggled to offset the degradation of slavery by developing personal qualities of which she could be proud, such as her honesty, physical strength, and industry. With the help of such compensations, Truth, unlike Douglass, reined in her rebellion against slavery and, along with accepting her status as a slave, evidently accepted the idea that slaves did not learn to read and write. She also struggled against her ignorance and dependence by developing a bravado which, as it gradually evolved into her public-speaking persona, allowed her to spin myths about herself to cover up feelings of inferiority, and to adopt a tone of disdain about learning. Thus, the broader effects of slavery on Truth's mind and emotions may have contributed significantly to her continued illiteracy. Is this, then, a sufficient explanation?

In her old age, Truth was still declaring, much as she had often declared earlier, that she "never had an opportunity" to learn to read. As we have already seen, however, some opportunities for Truth to learn to read and write were available for her while she was still a slave, whether or not she reached for them, and certainly they existed abundantly after she was freed. Opportunities surrounded her in Ulster County, Manhattan, and Northampton. Moreover, from 1850, when she began to speak publicly as a reformer, she came to know many reformers who had taught schools for blacks and would likely be open to teaching her, including Lucy Stone with whom she shared the platform at women's rights conventions; the Ohio abolitionist editor Marius Robinson, who publicized her speech-making; abolitionist lecturer Lucy Colman, who took her to the White House to visit President Lincoln; and her close Michigan friend of her later years, Frances W. Titus. For her part, Truth, in an 1856 discussion with the white Garrisonian Henry C. Wright on the proper role of abolitionists in reaching down to the uneducated, seemed at least tentatively open to having abolitionists teach her: "Suppose I want to learn to read," she asked, who will "learn me? Will friend Wright come down to teach me?"[4]

According to a story that has not been authenticated, in Ohio in the early 1850s editor Robinson tried to teach Truth to read, but she failed to learn. She was probably about fifty-five years old at the time, but, according to this story, she told Robinson: "My brains is too stiff now." Long afterward, an abolitionist pastor reported that Truth had tried to learn to read once when she was said to be too old. This might refer to Robinson's attempt to teach her or to another such attempt.[5]

Despite the many opportunities she seemed to have to learn, we have no clear evidence that at any time in her life Truth herself took the initiative to learn to read or write. It may be that Truth found her role in life satisfying enough to take the force out of any impulses to seek learning that she may have had. It may be that those who wrote letters for her did not interfere enough with what she wanted to say to push her into learning to write for herself. (It was such interference that finally pushed the black Methodist evangelist Rebecca Jackson to learn to write in about 1830.) It also may be that Truth ran into so much frustration in trying to learn that she quickly gave up.

As we have already observed, when Truth was a slave, according to her master's daughter, it was "almost impossible to teach her anything," and after she was liberated, there was a hint that Truth had trouble reading the letters of the alphabet. In 1874 she was reported to be "ignorant of the alphabet," seeming to confirm that she still could not read letters. A pastor who talked with her in Kansas in 1879, quoted her as explaining why she failed to learn: "The letters all got mixed up and I couldn't straighten them out." In 1880, three years before she died, Truth apparently tried to sign her name of "Sojourner" in capital letters, in an autograph that a museum has preserved; the museum calls this her "only known signature." The first two letters are recognizable as *S* and *O*. The third could be an upside-down *J*. The last three could be *S O J* in reverse. In 1881 she said she still could not read or write, or "even spell my own name if it was before me."[6]

Because Truth found that she could not learn to read or write the letters of the alphabet, and that they seemed to become jumbled before her eyes, it seems probable—a probability that is not known to have been directly proposed in previous studies about Truth—that Truth had a learning disability which at the time might not have been understood. Perhaps she had irregular visual perception that jumbled the letters of the alphabet for her, more of a problem than her glasses could correct. (During much of her life, Truth recalled in her old age, she had worn glasses for ironing.)[7] Such a perceptual disability could have seriously frustrated her in her attempts to learn to read or write. Today experts believe that perhaps 10 to 15 percent of Americans have reading disabilities, but they also believe that with determination and appropriate guidance, these disabled can usually learn to read. In her time, the appropriate guidance was not likely to be available. Perhaps the cause of her not learning to read, then, can best be understood as the interaction of her experience of slavery, the development of her character, and her probable learning disability.

When she was young, Truth seemed to allow her lack of learning to lead her to undervalue education. After she became a public speaker for reform, she displayed signs of negative attitudes toward intellectual education, perhaps disdaining it because it was beyond her reach. Speaking in a church, she ridiculed "Greek-crammed" preachers. Speaking at a college, she ridiculed the students for writing down notes on what she said, advising them instead to keep notes as she did in her head.[8]

At least she clearly came to respect certain kinds of education. She encouraged her son to study navigation. During the Civil War when she called on President Lincoln, and he proudly showed her a Bible given him by blacks, she told him that she grieved that slaves had been prevented from learning to read the Bible. Afterward, as we shall see, she campaigned for freed slaves to educate themselves so that they could become self-supporting.

For her personally, instead of allowing her illiteracy to weigh her down as much as it might have, she learned to use it to her advantage. To avoid clashing with someone over religious doctrine, she would say that if she could read the Bible she might see the matter differently. As a speaker, she would play provocatively with her illiteracy, as in this one-liner that won her applause: "I tell you I can't read a book, but I can read de people." Remarkably, she seemed to be able to use her illiteracy to lift herself up into a high pulpit from which she then could more effectively scold an audience, as she did once thus: "With all your opportunities for readin' and writin', you don't take hold and do anything."[9] For many of Truth's listeners, her lack of literacy and culture contributed to her fascination, and of course, shrewd as she was, she knew it, and played it up.

Her speech—delivered in a robust voice, so deep that some of her enemies suspected that she was a man—evidently consisted of a unique combination of elements, which varied from time to time, including, as different observers understood it, a guttural Dutch accent from her early childhood, the broken English of white illiterates, black dialect (but not, she insisted, Southern black dialect), and standard English. In her early years as an agitator for reform, the New York *Tribune* said her English was "tolerably correct," but her "homely" expressions "enhanced" her style. A British journalist who met her in Washington during the Civil War, and knew she sometimes spoke in "broken negro dialect," reported that she was "able to speak in correct and beautiful English" when she chose. Similarly, a Chicago journalist who interviewed her in 1879, reported that in conversation her language "is grammatically correct, and she can say what she means as well as the most learned college professor." In a conversation in 1881, evidently far from using black dialect, she spoke, according to another Chicago journalist, "with unusual clearness and distinction . . . ordinarily using a strong, sinewy Anglo-Saxon diction." However, in her speeches over many years, despite her association with many cultured people, she did not usually seem to choose to use more standard English. Some of her friends, like Garrison and Pillsbury, may have advised her to speak in a black style, much as when Frederick Douglass was beginning to be an antislavery speaker, they advised him to do, to make him seem more believable.[10] Douglass did not follow such advice, but Truth seemed to have found on her own that it worked for her. She seemed to keep her speech considerably homely, ungrammatical, and in dialect because she found her audiences liked it that way; it made her more picturesque to them, more bewitching, more memorable. In a sense she molded her public image around her illiteracy, using it to dramatize herself and shape her life, turning her illiteracy from a handicap into a significant element of her charm.

As the perceptive Douglass recalled, "She seemed to please herself and others best when she put her ideas in the oddest forms." In 1867 Truth complained to a New York newspaperman that he was not reporting her words accurately, but she admitted "good-naturedly," he said, that her speech was difficult to record because she was speaking in "an unknown tongue." In 1871 when she spoke in Boston, the Boston *Post* reported that although her pronunciation was so outlandish that she pronounced her own name as "Sojoum' Trute," nevertheless her "inimitable patois" enhanced the "piquancy of her remarks."[11]

Also contributing to her fascination was her exotic new name of "Sojourner Truth," which surely only someone with a sense of theater could have relished for herself. Also contributing was that she stood nearly six feet tall, and was exceedingly black—one of "the blackest women I ever saw," recalled one of her friends; "hideously black," said a New York *World* report that Truth, in a curious reaction, said she especially liked because it was witty and light.[12]

Truth spoke largely from her own experience, but what she said reflected an awareness of current clashes of thought, and she was sometimes able to cut through them with startling flashes of insight of her own. Truth was very articulate, if not in as ordered, sequential, and linear a fashion as Douglass. Her thinking was more free associative. It lent itself to sudden leaps, to metaphor, poetry, and parable.

She spoke extemporaneously, she said, not knowing what the Lord would put into her mouth, explaining, "I go to hear myself as much as anyone else comes to hear me." She spoke some phrases deliberately, emphasizing them, but raced through others, and often interrupted herself with droll asides. As she recalled, she did not always have natural "stops" in her flow of speech. According to a Quaker friend, however, Truth had "magnetic power over an audience." According to the Detroit *Advertiser,* she had both "a heart of love" and "a tongue of fire." According to women's advocate Lucy Stone, Truth spoke "with direct and terrible force, moving friend and foe alike."[13]

In other aspects of her life, however, her illiteracy continued to handicap her. Once she conceded that it was "hard work" to get as many letters written for her as she wanted. In another instance, thanking a correspondent for her "kind words," Truth replied, as a friend wrote it down for her, "Oh, if I could but write and answer them myself!"[14] More importantly, her illiteracy affected her opportunities for leadership. During the time she was a slave, most blacks in New York State were illiterate, but by 1850 about 50 percent of the blacks in the state had become literate, and by 1880 about 80 percent, and similarly in the North at large. Under these circumstances, her opportunities for leadership among blacks as well as whites were limited. Partly because she could not read or write, her participation in reform movements remained marginal. She never became part of the decision-making inner councils of either the abolitionist or women's rights movement, as Douglass sometimes did. Also partly because she could not read or write, she could not function well in the world of earning or handling money, which helped to keep her poor.

Nevertheless, Truth usually adopted a tone of jaunty acceptance of her illiteracy. She declared, "I don't read such small stuff as letters, I read men and nations." She also insisted, "I know and do what is right better than many big men who read." According to Lucy Stone, Truth often even said that "all the great trouble of the world came from those who could read, and not from those who could not," so she "was glad she never knew how to read." This suggests that Truth protected herself in a manner not uncommon among children who suffer from learning disabilities: Instead of admitting that she could not learn, she said she did not want to learn. In fact, to the distress of Frederick Douglass, she seemed to revel in being uncultured. She "seemed to feel it her duty," Douglass recalled, "to ridicule my efforts to speak and act like a person of cultivation and refinement. . . . She was a genuine specimen of the uncultured negro. She cared very little for elegance of speech or refinement of manners." Truth seldom indicated that she felt oppressed by being illiterate or uncultured or inelegant. According to Harriet Beecher Stowe, Truth conveyed "almost an unconscious superiority."[15]

Her overwhelming faith that God had called her to a special mission to set the world right side up, seemed to help to convince her that her illiteracy was another God-given trait, like her blackness and her womanhood, which fashioned her beautifully to carry out her mission.

6

Her Famous Akron Speech

"Between a hawk and a buzzard."

Sojourner Truth delivered a provocative speech at a women's rights convention in Akron, Ohio, in 1851. The haunting "Ar'n't I a woman?" question, which Truth is reported to have used dramatically again and again in the speech, has become in our time a familiar slogan in the women's rights movement. Moreover, the speech and the circumstances surrounding it have become significant not only in interpreting Sojourner Truth but also in interpreting the formative years of the struggle for both black and women's rights in America.

Truth's speech has almost invariably been presented as reported by Frances D. Gage. Since Gage was the presiding officer of the Akron convention, her report has seemed on the surface to be reliable. Considering how important the speech has become, however, it is significant to inquire whether Gage was justified in claiming that the convention received Truth with hostility, "hissing" her; whether Gage was accurate in reporting what Truth said in her speech, including the famous words, "Ar'n't I a woman?"; and whether Gage was correct in reporting the "magical influence" of Truth's speech in "turning the whole tide" of the convention from being "mobbish" into a victory for women's rights.

Gage's report has customarily been quoted either from the 1875 edition of Truth's *Narrative* or from the 1881 monumental *History of Woman Suffrage* by Elizabeth Cady Stanton and her friends.[1] However, both Truth's *Narrative* and Stanton's *History* fail to cite where Gage's report was originally published. Moreover, both omit from Gage's report two significant admissions by Gage: that she wrote the report twelve years after Truth gave her speech, and that the report gives only a "faint sketch" of it.

Gage's admissions could have served as a warning that her report might be less than accurate. However, almost all commentators on Truth, either not knowing of or not paying attention to Gage's admissions, seem to assume that her report is accurate. One of Truth's biographers even made the naive claim that Gage preserved Truth's speech "in its pristine form, so that we know exactly the kind of language and dialect she employed, and what it was in her speeches that brought people of the highest grade of intelligence and training under her spell."[2] As far as is known, no one has seriously attempted to check the accuracy of Gage's report until now.

As hardly any recent commentators seem to have been aware, Gage published her report on Truth's speech in 1863, in the *National Anti-Slavery Standard* of May 2. At that time, if Truth thought Gage's report inaccurate, she could have said so. Or in 1875, when Gage's report was about to be reprinted in a revised version of Truth's *Narrative,* if Truth thought Gage's report inaccurate, she could have prevented it from being reprinted. After all, Truth's *Narrative* was published and republished with her active involvement.

But since Truth never learned to read, she could not easily check the reliability of reports of her speeches. In any case, her focus in telling the story of her life was not on factual truth about her life, but on the moral truth that could be learned from it. Truth may have felt that the way Gage reported her speech, even if in her memory not entirely accurate, was at least well intentioned, and in line with what Truth wished she had said. Moreover, Truth often seemed willing to let friendly myths develop about her, myths that might make her a more fascinating advocate of the causes she supported.[3]

Why did Gage publish her report of Truth's speech only in 1863, twelve years after the speech was given? The occasion for her publishing it then, Gage explained in a part of her report, which was omitted in both Truth's *Narrative* and Stanton's *History,* was that Harriet Beecher Stowe, the well-known novelist, had just published in the *Atlantic Monthly* her account of Truth's visit to her.[4] Stowe's account, published during the Civil War when national attention was considerably focused on blacks, made Truth into an intriguing figure for many Americans for the first time. Gage, in her account of Truth's Akron speech, recalled that Stowe's article brought "vividly to my mind" the scene of Truth's Akron speech.

Frances Dana Gage, as she grew up in southern Ohio near the Virginia border, had been encouraged by her New England-born parents to help slaves escape. By the time of the Akron convention in 1851, Gage was already, like Truth, a dedicated advocate of both blacks' and women's rights. Gage was also a writer of both poetry and fiction.

Gage does not tell us what sources she used in writing her account of Truth's speech, except that by her using such phrases as a "faint sketch" and "vividly to my mind" she hinted that she used her memory. If Gage did in fact use her memory, how accurate would it have been after twelve years? Perhaps she also used notes that she had made at the time of the convention. If she did, especially since she said she was presiding over the convention at the very time that Truth was speaking, her presiding could have limited her ability to record Truth's words in accurate detail.

In her report, Gage took pains to portray the atmosphere of the woman's rights convention at which Truth spoke. Woman's rights, Gage wrote, was a "wondrously unpopular cause." The leaders of the woman's movement at the convention were "staggering under the weight of disapprobation already laid upon them," and so "many of them" were "almost thrown into panics" [sic.] on the first day of the convention when they saw Truth, "a tall, gaunt black woman in a gray dress and white turban," enter the crowded church where the meeting was held, and "walk with the air of a queen up the aisle." Repeatedly "trembling" women asked Gage not to let Truth speak because it would "ruin us" to "have our cause mixed with abolition and niggers." On the second day, according to Gage, opponents of women's rights, especially bombastic clergymen, "were seeming to get the better of us." When Gage finally let Truth speak, "some of the tender-skinned friends" of the cause were "on the point of losing dignity," and the atmosphere of the convention was "mobbish" and "betokened a storm."

Contemporary reports about the convention are available, including twenty-seven descriptions of it published soon after it occurred, to check whether they portray the public reaction to the convention and the mood of the convention itself much as Gage did twelve years later. The individual authors of eight of these descriptions are known by name; all eight were themselves advocates of women's rights and active at the convention, and five of the eight were women. However, the twenty-seven descriptions were in publications of various political persuasion, some sympathetic to reform, some not.[5]

In regard to Gage's claim that the woman's rights movement was "wondrously unpopular," we note that in Akron, a bustling little town, the Universalists offered their Greek-pillared stone church to house the convention, and a local newspaper welcomed its coming. Afterward several newspapers noticed the courtesy of Akron citizens to the convention, one praising them for their "urbanity and generous hospitality," another noting that an Akron lawyer entertained members of the convention at his house. Editor Jane Swisshelm, a leading figure in the convention, reported afterward in her Pittsburgh *Saturday Visiter* that the proprietor of the Akron temperance hotel where she stayed was so kind as to decline to bill her for her lodging.[6]

Did Gage exaggerate popular hostility to the convention? It is true that a correspondent of a fashion-conscious New York weekly, the *Home Journal,* was shocked that ladies of the convention took off their hats at one session, and feared that what the convention advocated would render it "impossible for man to rule his household" as the Bible says he should. It is also true that a few newspapers such as the Cincinnati *Gazette* sneered at the women of the convention as "old maids," and at the men who attended to support the women's cause as thereby becoming women. But Gage herself seemed to have described the general newspaper reaction to the convention fairly accurately when she wrote soon after the convention—in sharp contrast to what she wrote in 1863—that "the great press, in mass, have noticed" the convention, "and few have sneered at or abused it."[7]

In contrast to Gage's claim in her 1863 report that the convention leaders were "staggering," fearing being overwhelmed by "mobbish" opponents of women's rights, one of the convention secretaries wrote at the time that the convention was a "pleasant social gathering." Garrison's Boston *Liberator* reported that at the session at which Truth spoke, as at other sessions, "all faces" were "beaming with joyous gladness." Near the end of the convention, one of its prominent speakers, Emma R. Coe, congratulated the convention that its "spirit of harmony" had not been interrupted by "one discordant note." The Cleveland *Herald* (Whig) reported that, although nearly half of the audience at the convention were men, you did not see "the sly leer, the half uttered jest, that you might imagine." One of the convention's vice-presidents, Celia M. Burr, wrote that in the discussion over the resolutions, nearly all the men present, far from opposing women's rights, were for such rights in more extreme form than most of the women were. Jane Swisshelm reported in her newspaper that the danger to the convention derived not from the possibility that opponents of women's rights might take over the convention, as Gage later claimed, but from presiding officer Gage's not knowing parliamentary rules, and from the extremism of some advocates of women's rights, including Truth.[8] In fact, none of these twenty-seven descriptions published at the time, despite their many different points of view, gives the impression, as Gage did twelve years later, that there were "mobbish" opponents of women's rights present, much less that the convention or its leaders were ever "staggering," or about to panic, or about to be overwhelmed by these opponents.

It is easy to believe that some of the women at the convention might have been anxious about what they were doing in this early period of the women's rights movement, when women were often considered "indelicate" if they spoke in public on any subject at all. It is also possible to believe that Gage might have been more anxious than many other participants because she was the presiding officer, and, because, as she explained to the convention, she had never before attended a public business meeting, much less presided at such a meeting. However, Gage herself, two years after the Akron convention when she was presiding over a national women's convention held in Cleveland, said that while women had held many conventions at which everyone was given liberty to speak —and she mentioned the Akron convention as one of them—"no one has had a word to say against us at the time."[9] This was in direct contradiction to what Gage later claimed in her 1863 report, that opponents spoke up in the convention and threatened to take it over.

In her 1863 recollections, Gage portrayed the leaders of the convention as feeling that the uncouth, very black Truth, when she walked into the convention, was an alarming intruder. It is true that at the time many Ohio whites, like many whites in many other Northern states, expected blacks to attend separate schools, and, if they attended church with whites, to sit separately. Nevertheless, both the Ohio and the national women's rights movements were allied with the movement to abolish slavery. In fact, women's rightists often compared the condition of women with that of slaves, as they did both at this convention and at the 1850

Worcester convention. Indeed, though some women were reluctant to admit it, the women's rights movement to a considerable degree was an outgrowth of the movement to abolish slavery, as the Salem, Ohio, *Anti-Slavery Bugle* claimed. As one would expect, many of the leaders of the convention were active abolitionists, including Gage herself, editor Marius Robinson of the *Bugle,* and editor Jane Swisshelm. Moreover, Akron was located in the belt of Yankee settlements that especially spawned the movements for both blacks' and women's rights, the belt that stretched from Boston west across central New York State into northern Ohio and beyond. In addition, the call to the convention, like much women's rights news, was published in abolitionist newspapers, and the call had welcomed "all the friends of Reform, in whatever department engaged," to come to give us "counsel." [10]

Also, as Gage did not say but as many of those at the convention were likely to know, some white abolitionists made a point of opening their meetings to blacks, and sometimes a few blacks participated, if uneasily. Moreover, as Gage also did not say but as many of the convention were likely to know, blacks had been present at all three of the major women's rights conventions that preceded the one at Akron: Frederick Douglass had played a significant role at the first woman's rights convention, held in 1848 in Seneca Falls, New York; Douglass had also been present in the spring of 1850 at the first Ohio women's rights convention, held in the abolitionist citadel of Salem (the call to this convention had explained that its purpose was to secure "equal rights" to "all persons" without regard to "sex or color"); [11] and as we have seen, both Douglass and Truth had spoken at the national woman's rights convention held in Worcester, Massachusetts, in the fall of 1850. Also it is likely that some members of the Akron convention had already become aware of Truth's startling effectiveness as a speaker by reading periodicals that advocated both black and women's rights, such as the Boston *Liberator,* New York *National Anti-Slavery Standard,* and the Salem, Ohio, *Anti-Slavery Bugle,* all of which had praised Truth within the past year.

Gage, in her report, said not only that "trembling" women urged her "again and again" not to let Truth speak, but also that when Truth got up to speak, she was hissed. Many writers, including Eleanor Flexner, in her classic history of the American women's rights movement, have followed Gage in highlighting this supposed hostility to Truth. In fact, recent works on blacks' and women's history argue that black women encountered hostility from the white women's rights movement, and the major evidence they offer to substantiate this argument is the supposed hostility to Truth that Gage described at the Akron convention. One recent work on women's history, in arguing that women's rights conventions in general were racist, charges that at such conventions, "on every occasion Sojourner Truth spoke, groups of white women protested," but the only evidence it offers to support this claim is the alleged hostility to Truth at Akron.[12] In fact, there is no available evidence that white women feminists protested when Truth spoke at other women's rights conventions, as at Worcester, Massachusetts, in 1850; Massillon, Ohio, 1852; New York, 1853; Rochester, 1866; New York, 1867; New York, 1870; Providence, 1870; and Rochester, 1878. This lack of evidence reinforces doubts that Gage's account of hostility to Truth at Akron is accurate.

Since the women at the Akron convention were generally well-dressed, educated, middle-class whites, it is certainly possible that some of them were uneasy about the presence of a strangely dressed, illiterate ex-slave who was selling a book about herself. Also Jane Swisshelm hints of something other than easy acceptance of Truth when, in describing leading participants at the convention, she describes Truth as "a large Negro woman who was there selling books" without giving her name, while giving the names of at least nine white participants. Hannah Tracy, one of the secretaries of the convention, in her recollections long afterward, also hints of something other than easy acceptance of Truth. According to Tracy, she and Gage met Truth in an Akron hotel shortly before the convention began. The young reformer-journalist Lucius A. Hine, who was in the room at the time and who was to be one of the convention vice-presidents, was amused at the awkwardness of Gage and Tracy when Truth told them she was attending the convention. Though both Gage and Tracy bought from Truth a copy of her *Narrative,* Tracy recalled, "I fear we did not feel ready to give her as royal a welcome as her merits deserved, for Mr. Hine sat grinning behind his newspaper in the corner of the room."[13] These instances probably suggest more discomfort with Truth than hostility to her, though perhaps at times there is only a fine line between the two.

Truth herself, just after she left Akron, sent a letter to Amy Post, the abolitionist-feminist friend with whom she had recently been staying in Rochester: "On Tuesday [I] went to Akron to the Convention where I found plenty of kind friends, just like you, & they gave me so many kind invitations I hardly knew which to accept of first. . . . I sold a good many books at the Convention." Truth said nothing about meeting any hostility at the convention.[14] Nor do any of the twenty-seven available descriptions of the convention published soon after it occurred mention that Truth was hissed or otherwise met hostility at the convention.

Gage said that "trembling" women at the convention had repeatedly urged her not to let Truth speak because "it will ruin us. Every newspaper in the land will have our cause mixed with abolition and niggers." When Truth did speak, did this prove to be true? Although the New York *Herald* had tried to smear the Worcester convention because blacks spoke at it, it is not clear that any of the twenty-seven available descriptions of the Akron convention published at the time, most of them in newspapers, tried to smear the women's rights cause because the convention allowed the black abolitionist Truth to speak.

Turning to the content of Truth's speech, we compare Gage's 1863 "faint sketch" of its content with the only other available reports of its content. There are four such reports. Counting only the parts of them that relate strictly to content, they range from as brief as one sentence to as long as Gage's report. They were all published in 1851 soon after the event, and all in reformist papers.[15] First we select key ideas in Gage's report of the content, and then check to see whether these ideas turn up in the other four reports.

Several of the key ideas do turn up in at least one of the other four reports. For example, according to Gage, Truth replied to a clergyman, who had argued that women should not have the same rights as men because Christ was not a woman, by saying that Christ came from God and a woman, without the help of man. This idea is in both the New York *Tribune* and the Salem *Anti-Slavery Bugle,* though neither says it was in reply to anyone, and neither uses the language or dramatic fervor in expressing it that Gage reported. For another example, according to Gage, Truth said that if the first woman God ever made turned the world "upside down" by herself, then surely all the women present should be able to set it "right side up again." This idea also is in both the *Tribune* and the *Bugle,* and in similar language. For still another example, according to Gage, Truth said that she could do as much farm work as a man.

This idea appears in all four of the other reports, though in language very different from that in Gage's report. Thus we can be reasonably sure that Truth included these particular key ideas in her speech, if not expressing them in the manner that Gage reported.

However, several other key ideas in Gage's report of Truth's speech do not appear in any of the other four reports. For instance, according to Gage, Truth, speaking about man's traditional deference to women, said that although she was a woman, nobody ever helped her into carriages, or over mud puddles, or gave her the "best place." Also according to Gage, Truth said she could bear the lash as well as a man. Since neither of these ideas appears in any of the four reports, we have to doubt whether Truth expressed them.

Moreover, according to Gage, Truth said that she had "borne thirteen chillen," and had seen almost all of them sold away from her. Not only does no statement about her children appear in any of the other four reports, but also it has been widely recognized that she probably had only five children and only one of them was sold away from her. This conspicuous error in Gage's report could have provided a red flag to students of Truth, suggesting doubts about the reliability of Gage's account in general. However, some writers, in quoting Gage's report of what Truth said, covered up Gage's error by arbitrarily altering the figure of thirteen children to five, without giving any hint of uneasiness about doing so.

Also according to Gage, Truth said that when her children were sold away from her and she "cried out with a mother's grief, none but Jesus heard." Not only did none of the other four reports of the content of her speech say that she said anything like this, but in fact, as we have seen, many persons had heard her grief at the loss of her son Peter and had acted to help her. Especially because Truth had already named some of these persons in her *Narrative,* it seems unlikely that she would make such a false and ungrateful statement as this.

Next we consider the most outstanding expression of Truth's speech as Gage reported it, the well known "Ar'n't I a woman?" question. In recent years the passage in which this question appeared has made such an impression on readers of Gage's report, that often after translating "Ar'n't" into the more familiar "Ain't,"[16] they have called Truth's whole speech the "Ain't I a woman?" speech, and the "Ain't I a woman?" expression has often been used on the stage, on women's liberation posters, and in the titles of articles, chapters, and books.

The "Ar'n't I a Woman?" expression, as Gage reported it, was undoubtedly an adaptation of the motto, "Am I not a Woman and a Sister?," which had for many years been a popular antislavery motto. It had long appeared in antislavery literature, often accompanied by a picture of a black slave woman in chains.[17]

We have already found reason to doubt that several of the key ideas in this "Ar'n't I a woman?" passage are really Truth's, but here is the passage in full, from Gage, to give the reader the chance to feel directly the impact of the "Ar'n't I a woman?" question. Gage reported that Truth repeated the question four times:

"Nobody eber helps me into carriages, or ober mud-puddles, or give me any best place"; and, raising herself to her full height, and her voice to a pitch like rolling thunder, she asked, "And Ar'n't I a woman? Look at me. Look at my arm," and she bared her right arm to the shoulder, showing its tremendous muscular power. "I have plowed and planted and gathered into barns, and no man could head me —and Ar'n't I a woman? I could work as much and eat as much as a man (when I could get it), and bear de lash as well—and Ar'n't I a woman? I have borne thirteen chillen, and seen 'em mos' all sold off into slavery, and when I cried out with a mother's grief, none but Jesus heard—and Ar'n't I a woman?"

If Truth really repeated the question "Ar'n't I a woman?" four times, in such a haunting litany as Gage presented, it is difficult to believe anyone seriously attempting to report her speech at the time would omit it. However, none of the four 1851 reports of her speech says that Truth used this question. The one that comes closest to doing so, in the *Bugle,* asserts that Truth, after saying that she had "plowed and reaped and husked and chopped and mowed," merely asked, "Can any man do more than that?"; and the *Bugle* does not say that she repeated the question.

If Truth asked the question "Ar'n't I a woman?" four times, with such persuasive power as Gage indicates, would it not be natural for Truth to repeat the same question in other speeches? In Truth's time speakers often repeated their speeches, or parts of them, there being no television to make a speech stale from one delivery. In fact, Truth did repeat ideas or expressions she found effective. She repeated one of the key ideas that we have seen she expressed at Akron, as authenticated by reports at that time, the idea that women, having caused Adam's fall, and thus having turned the world upside down, could now turn the world "right side up."

According to her *Narrative,* Truth had already been approaching this idea in her conversation by early in 1850. Truth had also already used this idea, as we have seen, in her speech at the Worcester women's convention in the fall of 1850; after using it at Akron in 1851, she again used it in a speech in New York in 1853; and according to newspaper reports at those times, she used similar expressions in each of these speeches.[18] But there is no available evidence that Truth in other speeches ever repeated the question "Ar'n't I a woman?," or any equivalent, if indeed she ever said it at Akron in the first place.

If Truth asked this question at Akron rhythmically, four times, as Gage claims, would it not be natural for Truth to use other rhythmic repetitions, in similar parallel grammatical constructions, in other speeches? An examination of available reports of Truth's other speeches indicates that Truth was not given to such rhythmic repetition. On the other hand, an examination of Gage's speeches and writing indicates that Gage was indeed given to it. For instance, in the speech Gage gave at the Akron convention, which was printed in the proceedings probably as written out by Gage herself, there were rhythmic parallel sentences in a series, each one beginning with "So it"; there were also rhythmic parallel phrases such as "the sunshine more glorious, the air more quiet, the sounds of harmony more soothing, the perfume of flowers more exquisite"; and there were many rhetorical questions, including in one passage six in a row. Also in a letter to abolitionist editor Garrison, published shortly before Gage published her account of Truth's Akron speech, when Gage was in the Carolina sea islands caring for recently freed slaves, Gage artfully repeated the word "reading" five times in the following sentence: "I was reading [Wendell] Phillips's speech in South Carolina—reading it on one of the Sea Islands—reading it with the bowed and broken slaves of two years ago now walking erect, chainless and masterless all around me—reading it in sight of the great fleet which is (God helping the right) to take Charleston—reading it with the mocking-birds singing roundalays in this old secesh [secessionist] garden, among the budding and blossoming roses and jessamines." Undoubtedly, for Gage as a poet, using such rhythmic repetition was natural. As one commentator has said, in her poetry she was given to "swinging rhythm."[19]

Does it not seem possible, even probable, that Gage, the poet, invented the powerful "Ar'n't I a woman?" litany and imposed it on what Truth really said? Could Gage's statement that in her report of Truth's speech she was giving but a "faint sketch" of it be in effect an apology for her having invented much of this and other passages?

Finally we consider the impact of Truth's speech on the convention. According to Gage, "I have never in my life seen anything like the magical influence [of Truth] that subdued the mobbish spirit of the day, and turned the jibes and sneers of an excited crowd into notes of respect and admiration." Truth "had taken us up in her great, strong arms and carried us safely over the slough of difficulty, turning the whole tide in our favor."

If Truth really had such a "magical influence" that she "turned the whole tide" in the convention from "mobbish" hostility to support of women's rights, is it not likely that Truth herself, in her letter in which she reported attending the convention, would at least have hinted so? Or that Gage, in her comments on the convention published soon after it was held, brief though they were, would have suggested so?[20] Or that, even if some commentators might be reluctant to concede so much influence to an illiterate black woman, at least one of the twenty-six other available descriptions of the convention published soon after it was held would have suggested it?

In fact, neither Truth nor Gage in these statements said anything about Truth's having any impact on the convention. Among the nine descriptions of the convention that mention Truth, the Akron *Summit Beacon* said that Truth "won upon all by her quaint utterance of good hard sense"; but it also seemed to say that Truth was merely one of at least fourteen "stars" at the convention, along with Gage, Jane Swisshelm, Celia Burr, Emma R. Coe, and Emily Robinson. The lengthy official proceedings, signed by Gage as convention president and by three convention secretaries, mentioned Truth only once, saying that she participated in a discussion without saying what she said or that she affected anyone. The *Anti-Slavery Bugle* claimed that the convention had many stars, but "no mighty sun eclipsed all lesser lights." The New York *Daily Tribune,* referring to the second day's morning session, reported that Truth "delighted her audience with some of the shrewdest remarks made during the session"; but altogether the *Tribune* gave more space to three other participants in the convention, including Gage and Swisshelm. The

1. Rondout Creek, Near Kingston, NY. Truth was born and often lived as a slave near the creek. The Catskill Mountains show in the distance. Painting by local artist Joseph Tubby, 1830s? (From New York State Office of Parks, Senate House State Historic Site, Kingston.)

4. Broadway, New York, Where It Crosses Canal Street, in the 1830s. Truth often lived on Canal Street at this time. Etched by Horner. (From the Museum of the City of New York.)

Facing page: 2. Ulster County Court House, Kingston, NY. Truth took legal action here to recover her son from slavery in Alabama. (From F. W. Beers, *County Atlas of Ulster,* 1875.)

3. Robert Matthias, the Authoritarian Leader of the New York Commune Truth Joined. (From W. E. Drake, *The Prophet! . . . the . . . case of . . . Matthias,* 1834.)

5. Brooklyn Ferry, about the Time Truth Took It to Begin Her Wandering as an Evangelist. Engraving by William Bartlett. (From New York State Historical Association, Cooperstown.)

6. The Northampton Association's Factory and Boarding House Building. Truth was in charge of the laundry in the basement. (From Sheffield, *History of Florence,* 1895.)

SOJOURNER TRUTH.

7. The Earliest Known Picture of Sojourner Truth. (From the frontispiece of her *Narrative,* Boston, 1850.)

8. Truth's "Only Known Signature" (dated April 23, 1880, by someone else). It suggests she had problems in visual perception. (From Battle Creek Historical Society.)

9. Universalist Church, Akron, OH. Here, in 1851, Truth pled for women to have a chance to set the world "right side up." (From Samuel A. Lane, *Fifty Years . . . of Akron,* 1892.)

10. Sojourner Truth at a Wash Tub. Pencil sketch by art
student Charles C. Burleigh, Jr. (born 1848), son of a
prominent New England abolitionist family. (From Historic Northampton, Northampton, MA.)

11. The Libyan Sibyl, Inspired by Truth. Sculpture, 1860–61, by William Wetmore Story. (From Metropolitan Museum of Art, Wolf Foundation [1979.266].)

13. Slaves Freed by the Emancipation Proclamation, Seeking the Protection of a U.S. Army Camp. Drawing by A. R. Waud. (From *Harper's Weekly,* Jan. 31, 1863.)

14. Sunday Prayer Service at Freedman's Village, Arlington, VA. Truth worked as a counsellor here. (From Library of Congress.)

Facing page: 12. Sojourner Truth, 1864. Photograph by Randall, Detroit. (From State University College, New Paltz, NY.)

FREE LECTURE!

SOJOURNER TRUTH,

Who has been a slave in the State of New York, and who has been a Lecturer for the last twenty-three years, whose characteristics have been so vividly portrayed by Mrs. Harriet Beecher Stowe, as the African Sybil, will deliver a lecture upon the present issues of the day,

At   On

And will give her experience as a Slave mother and religious woman. She comes highly recommended as a public Speaker, having the approval of many thousands who have heard her earnest appeals, among whom are Wendell Phillips, Wm. Lloyd Garrison, and other distinguished men of the nation.

☞ At the close of her discourse she will offer for sale her photograph and a few of her choice songs.

16. Truth's House, College Street, Battle Creek. (From Chicago *Semi-Weekly Inter-Ocean,* Sept. 25, 1893.)

Facing page: 15. "Free Lecture! Sojourner Truth." Broadside, 1870s? (From State Archives of Michigan.)

17. Sojourner Truth. In her bag she often carried copies of the *Narrative* of her life to sell. Photographer and date unknown. (From State University College, New Paltz, NY.)

18. "Woman's Emancipation." Cartoon Ridiculing Women for Dressing and Smoking Like Men. (From *Harper's New Monthly Magazine*, August, 1851.)

19. Playing for a Juba Dance. (From *White's New Illustrated Melodeon Song Book*, New York, 1848.)

20. The Adventists' Sanitarium, Battle Creek, in the early 1880s. Truth occasionally spoke to the patients in their "great parlor." (From Seventh Day Adventist General Conference, Silver Spring, MD.)

Liberator wrote that Truth "spoke in her own peculiar style, showing that she was a match for most men," but then the *Liberator* gave more space to at least five other participants in the convention, including Swisshelm and Coe.[21]

It is clear from these reports that Truth made a significant impact on some of those attending the convention. But none of these reports, whether pro- or antireformist, gives the impression, as Gage did, in her report twelve years later, that Truth was the one "magical" star of the convention. None goes so far as to claim, like Gage, that Truth turned "the whole tide" of the convention.

Gage published her report on Truth's speech in 1863 during the Civil War, when the women's rights movement was temporarily suspended, and its leaders, including Gage, were concentrating not on women's rights but on winning the war for the Union and freeing the slaves. It was an inopportune time to publish an article that focused on women's rights. Gage may have deliberately published it at this time anyway because she believed that human rights advocates at this time, with all of their legitimate concern for justice to the slaves, needed to be reminded —as Stowe had not reminded them—that the black and women's causes should be tied together, and that the tie was personified in Truth.

When Gage's report first appeared, it was scarcely noticed, being focused too much on the unfashionable subject of women's rights, and written by a comparatively little known author, and published in an obscure abolitionist periodical. By comparison, the article that had occasioned Gage's report, Stowe's article on Truth, had won much attention because it was largely focused on the then more fashionable subject of blacks, was written by a famous author, and was published in the prestigious *Atlantic*.

After Gage's report was republished in Truth's *Narrative* in 1875, and again in Stanton's *History of Women Suffrage* in 1881, it began to be noticed a little more. Later in 1881 the crusading Boston woman's rights periodical, *Woman's Journal,* edited by Lucy Stone, quoted the report, saying that it "will bear to be printed many times more." When Truth died in 1883, two major newspapers quoted the report, including the "Ar'n't I a woman?" passage: The Springfield *Republican* said that it showed "how powerful and original" Truth had been; the Detroit *Post and Tribune* declared, "There is not in all the annals of eloquence a more striking passage."[22]

However, from the 1860s all the way through the 1910s, in available writing about Truth, there were many times more references to Stowe or her article about Truth than to Gage or her article about Truth. From the 1920s, when women began to exercise their new right to vote nation-wide, through the 1960s, when black activism was strong, Gage's article began to catch up, but references to Gage or her article were still fewer than to Stowe or her article. It was only in the 1970s and 1980s, in a period of heightened concern about both black and women's rights and the relation between the two, that references to Gage or her article for the first time exceeded references to Stowe or her article.

Gage's report, gradually becoming well known, wove myths about Truth, myths that helped to build up Truth into a heroic figure. Never-theless, we must ask whether the frequent uncritical use of Gage's report in recent years has led to misleading interpretations not only about Truth and her place in history, but also about early black–white relations at large.

When we compare Gage's 1863 report of Truth's speech with available reports written in 1851 soon after the event, the comparison suggests that we should heed Gage's own warning that she had "given but a faint sketch" of Truth's speech. The comparison suggests that, unless evidence to the contrary turns up, important parts of Gage's report regarding the atmosphere of the convention, the contents of Truth's speech, and the effect of the speech on the convention should be considered false. The comparison suggests that Gage, the poet, intended to present the sym-bolic truth of Truth's words more than the literal truth; that Gage, the novelist, imagining that Harriet Beecher Stowe was looking over her shoulder, felt pressed to make Truth's story more compelling than it was; that Gage, the passionate advocate of blacks' and women's rights, embel-lished her report to strengthen the causes she favored, imposing her own ideas and expression on what Truth said. Disappointing as it may be, the comparison makes it unlikely that Truth asked the thrilling question, "Ar'n't I a woman?", the principal words by which Truth is known today.

If we depend on contemporary accounts as more likely than Gage's to be reliable, then we perceive that when Sojourner Truth began to speak, there were no signs of panic, no hissing, no mobbish opponents whom she could overcome. Then we find that Truth's words, unadorned, if less dramatic and smooth than Gage wanted them to be, did not make her the one star of the convention, as Gage indicates, but nevertheless made her impressive.

When Truth's biographers, following Gage, say that she turned the convention around from opposing to favoring women's rights, we have to suspect that they may be telling us more what Gage wanted us to believe than what really happened. When recent writers on women's and blacks' history claim that white women advocating women's rights were hostile to black women's participation in the women's movement, and they base their claims especially on Gage's account of the supposed hostility to Truth at Akron, we have to wonder whether they are distorting history. Unless evidence to the contrary turns up, we have to regard Gage's account of Truth's asking the "Ar'n't I a woman?" question as folklore, like the story of George Washington and the cherry tree. It may be suitable for telling to children, but not for serious understanding of Sojourner Truth and her times.

If friends and students of Truth wish to reassess their views, they might stop depending on Gage's report as if it were reliable, and depend instead on the reports of the speech that were published at the time, especially the fullest one, in the *Bugle*. If not as dramatic as Gage's report, the *Bugle* report is terse, portrays Truth as speaking in a folksy style that rings true, attributes to her some of the same provocative ideas that Gage's report attributed to her, and is much more likely to be authentic:

One of the most unique and interesting speeches of the Convention was made by Sojourner Truth, an emancipated slave. It is impossible to transfer it to paper, or convey any adequate idea of the effect it produced upon the audience. Those only can appreciate it who saw her powerful form, her whole-souled, earnest gesture, and listened to her strong and truthful tones. She came forward to the platform and addressing the President said with great simplicity:

May I say a few words? Receiving an affirmative answer, she proceeded; I want to say a few words about this matter. I am a woman's rights [sic.]. I have as much muscle as any man, and can do as much work as any man. I have plowed and reaped and husked and chopped and mowed, and can any man do more than that? I have heard much about the sexes being equal; I can carry as much as any man, and can eat as much too, if I can get it. I am as strong as any man that is now.

As for intellect, all I can say is, if woman have a pint and man a quart—why can't she have her little pint full? You need not be afraid to give us our rights for fear we will take too much—for we won't take more than our pint'll hold.

The poor men seem to be all in confusion and don't know what to do. Why children, if you have woman's rights give it to her and you will feel better. You will have your own rights, and they won't be so much trouble.

I can't read, but I can hear. I have heard the Bible and have learned that Eve caused man to sin. Well if woman upset the world, do give her a chance to set it right side up again. The lady has spoken about Jesus, how he never spurned woman from him, and she was right. When Lazarus died, Mary and Martha came to him with faith and love and besought him to raise their brother. And Jesus wept—and Lazarus came forth. And how came Jesus into the world? Through God who created him and woman who bore him. Man, where is your part?

But the women are coming up blessed be God and a few of the men are coming up with them. But man is in a tight place, the poor slave is on him, woman is coming on him, and he is surely between a hawk and a buzzard.[23]

7

Confronting Douglass

"Is God gone?"

In 1860 Harriet Beecher Stowe published an arresting story about Truth's confronting Frederick Douglass. According to Stowe, Douglass was speaking and Truth sat in the front row of the audience:

Frederick Douglass, fired with the wrongs of his race, and the despairs of the white race, declared that there was neither hope nor help for the slave but in their own right arms.

In the pause that followed this appeal, Sojourner lifted her dark face, working with intense feeling, and said in a low, deep voice, which was heard in every corner of the room, "Frederick, is God dead?"

Stowe told the story as a rebuke to the President of the United States, James Buchanan. He had proposed to stop the "agitation" against slavery by amending the Constitution to make clear that it legalized slavery. Stowe concluded her story:

Let that old black slave-woman's question ring through the nation, as then it rang through Faneuil Hall. To all who hope or dream to put down agitation by a covenant with death and an agreement with hell, old Africa rises, and raising her poor maimed, scarred hand to heaven, asks us—"Is God dead?"

Stowe originally published the story in the New York *Independent,* and then relishing it, republished it three years later in the *Atlantic*

Monthly. The story was often retold in Truth's time. Truth's friend William Still retold it in the Philadelphia *Bulletin* of July 28, 1876, commenting: "There is but little room to fear that history will ever allow" Truth's "Is God dead?" question "to go into oblivion." When Truth died in 1883, the Rochester *Evening Express* pointed to "Is God dead?" as her "most striking" saying. Afterward, "Is God Dead?" was carved on her tombstone. In 1913 W. E. B. DuBois retold the story in a black historical pageant. In 1942 the Detroit *Free Press* declared that her "Is God dead?" cry had become "the battle-cry of faith and hope for Negroes everywhere."[1]

When Stowe retold the story in 1863, she emphasized that Douglass believed blacks must turn to violence. Douglass, she said, ended his speech by insisting that blacks "had no hope of justice from the whites, no possible hope except in their own right arms. It must come to blood; they must fight for themselves, and redeem themselves, or it would never be done."

In this second telling, Stowe was more specific about Truth's effect on the audience:

Sojourner was sitting, tall and dark, on the very front seat, facing the platform; and in the hush of deep feeling, after Douglass sat down, she spoke out in her deep, peculiar voice, heard all over the house, "Frederick, is God dead?"

The effect was perfectly electrical, and thrilled through the whole house, changing as by a flash the whole feeling of the audience. Not another word she said or needed to say; it was enough.

Since the time Stowe told this story, there has been widespread doubt about where and when this incident occurred, and indeed some doubt whether it occurred at all. Stowe first heard the story from Wendell Phillips. However, Phillips did not claim to have been present when the incident occurred, and neither Phillips nor Stowe gave any indication as to when it occurred. According to Stowe, the incident took place in Faneuil Hall, Boston. Many have followed Stowe in placing it in Boston, but others have placed it in the West. Historians have recently reported the story to be "considered apocryphal."[2] Is this another story—like Gage's story of the "Ar'n't I a woman?" speech—which is so likely to be untrue that we should not use it?

In this instance, it has been possible to establish with certainty that

Truth's confrontation with Douglass did indeed occur and, further, to trace it to Sunday evening, August 22, 1852, in a Friends meeting house, in Salem, Ohio. In fact, significant reports of this meeting were published at the time in five antislavery newspapers, reports that apparently disappeared from view for many years until uncovered for the present study. These reports together give us a more accurate story of what Truth said and what effect she had on the meeting than has been available in studies of Truth before, and give the story a surprising twist.[3]

Soon after the incident occurred, Douglass, reporting on the meeting for his own Rochester newspaper, failed to report Truth's question to him at all. Since the question was embarrassing to him, perhaps it is natural that Douglass would not report it.

However, Oliver Johnson, an experienced journalist, reporting on the incident at the time for his antislavery weekly, the Philadelphia *Pennsylvania Freeman,* told us what Truth's question to Douglass was. According to Johnson, Truth's question was not exactly "Is God dead?" after all. The Friends meeting house "was crowded to its utmost capacity," Johnson wrote—about 1,000 people were there, mostly, as Douglass called them, "hard-handed farmers" and their families. Douglass, Johnson wrote, was eloquent, "one who never fails to command the close attention of his audience." He had brought the audience to a "high pitch of excitement" when, according to Johnson, Truth asked, "Is God gone?"

This "Is God gone?" expression, in the course of being repeated verbally over several years, might well have become the smoother, more sophisticated "Frederick, is God dead?" that Stowe reported later. Both Douglass and Johnson, in later years, when they heard the story as Stowe told it, accepted the "Frederick, is God dead?" version as conveying the sense of what Truth said. But the version recorded at the time—"Is God gone?"—is more likely to be accurate.

Did Truth's question have an "electrical" effect, as Stowe said? Reporting on the meeting at the time, Johnson wrote that Truth's question had an effect that was, among other things, "startling." Later Johnson wrote that when Truth "interjected" her "solemn question," "no bullet ever went to its mark with greater accuracy than that with which this interrogatory pierced the very heart of the question, and Douglass stood demolished and silent." Douglass himself later testified to the effect of Truth's question, "We were all for a moment brought to a stand-still, just as we should have been if someone had thrown a brick through the window."[4]

Two other of the reports written at the time tend to substantiate much of Johnson's original report. They describe Truth as thrusting at various speakers with a "single question." One of these reports was in the Salem, Ohio, *Anti-Slavery Bugle,* the weekly newspaper of the Garrisonian abolitionist society that ran this meeting. The other was in Garrison's Boston *Liberator* and was written by Parker Pillsbury, who attended the meeting.

The *Bugle,* in its report, described Truth as asking powerful "single questions" of speakers who were "politicians." From the *Bugle*'s Garrisonian perspective, Frederick Douglass had once occupied the high ground of a moral suasionist—when he had held that abolitionists should strive to abolish slavery only by appealing to consciences—but had degraded himself into a "politician," because he had come to advocate the use of political and physical force; he even toyed with supporting John Brown's use of guns. The *Bugle* wrote: "Sojourner Truth would sometimes throw in the way of the politicians a most ugly difficulty—a whole argument, with premise, conclusion and application, in a single question."

Like the *Bugle,* Pillsbury, for the *Liberator,* called Truth's device a "single question." Pillsbury also called it a "single dart," and said she directed it specifically at Douglass: "In two or three instances, poor old Sojourner Truth, the slave woman, pierced him through and through with a single dart, sent with that fearful aim and precision for which she is so eminently distinguished."

What did Truth mean by her famous question, whether in the original 1852 form of "Is God gone?" or, as it later became known, "Is God dead?"?

After Truth asked her question, similar expressions became well known in other contexts. One of these expressions was the philosopher Friedrich Nietzsche's "God is dead." He first used it in 1882 to assert that there is no God to give meaning to human existence, and therefore humans themselves must give whatever meaning there is to their existence. The same "God is dead" expression became popular in the 1960s in the "God is dead" theological movement. Some theologians used this expression to mean that the traditional God—in the sense of a patriarch with a beard who sat on his throne in heaven—is no longer meaningful in our time, so we need to envision God differently. In both these cases the expression meant a denial that God, or at least a God of a certain kind, lives.

However, Truth, by her question "Is God gone?", was insisting to the contrary that God lives. But to understand it so still does not adequately explain what she meant by her question.

According to a broad interpretation of what Truth meant, which has been given over many years, Truth was urging faith in God: She was urging Douglass not to despair, but to have faith that God will abolish slavery. A more specific interpretation, also given over many years, and not necessarily contradictory to the broad one, is that Truth's particular concern was the issue of violence. This view maintains that Douglass, in saying that slavery could only be abolished by blood, was endorsing violence, while Truth was insisting that God wants slavery to be destroyed without blood, and thus was repudiating violence.

In line with the first, broad interpretation, that Truth, by her question, was emphasizing faith in God, Lucy Stone commented long afterward, that Truth meant to insist that if God is on our side, we cannot fail. Similarly in line with this broad interpretation, during World War I a writer in a New York newspaper used Truth's question to support "faith" as opposed to "despair," and in particular faith that "our boys" will win the war (certainly this use of Truth's question was not interpreting it as insisting on nonviolence). Additionally in line with this view is the recent suggestion by an African-American scholar, that Truth's "outburst" against Douglass had "little" to do with divisions among abolitionists over whether violence was justified as a means of abolishing slavery, but much to do with whether God was involved. Truth, the scholar explained, believed that God had helped her through her struggles so far, and so was upset when Douglass seemed to insist that God had no part in the struggle to abolish slavery.[5]

Truth and Douglass by this time had differing conceptions of God. Douglass was coming to believe that God is remote and depends on humans to carry out His will for justice. Truth, however, as an evangelical, believed in a personal, easily accessible God, who actively intervenes for justice. Thus Truth, in asserting that God lives, could be understood as calling for reliance on God to intervene to destroy slavery, no matter how inadequate human efforts to destroy slavery were.

Moving to the more specific interpretation—that Truth's primary concern was the issue of violence—we note that in 1860, when the peace-conscious antislavery editor William Goodell republished Stowe's first account of the "Is God dead?" story in his New York *Principia,* he used the story to advocate peaceful means to abolish slavery. Goodell commented: "Give us but seven thousand men, with the faith of Sojourner Truth, and not many months would intervene before politicians even, would discover the peaceful solution of our national problem."[6]

More directly supporting the view that Truth was primarily concerned about the issue of violence was Douglass himself, whose testimony deserves weight. In his memoirs Douglass wrote that what he had said at Salem was to express his "apprehension that slavery could only be destroyed by bloodshed," and that what Truth meant by her question was that she opposed bloodshed. Calling Truth "my quaint old sister," he explained that she "was of the Garrison school of non-resistants, and was shocked at my sanguinary doctrine."[7]

Moreover, Oliver Johnson's account of the incident, written immediately after it occurred, interpreted Truth to mean that she opposed bloodshed:

Mr. Douglass, in the course of his speech, took occasion to glorify Violence as in some circumstances far more potent than Moral Suasion. He contended, in fact, that there were cases that could not by any possibility be reached by the latter. In this connection he referred us to the abject condition of the people of Russia, and ridiculed the idea that anything short of the shedding of the blood of the tyrants could afford relief.

When his argument on this point had reached its climax, and the audience had been wrought to a high pitch of excitement by his rhetoric—in answer to his exclamation, "What is the use of Moral Suasion to a people thus trampled in the dust?" was heard the voice of Sojourner Truth, who asked, with startling effect, "Is God gone?"

Mr. Douglass stood for a moment in silence, and seemed fully conscious of the force of the question; and when he replied he could only affirm that God was present in the mind of the oppressed to stimulate them to violence! Sojourner's arrow, however, was sped by more than human power, and it pierced with deadly effect the Atheism which teaches that the Sword is mightier than the Truth. It was indeed sublime to see the plausible sophistry of Mr. Douglass rendered powerless by a simple question from the mouth of an illiterate woman.[8]

Unlike Johnson, Stowe, in her telling of the "Is God dead?" story both times, did not clearly identify nonviolence as Truth's primary concern. Nevertheless, as became well known, Stowe, in writing her novel *Dred* (published 1856) in the years after Truth had visited her, based one of her major characters, Milly, on Truth, and she made Milly clearly nonviolent.[9]

Milly, like Truth, is a majestic black slave woman who has spiritual depth. Like Truth, she influences both the blacks and whites around her. Like Truth, she has overcome her earlier desire that God kill whites for holding slaves, and has learned to forgive them. When a slave named Dred plans a slave insurrection, Milly, saying Christians should love their enemies and leave vengeance to God, persuades him at least to postpone his plans. We do not know whether Stowe, at the time she wrote *Dred,* already knew the "Is God dead?" story, but at any rate Stowe in this novel interpreted Truth as distinctly nonviolent.

As a slave Truth had been whipped, which one might suppose could have accustomed her to regard violence in human relations as natural, and perhaps to be violent herself. Indeed, when her children were young, Truth recalled, if they did wrong, she would whip them. Yet there are also signs that she could be gentle and forgiving. Although as a slave she had sometimes prayed to God to punish slaveholders by killing all whites, when she escaped from Dumont, she made clear she was protesting against him but did not wish to hurt him. Also when soon afterward she experienced her religious conversion, she interpreted it as her turning from hating to loving whites.

However, when she was living in New York City, and was trying to find some way to keep Peter out of trouble, she urged him to go to sea on board a "man-of-war." [10] As noted earlier, she tolerated Matthias as head of the Kingdom in his occasional whipping of its members, including herself. Also when the police came to arrest Matthias for lunacy, she physically tried to deter them from what she felt was unjustified violence to Matthias. Moreover, she later tried to prevent Folger from fighting Matthias by holding Folger against a door. In these last two examples, she was practicing only the defensive "violence" of protective restraint rather than aggressive violence.

In 1844 when Truth joined the Garrisonian-related Northampton community, she found the ideas of nonviolence freely circulating around her. Having already often been inclined to be forgiving, probably she was ready to listen to these ideas. Garrison had helped to see to it that when the American Anti-Slavery Society was founded in 1833, it was pledged to abolish slavery by nonviolent methods. Garrison and some of his abolitionist associates had founded the Nonresistance Society in 1838 to teach the principles of nonviolence; Henry C. Wright, who at one time was an agent of the Northampton Association, was the society's general agent; George Benson, a leader of the Northampton community who took a special interest in Truth, had for several years been a vice-president of the society. The Northampton Association itself was not formally pledged to nonviolence or to any other creed, but its school forbade corporal punishment, and Garrison, on one of his visits to the association, told the members that he took it for granted that they were "generally antislavery, anti-war, and temperance men." One of Truth's biographers, Hertha Pauli, writing in the 1960s when Martin Luther King had made Americans aware of nonviolent protest as a means of bringing about basic social change, claimed that while Truth struggled for freedom by nonviolence, "she never heard the slogans of nonviolence." However, while the specific slogans used in the 1960s were different from those used in Truth's time, Truth heard "slogans of nonviolence" at the Northampton community and elsewhere from many abolitionists like Garrison, Parker Pillsbury, and Lucretia Mott. Truth heard slogans, especially biblically based ones, such as "overcome evil with good," abolish slavery not by "carnal weapons" but by "moral suasion," and overthrow prejudice "by the power of love."[11]

In 1852 when she was speaking against slavery, she sometimes sang an antislavery song of her own composition, which included these verses:

> Yet those oppressors steeped in guilt—
> I still would have them live;
> For I have learned of Jesus
> to suffer and forgive.
>   I want no carnal weapons,
> No enginery of death;
> For I love not to hear the sound
> Of war's tempestuous breath.[12]

About two weeks after she had confronted Douglass with the question, "Is God gone?" she again showed her concern for using peaceful means in the struggle against slavery, this time in Cleveland in September, 1852, at an Ohio state convention of blacks. The convention was discussing how far fugitive slaves should go in using violence to help themselves escape. According to the official proceedings of the convention, many delegates argued that if the slave catchers used violent "carnal weapons," then the fugitives, to prevent their being caught, were justified in using them too; Truth was the only one reported as "urging peace and forbearance."[13] This reinforces the belief that at the Salem meeting Truth was concerned about the issue of violence.

Speaking at a woman's rights convention in New York in 1853, Truth said that while Esther, in pleading to the Persian king for the rights of the Jews, caused Haman to be hanged, she herself, in pleading for the rights of women, did "not want any man to be killed."[14]

In the whole decade before the Civil War, while abolitionists became increasingly disturbed that their nonviolent struggle to abolish slavery was not effective enough, Truth is never known to have endorsed slave revolts as a means of abolishing slavery.

Once the Civil War broke out, however, it became difficult for Truth, as for nearly all abolitionists who had once been nonviolent, to remain nonviolent. Was Douglass right after all that slavery could only be ended by bloodshed?

Early in the war, in June, 1861, Truth retained only a hint of faith in nonviolence. Speaking in Indiana, she ran into trouble from anti-black Democrats who insisted on trying to enforce an Indiana law—of questionable constitutionality—that forbade blacks to come into the state. These Democrats had Truth arrested. A pro-Union military unit called the Home Guard took her into custody to protect her from being jailed. When she nevertheless insisted on speaking in the Steuben County court house as planned, her friends advised her to carry a sword or pistol to protect herself, but she replied, "I carry no weapon; the Lord will reserve [preserve] me without weapons. I feel safe even in the midst of my enemies." But she accepted the escort of the armed Home Guard, so that when she marched into the court house to speak, she was protected, she recalled, by "flashing bayonets."[15]

Already by this time, even though it was not at all certain that the war would lead to the abolition of slavery, Truth was saying that if she were "ten years younger," she "would fly to the battle-field, and nurse and cook for the Massachusetts troops, brave boys! and if it came to the pinch, put in a blow, now and then."[16]

During the war, Truth continued to support the Union soldiers ardently. She encouraged black enlistment, and when one of her grandsons enlisted, she gave him her enthusiastic blessing for helping "to redeem de white people from de curse dat God has sent upon them." Although Truth's friend the Quaker Lucretia Mott deliberately avoided visiting the army camp for black soldiers that had been established near her home in

Philadelphia, because she feared it would be interpreted to mean that she supported the war, Truth, after Michigan established a camp for black soldiers in Detroit, collected food for them in what was then her home town of Battle Creek, and delivered it in person to the soldiers in their camp. Truth declared in a letter soon afterward, "If I were ten years younger, I would go down with these soldiers here & be the Mother of the Regiment!" About the same time she was quoted as saying that "if she were only ten years younger," she would be "the Joan of Arc to lead de army of de Lord; for now is de day and now de hour for de colored man to save dis nation." [17]

A few of the heretofore nonviolent abolitionists found themselves uncomfortable as they tried to reconcile their belief in nonviolence with their inclination to support the Union cause in the war. Parker Pillsbury and Abby Kelley Foster, for example, continued to advocate freeing the slaves by voluntary choice, believing that freeing them instead by military necessity, as an act of war—as Lincoln did in his Emancipation Proclamation —would perpetuate white hatred of blacks. Garrison, although supporting the Union cause, took an interest in men who became conscientious objectors to military service—one of his own sons became such an objector.[18] But Truth showed no signs, as far as available evidence indicates, that she agonized over reconciling her nonviolence with her support of the war. The opportunity that the war provided to abolish slavery appeared to her of such overriding importance that she seemed to abandon her nonviolence.

8

Northampton to Battle Creek

"Come spirit, hop up here on the table."

When Truth acquired her house in Northampton in 1850, it was the first time she had a house she could share with her children. Though earlier she had several times been willing to go away from her children, at this time she invited all three of her daughters to live with her. By this time all of them were legally free to come.

Sophia, the youngest of the three, had been freed, at least informally, at the same time as Sojourner herself, the Van Wagenens having bought both of them in effect to free them from Dumont. In 1850, almost immediately after Truth acquired her house, Sophia came to live with her, but did not stay long. She soon married in Medina, in western New York.[1]

Elizabeth was legally freed from serving Dumont only in about 1850 when she reached the age of twenty-five. She is believed to have married and had a child, Samuel Banks, in about 1852, in New Bedford.[2] But soon afterward she came to live with her mother in Northampton.

Diana, the eldest daughter, probably reached the age when the law no longer required her to serve Dumont in about 1841. But Diana continued working for Dumont until 1849, when he moved "west" with some of his sons. By 1850 Diana was living in Northampton with her mother, trying to support herself by taking in washing.[3]

By April 1853, however, Diana was ill. Truth, in concern, wrote from Northampton to Mrs. Mary K. Gale, a white abolitionist friend, in Medway, Massachusetts, about seventy miles to the east. From the letter it is apparent that Gale had found work with a neighbor for Elizabeth, but now Truth felt obliged to call Elizabeth home:

Florence, Northampton, April 14th, 1853

My dear Mrs. Gale, Dear beloved friend,

I arrived in Boston and received a dispatch dated April 3d saying that my daughter Diana was laying dangerously ill at my home in Northampton, and wishing me to come as soon as possible. The neighbors have kindly watched over her until my arrival and are still kind. She is still very sick, with pleurisy and lung fever, and the doctor says she will scarcely be fit to leave in two months if she gets along well.

The dispatch was sent to Mr. Garrison, and I started as soon as possible after I learned how things were. Diana cannot help herself at all.

I want to have my daughter Elizabeth come here and take care of her awhile, and then I can go to New York, and other places and do the business that is necessary I should do as soon as it is proper for me to leave her. The neighbors and friends think this is the best course I can take, and I want her to be sure and come soon, after she gets this, by all means come Monday or Tuesday. It is impossible to get help in this place. Mrs. Anthony has been very kind and has taken good care, but she cannot stay, and Elizabeth must come. Diana is very anxious that she should come and I pray you let nothing prevent her coming Monday or Tuesday. If she does not come I shall expect a letter Tuesday.

If she has not money if Mrs. Gale will see that she has enough to bring her here, I will satisfy her when I come that way. Will Mrs. Gale apologize to Mrs. Jenks and tell her that it is only necessity makes me call for her, but it does not take our Heavenly Father long to change our course, and make our pathway to differ from what we have calculated. Mrs. Gale will please read this letter to Mrs. Jenks, and they will understand.

Ever truly yours,
Sojourner Truth[4]

Probably Elizabeth did leave her work and come home, as Truth requested, for, as it turned out, Truth succeeded in getting away to attend to her "business," as she called it prosaically here. In May, Truth was attending conventions and speaking in and near Philadelphia, and in September in and near New York. She was speaking on slavery, women's rights, religion, and the story of her life, sometimes mixing all these together, and as usual she sold her books.

In May of 1855 or 1856, Truth wrote an unknown friend about her grandson, James Caldwell. Which of Truth's daughters was James's mother is not certain. At any rate, it was James whom Truth had taken with her when she visited Harriet Beecher Stowe in 1853. According to this letter, Truth apparently had placed James, who was about twelve or thirteen by now, out to service, but he was not doing well:

Florence [Northampton], May 12 [1855? 1856?]

Dear Friend,

I have this day got your letter. Have been in Conn. & did not stop long enough in any one place to write & have an answer.

I am very sorry Jimmy has troubled you. I did hope he would be a good boy & be a help and not a hindrance.

I will come for him just as soon as I can get my things fixed for a little so that I can leave home. I got home today, found Elizabeth sick. She had been quite sick but is better.

Dianna [sic.] is in Westfield living with Mr. [Gilbert] Haven, a Methodist minister she likes very much & they seem to [like] her.

I will try to get to your place in a week or ten days at most. I hope Jimmy will try to do the best he can until I can get there. Rest assured I am very sorry you have had such a burden imposed upon you.

With much gratitude for your kindness I remain thy friend & sister,

Sojourner Truth[5]

At the same time that Truth was enlarging her view of her mission to the world, she was enlarging her view of her responsibilities to her family, and finding that these responsibilities sometimes weighed heavily on her.

Meanwhile Truth was doing well enough in her lecturing, selling her book, and managing her finances to pay off the mortgage on her house. On November 1, 1854, Samuel L. Hill discharged the mortgage, acknowledging that it had "been fully paid." On January 18, 1856, she bought from Hill another lot next to her house for $25, as if she was still doing well financially, and expected to stay in Northampton.[6] However, she was soon allowing herself to be caught up in the great surge of New Englanders and New Yorkers who were migrating to the Middle West, dreaming of new beginnings.

In the fall of 1856, Truth was visiting the Battle Creek region of Michigan, where Eastern settlers were rapidly clearing the gently rolling land for growing wheat and fruit. She spoke in Battle Creek in October, 1856, at the annual meeting of the Michigan Progressive Friends (also known as Friends of Human Progress). On this occasion she met some ardent advocates of blacks and women, including Warren Chase, a Spiritualist, and several of Quaker background such as Henry Willis, the Merritt family, and Frances Titus, all of whom were to become her friends. In May, 1857, she was again in Battle Creek, speaking there and in the vicinity.[7]

On July 28, 1857 she bought a lot in Harmonia, about five miles west of Battle Creek proper.[8] Harmonia was a small Spiritualist community, its name being a popular Spiritualist term. Harmonia had been formed by Quakers-become-Spiritualists, particularly the Reynolds Cornell family. It was from the Cornells' son Hiram that Truth bought her lot.

The Cornells, like many Michigan Quakers, were originally from New York State. They had become members of the Battle Creek Quaker meeting in 1838, and had first settled in what was later to become Harmonia in about 1844, buying extensive land and gathering other Quaker farmers around them. It was not until several years later that the Cornells had become Spiritualists.

Truth herself once said that she came to Battle Creek because "old friends of mine from Ulster County, N.Y., had removed, and wanted me to follow," but who these friends were she did not say. It is now possible to identify these old friends as including—and perhaps entirely consisting of—the Cornells of Harmonia. Both Reynolds Cornell and his wife Dorcas had grown up in Quaker families in the part of Ulster County where Truth had lived as a slave. Dorcas Cornell's parents, the Alexander Youngs, had been part of the Quaker community in Poppletown that had helped Truth in recovering her son. Truth remembered those Quakers warmly. Reynolds Cornell's daughter Delia, who was one of the teachers in the Harmonia Seminary, recalled long afterward that before Truth settled in Harmonia, she visited the Cornells there as a guest, and was "greatly pleased to find that her hostess had been a neighbor to her in the days of her thraldom." The Cornells found that they and Truth shared not only common memories of people and the hilly landscape in Ulster County, but also common sympathies for reform causes, including antislavery and spiritualism. It would be understandable that the Cornells encouraged her to settle with them in Harmonia.[9]

On September 3, 1857, Truth sold her house and adjoining lot in Northampton for $740, thus making a tidy profit.[10] The low price—$40 —she paid for her lot in Harmonia suggests that she bought it without a house and then built one afterward. Her new house was evidently, like her house in Northampton, a modest one, because her Harmonia real estate was valued in the 1860 census at $900, less than that of several of her immediate neighbors.

Soon after moving to Harmonia, Truth had living with her in her new house at least one of her grandsons, five-year-old Samuel Banks. Her house was near the Cornells' houses, and near Hiram Cornell's school for children, called Bedford Harmonial Seminary, which was controversial because it was associated with Spiritualists. Her house was also diagonally across the street from the newly built house of Warren Chase, who had been the major figure in a utopian socialist community in Wisconsin, and a member of the state senate there. He was now one of the most prominent promoters of spiritualism in the nation. Unlike many Spiritualists, Chase considered himself an "infidel" Spiritualist, not a Christian one. Chase was pleased that in Hiram Cornell's school "students were not taught to pray and read the Bible," and sent his children to the school.[11]

No available evidence suggests that Truth would choose a community because it either discouraged reading the Bible or offered opportunities for farming. It has been suggested that she moved to the Battle Creek area because there was a black community there.[12] But we lack any indication that Truth particularly wished to live among blacks. In any case, she would be unlikely to move from Massachusetts to Michigan in order to be closer to blacks, for at the time in Michigan, as in Massachusetts, blacks made up less than one percent of the population, and both the Battle Creek and Northampton areas had insignificant numbers of blacks. Perhaps a reason Truth moved to the area was that there might be more opportunities for her children and grandchildren to find suitable work and education; Diana, Elizabeth, and James had all been obliged to fan out from Northampton to find work. It is not clear if the Battle Creek area was any more antislavery than Northampton, but Battle Creek, perhaps especially because of its Spiritualists and Quakers, seemed unusually tolerant of differences; the Battle Creek Quakers were of the Hicksite wing of Quakers, that is, the more tolerant wing. When Warren Chase decided to settle in Harmonia, he considered Battle Creek to be one of the most liberal towns in the state. When in 1868 Michigan voted on whether to adopt a new state constitution that would give blacks the equal right to vote, Michigan as a whole voted against it, but Battle Creek voted for it.

It is likely that Truth was drawn to the Quaker-related community of reformers in Battle Creek proper, including the Willises, Merritts, and Tituses. Truth had met Henry Willis by at least 1852 at an antislavery convention in Ohio. Afterward when Truth had spoken at the Progressive Friends convention in Battle Creek in 1856, it was Willis who suggested that a collection be taken up for her benefit, resulting in a "liberal contribution." Willis and his Quaker friends encouraged her to continue her public speaking, and also assisted her to find employment as a domestic to help support herself. One of the Merritt family claimed much later that his mother had brought Truth to Battle Creek to be his nurse.[13]

However, the fact that Truth chose to settle in Harmonia, the Spiritualist community, rather than in Battle Creek proper, is significant. In choosing to settle in Harmonia she was for the third time choosing to live in an intentional community, the first having been the Matthias community in New York, the second having been the Northampton Association. Evidently she felt a need, as she had before, to live in an community whose ideals she shared, and from which she could hope to secure at least emotional support. However, although both the Matthias and Northampton Association communities had been highly structured, the Harmonia community was scarcely structured at all. Participants lived in about a dozen separate houses, as separate families. They did not pool property, share work, or live by common rules. They simply came to live in the same community because they believed they would find it congenial to do so.

Frances Titus, who became a long-time Battle Creek friend of Truth's, in writing the 1875 version of Truth's *Narrative,* gave no explanation for Truth's move to Michigan. Titus did not even mention that Truth settled in a Spiritualist community. Possibly Titus, as sympathetic as she and many of her Battle Creek Quaker friends were to spiritualism, felt that linking Truth to spiritualism would not add to Truth's reputation. Since then, many other commentators on Truth, if they even knew about Truth's association with Spiritualists, have ignored it.

Truth had been fascinated by spiritualism as early as 1851, when she visited western New York where the spiritualist storm that swept America in the 1850s arose. In Rochester, Truth had stayed with the Posts, who were intimate neighbors of the Fox sisters whose spirit "rappings" were convincing many Americans that human communication with the spirits of the dead was a reality. Isaac Post, himself a medium, devised the alphabet system the Fox sisters used in communicating with spirits by rappings.

While staying at the Posts, Truth herself took part in a table-rapping seance. As a correspondent of the *Anti-Slavery Bugle* explained, the seance was:

> rendered very rich and piquant by the presence of that rare original, Sojourner Truth. Her matter-of-fact simple minded manner of seeking intercourse with spirits, was amusing beyond description. The sounds were faint and low, and given at long intervals, although a complete circle was formed around the table. Sojourner stuck to the belief they could be better heard on the table, and while she listened with all her soul, part of the time with her ear on the floor, called out very unceremoniously, "Come spirit, hop up here on the table, and see if you can make a louder noise." [14]

When Truth moved to the Battle Creek area, several of the Battle Creek Quaker families such as the Willises and Merritts had themselves become advocates of spiritualism—in fact so many of the Battle Creek Quakers were becoming Spiritualists in the 1850s that the Battle Creek Quaker meeting never recovered its strength. These Battle Creek Quakers-becoming-Spiritualists were also strong advocates of blacks and women, as were many Spiritualists. Yet in October, 1857, when Truth was one of the "principal speakers" at a meeting of the Michigan Progressive Friends —a meeting attended by abolitionists, temperance advocates, women's advocates, land reformers, socialists, and Spiritualists—according to the abolitionist Parker Pillsbury, the meeting was dominated by Spiritualists who, unlike the Merritts and Willises, were all too often "morbid" and "bigoted" and voted Democratic. [15]

In Truth's time, Spiritualists played a role similar to that of "New Age" religionists in the late 1900s. The general public often ridiculed Spiritualists, and conservative churches often attacked them; Seventh Day Adventists, who were strong in Battle Creek, were among those who attacked Spiritualists, claiming they talked not to spirits of the dead but to devils. Some abolitionist-feminists such as Lucretia Mott, Parker Pillsbury, and Frederick Douglass were skeptical of Spiritualists. Others tended to avoid identifying with them because they did not wish to antagonize the conventional church. But many abolitionist-feminists, including Garrison, Lucy Stone, and Paulina Wright Davis, despite being dubious of certain claims by particular Spiritualists, tended to believe that spiritualism not only reinforced the Christian belief in immortality, but also was a progressive development that went hand in hand with efforts to improve the status of blacks and of women. By the late 1850s most of the Progressive Friends—a movement especially of dissident Quakers in which Truth and many of her friends took part, in Battle Creek, Rochester, and elsewhere—had accepted spiritualism. By the 1860s the intermingling of Progressive Friends and Spiritualists was so pervasive that it was hard to tell them apart.

According to a recent student of the relation of nineteenth-century feminists to spiritualism, those who took "the most radical position" for women's rights "consistently" became Spiritualists.[16] One reason progressive women did so was that women could become leaders in the Spiritualist movement, as they scarcely could in the conventional church, because authority in spiritualism derived from individual spiritual experience rather than, as in the conventional church, from office or education. This may well have been one of the aspects of spiritualism that appealed to Truth, because her religious authority clearly came from her own experience. Also, although blacks were little related to the white spiritualist movement, they often brought from Africa belief in obligations to spirit ancestors, so that many blacks were likely to be at least somewhat open to spiritualism.

Battle Creek, partly because of the nearby Harmonia community, was a considerable center of spiritualism. Although many people who became Spiritualists remained in conventional churches, from at least 1857 for as long as Truth remained alive, there was a Spiritualist church in Battle Creek proper, and at least five of Truth's once-Quaker abolitionist friends were active in it: Henry Willis, Joseph Merritt, and three of his sons, Richard, Charles, and William Merritt. Not only did Warren Chase sometimes speak in this church, but visiting advocates of blacks' and women's rights, including such friends of Truth as Parker Pillsbury and Giles B. Stebbins, did so as well. While evidence is not available that Truth directly participated in this church, at least she was friendly with its colorful pastor, James M. Peebles, who bought property in Harmonia. He was an impressive man, six-feet-four-inches tall, "slim as a May-pole," with hair flowing over his coat collar, who said his purpose was not to destroy Christianity but to "give it broader scope." He thundered against slavery and whiskey, practiced hypnotism, befriended mediums, and promoted herbal medicines. In 1863 Peebles carried to New York City a letter from Truth to her abolitionist editor friend, Oliver Johnson, who was himself both a Progressive Friend and Spiritualist.[17]

Truth may have lived among the Harmonia Spiritualists comfortably for a time. According to her Harmonia neighbor Warren Chase, writing in 1863 in a widely read national Spiritualist weekly: Truth lives here in "quiet and health." "The neighbors occasionally give her a surprise party," and she often sings to us her "anti-slavery and religious songs, to the delight of all who hear them." Truth "amuses us" with "stories" of her experiences of slavery, "the most touching" of which was how her father died in his old age, alone in the cold, abandoned by his slave master. Chase considered Truth to be "the most remarkable and talented person without education, of any color, that I ever met with." Chase also considered Truth to be a Spiritualist: She "has long since discovered that much which she once attributed to God is the work of guardian spirits, one of which is no doubt her father."[18]

Despite her choosing to live in a Spiritualist community, Truth may have found spiritualism disturbing as well as attractive. Doubtless it was unsettling to her that some spiritualists like Chase were aggressively anti-Christian, and some others were not progressive about social issues. Perhaps also her wrenching experiences with Matthias's Kingdom had led her to be somewhat skeptical, and some of her more sophisticated abolitionist-feminists associates had led her in that direction as well. In any case, Truth is not known to have ever become one of the many Spiritualists who held seances, or went about speaking in a trance, or publicly advocated spiritualism. Truth is not known to have said in her speeches, as Spiritualists sometimes did, that she received specific messages from departed loved ones such as her father. Her available public references to spirits are few and ambiguous. For example, according to a Syracuse newspaper, she said that "the spirit of prophecy" had given her a specific message. At another time, according to a New York City newspaper, she said the "spirits" told her she was as "black as thunder," though why she needed the spirits to tell her that is not evident—perhaps she or the newspaper was spoofing. According to an unconfirmed story, when a false rumor went out that Truth was dead, one of her daughters came home stricken with grief, and was astonished to find her mother still alive to greet her at the door. Truth told her, whether facetiously or not: "Why, honey, chile, ef I was dead, doan you s'pose I'd sen' you word?" According to her perceptive abolitionist friend Lucy Colman, who was herself a Spiritualist sympathizer, Truth was "what the Spiritu-alists call mediumistic," but, Colman said, in seeming contrast to Warren Chase, that her "control," instead of being the spirit of someone who was dead, was God Himself. "She held almost hourly converse with, as she supposed, the God of the universe," Colman explained, "asked his opinion about any contemplated business that she proposed to do, and went by his direction."[19]

Many of Truth's family gathered around her in the Battle Creek area. By 1860 Truth had living with her in her house in Harmonia her daughter Elizabeth Banks, and two grandsons, Elizabeth's son Samuel Banks, about eight, and the grandson Truth had already often looked after, James Caldwell, about sixteen. About this time Elizabeth remarried, this time to William Boyd, and they soon had a son. By the late 1860s, Truth's other two daughters, Diana and Sophia, joined her in the Battle Creek area too, Diana with her husband Jacob Corbin, and Sophia with her husband Tom Schuyler, and their children.[20]

If the Harmonia Seminary was, as has been claimed, for a long time the only school in the Harmonia neighborhood, some of Truth's grand-children probably attended it. We know that blacks did attend there, because the black John Evans, later a barber in Battle Creek, did so.

However, considerable dissension grew up in the Harmonia commu-nity, which eventually helped to break it up. Evans recalled that Truth came to dislike Harmonia, and wanted to leave.[21] By 1860 Hiram Cornell and his family had left, by 1863 Reynolds Cornell and his family, and by 1864 Warren Chase and his family as well. By 1863 Truth often seemed to be staying not in Harmonia but in Battle Creek proper, and by at least 1867 Truth had moved permanently there, leaving her daughter Sophia and her family to occupy her Harmonia house. But Truth continued to relate herself to Spiritualists.

Battle Creek was only a village, almost unknown to the nation when Truth moved to the area. After Harriet Beecher Stowe made Truth well known by writing about her, Truth may have helped to put Battle Creek on the map, almost as much as did afterward the Adventists' Battle Creek Sanitarium, and the breakfast cereal industry that grew out of it, particu-larly the big Kellogg and Post companies.

In both Harmonia and Battle Creek proper, aside from her own family,

Truth primarily associated with whites, as she also had in Northampton. Although there were black churches in Battle Creek, she did not identify with them. Her grandchildren attended school primarily with white children and played primarily with whites. On summer evenings she took delight in strolling with one of her grandsons along the tree-shaded Battle Creek streets, ready to stop along the way to chat with her mostly white neighbors.[22]

Having her family around her meant not only joy for Truth but also burden. Several of them lived with her in her house in Battle Creek, as they had in Harmonia, and they were often poor, as she was herself. When they could find work in Battle Creek, various members of her family were employed as domestics, cooks, laborers, farm laborers, mechanics, or the like. At various times some of them went elsewhere to work, as if they could not find adequate work in Battle Creek. Her daughters Elizabeth and Sophia temporarily went back East, to work in the Rochester, New York, area, as did some of Truth's grandsons. Once Truth took her grandson Samuel to Toledo, Ohio, hoping to place him in work there.[23]

Truth's daughters, like herself, remained illiterate, and none of her family is known to have become especially well educated. None became known for identifying with reform or with either Quakers or Spiritualists. Elizabeth had trouble with her second husband, William Boyd, taking him to court in 1872 for deserting her, neglecting to support his family, and leaving them a burden on the public; he pleaded guilty. (One can imagine that Truth, with her successful experience in court cases, encouraged Elizabeth to take him to court.) Although a friendly visitor once reported that all Truth's grandchildren were "promising," Diana's son Jacob Corbin was sent in 1878 first to a "county house" and then to a state school for problem youths in Coldwater. When he was released the next year, he was indentured to Truth.[24] Truth's achievements stand out against her often pinched and troubled family life.

9

Underground Railroader?

"I'm on my way to Canada,
That cold, but happy land."

When Truth was in her old age, a reporter once asked her whether she had helped slaves escape through the Underground Railroad. She replied, "Yes, indeed, chile." But she gave no details and seemed to turn quickly to something else.[1]

Many twentieth-century publications have asserted that Truth participated significantly in the Underground Railroad without supplying details of where or when she did so. For example, a history of the Railroad claimed that Truth was one of the Railroad's "major personalities." The scholars Jane and William Pease claimed that Truth was as well known "on fugitive escape routes" as "on the lecture circuit." A study of women's power claimed that Sojourner Truth and Harriet Tubman both "went back time and again, with huge prices on their heads, to free other slaves on their own plantations," as if both Truth and Tubman had come from Southern plantations. An advertisement in *Ebony* magazine presented a picture of Truth as a commanding figure, underneath which the only claim it made for her fame was that she was "Leader of the Underground Railway Movement."[2]

It seems unlikely that Truth could have participated significantly in the Underground Railroad while she was a slave or soon after she was freed. In these years it is doubtful if she had yet developed the command of herself or the antislavery ideology to enable her to take such radical, dangerous action for others. Also, while she was still living in Ulster County and in New York City, she lacked a home of her own in which to hide slaves, and is not yet known to have become close to anyone active in the Railroad.

It was only in 1844, when Truth settled in the utopian Northampton Association, that she first clearly came close to Underground Railroaders. One of the impressive members of the Northampton Association, the black David Ruggles, had previously been the principal agent of the Underground Railroad in New York City, hiding fugitives and planning how they would move on up the Hudson River or into New England. After the association broke up, Ruggles established a water-cure spa in Northampton, and secretly used it to hide fugitive slaves. Also operating an underground station in Northampton was Samuel L. Hill, a leader of the association and a major benefactor of Truth. Possibly she saw fugitives in Ruggles's or Hill's care, and even helped feed or nurse them, but there is no evidence that at any time during the thirteen years Truth lived in Northampton, she took any part in the Underground Railroad.[3]

By the time Truth began to speak publicly against slavery, she owned a house of her own, and she had developed a thoroughgoing opposition to slavery that encouraged her to care about fugitive slaves. In 1851 Truth said those who supported the law by sending fugitive slaves back to their masters "did not know God."[4] In 1853, when Truth spent several days with Harriet Beecher Stowe in Andover, Massachusetts, Truth was fond of singing a song about a fugitive slave, a song that Harriet Tubman sang when she was guiding fugitives north:

> I'm on my way to Canada,
> That cold, but happy land;
> The dire effects of slavery
> I can no longer stand.
>
> O righteous Father
> Do look down on me,
> And help me on to Canada,
> Where colored folks are free![5]

While Truth was travelling, she stayed in Rochester, New York, with Isaac and Amy Post, who hid fugitive slaves on their way to Canada.

Frederick Douglass, who lived in Rochester much of the time, sent fugitives to the Posts. The Rochester abolitionist Lucy Colman claimed that nearly all the fugitives who fled from anywhere in the States to Canada knew Amy Post's name. Truth might have seen fugitives in Rochester, and perhaps incidentally helped them. But neither the Posts, Douglass, Colman, nor anyone else likely to be familiar with the Railroad in Rochester is known to have claimed that Truth assisted in it in any way.[6]

Truth was so well known among persons who were likely to be involved in the Underground Railroad, or who were likely to comment on it afterward, that if any shred of hard evidence turned up connecting her to it, they would be likely to mention it. Among the many other persons Truth came to know in her travels who assisted fugitive slaves in varying degrees were the Unitarian pastor Samuel J. May, of Syracuse, New York; the voluble Stephen and Abby Foster, Worcester, Massachusetts; antislavery editor Marius Robinson, Salem, Ohio; and the dominant figure in the Underground Railroad in Philadelphia, the black William Still. Nevertheless, evidence is lacking that Truth assisted any of these friends, or anyone else she visited in her travels, in harboring fugitives, in protecting them, or in guiding them on their way farther north. This is so although Truth spoke on the same platform with many of these friends, visited many of them in their homes, and admired many of them warmly. This is also true even though in her speaking she often recounted experiences of her own life, which would seem to have made it natural for her, at least by 1865 when all slaves had been freed and there was scarcely need any longer to protect Railroad secrets, to say publicly that she had worked in the Railroad, if she had.

In 1857 when Truth moved her permanent home from Northampton to Battle Creek, she might have done so, it has been hinted, because Quakers invited her there to participate in the Underground Railroad. A Detroit newspaper claimed in 1915 that while Truth was living in Battle Creek, she "helped hundreds of slaves" escape to Canada, and that it was an "open secret" that she did so.[7] Others have made similar claims.

Battle Creek was an important station on the Railroad. By the time Truth settled in Battle Creek, however, its most active Railroad days were already over, better routes having developed from the Ohio River to Canada that bypassed Battle Creek. The black Harriet Tucker recalled afterward that her family sheltered fugitives in Battle Creek in association with the Quaker Erastus Hussey, but she made no mention of Truth's participating. Erastus Hussey himself, the major figure in the Battle Creek Railroad, recalled those who worked with him in the Railroad, but did not mention Truth. In his recollections, the black William Lambert, an outstanding Railroad figure in Detroit—where some of the fugitives who passed through Battle Creek were also likely to pass en route to Canada—named many co-workers, but not Truth. Berenice Lowe, a close student of Truth's life in Michigan, wrote in 1956 that Battle Creek Quakers "may have found work for Sojourner to do" in the Railroad. "Casual newspaper biographies mention that this is so, but there is no proof."[8]

Moreover, the *Narrative* of Truth's life, in its various versions, except for reprinting a newspaper report of Truth's offhand claim that she helped in the Railroad, did not claim that she worked with the Underground Railroad.[9] This is true even though the *Narrative* was written with Truth's assistance, considerably from her own recollections. This is also true even though its authors, Olive Gilbert for the earliest editions and Frances Titus for the later ones, were themselves familiar with Truth's life in Northampton and Battle Creek. If Gilbert, because she wrote in 1850, had been restrained by the desire to protect both Railroad secrets and Truth herself, certainly Titus, writing about 1875 and later, after all slaves had been freed, would not have been similarly restrained.

In addition, most histories of the Underground Railroad do not claim that Truth participated. Also significantly, some writers who have written about Truth's life in detail have insisted flatly that Truth did not participate in the Railroad, notably Saunders Redding and Hertha Pauli.[10] The absence of any specific details to indicate that Truth participated anywhere in the Railroad is impressive. Despite Truth's offhand claim that she participated, and despite claims by many recent writers that she participated extensively, we conclude that she did not participate significantly in the Underground Railroad.

Why, then, did Truth not participate significantly in the Railroad? Would not participation have been natural for her? It was down-to-earth, person-to-person action such as might be expected of her. It would help some of God's most unfortunate children to recover the freedom she believed God gives His children as a matter of right.

Did Truth not participate in the Railroad because she feared she might be too easily identified, caught, and imprisoned, as her friend David Ruggles had been? She might have been easy to catch because she was conspicuous not only as a public speaker but also as a very black woman who was nearly six feet tall. Yet when she was speaking against slavery in Indiana, and supporters of slavery threatened to burn the building where she was speaking and "blow out our brains," she insisted on continuing to speak.[11] Fear does not seem to be a likely reason for her not participating in the Railroad.

Perhaps Truth felt that becoming part of the Railroad would force her to trust other people too much for her safety when, from experience, she knew she could be wrong in her judgment concerning which people to trust. She might also have believed that God had called her to speak out for freedom, while He called others to do other important work, like that of the Railroad.

Possibly also Truth hesitated to defy law directly. It is true that she, like many abolitionists, had learned to abhor the U.S. Constitution for its support of slavery. As Truth once explained, when she took hold of the Constitution, and looked in it for her rights as a black, she found none there. So she asked God, "What ails dis Constitution?" God replied to her, she reported, "Sojourner, dare is a little weasel [weevil] in it."[12] However, as we have seen, certain laws had helped her in ways that inclined her to regard law favorably, such as the laws that freed her from slavery, recovered her son from Alabama, and protected her from the Folgers' charges. She might have had more respect for law than many abolitionists who were willing to defy the law by taking part in the Railroad.

Finally, Truth may not have participated significantly because in some respects she was too outspoken, too open, or too individualistic. Particularly after her reformist speaking career was well launched, she freely scolded all kinds of people, both blacks and whites, associates and enemies. Perhaps she would not have been as good at keeping secrets as Railroaders needed to be. She was somewhat of a loose cannon; who knew what she would say next? She herself did not seem to know, explaining once, "De Lo'd just puts de words into my mouth." She usually went about speaking on her own, as, she boasted, a "free agent."[13] Strikingly, once she left New York, even though she joined intentional communities, she avoided identifying with organizations: There is no convincing evidence that she ever became an agent or officer of an anti-slavery society, a women's rights society, a temperance society, a women's club, or a church. If she was too individualistic to tie herself to such organizations as these, she might have deliberately shied away from tying herself in any significant way to such a shifting, shadowy, illegal network as the Underground Railroad.

10

Romanticized: Libyan Sibyl

"I don't wan' to hear about that old symbol."

At the world's fair in London in 1862, a statue inspired by Sojourner Truth became a center of attention. Harriet Beecher Stowe had played a role in the statue's creation.

Several years earlier when Stowe had been visiting Rome, she attended a breakfast at the house of the sculptor William Wetmore Story, of Massachusetts, a son of a U.S. Supreme Court Justice. Story was then working on a statue of the African queen, Cleopatra. Striving to find a style that was distinctly his own, Story rejected the idea of portraying Cleopatra in a conventionally elegant, cool Greek style, choosing instead, it seemed to Stowe, to portray her as having "slumbering weight and fullness of passion" like a "heavy thunder-cloud" that "is charged with electricity."

At the breakfast, Stowe happened to tell Story about another "African" woman, Sojourner Truth, whom Stowe remembered vividly from Truth's visit to her in Andover. What Story learned about Truth, as he listened, appealed to his imagination. According to Stowe, it "led him into the deeper recesses of the African nature—those unexplored depths of being and feeling, mighty and dark as the gigantic depths of tropical forests, mysterious as the hidden rivers and mines of that burning continent whose life-history is yet to be." Stowe romanticized Africa, Africans, and Sojourner Truth, and Story warmly responded. A few days later Story told Stowe that he had conceived of a statue to be based on Truth that he would call the "Libyan Sibyl," after the name of a character from classical mythology.

Two years later, Stowe, again in Rome, found that Story had finished sculpting his Cleopatra, and was already moving on to another African statue, his Libyan Sibyl. Story invited Stowe to visit him again, "and repeat to him the history of Sojourner Truth." Stowe did so, and Story showed her a clay model of his Libyan Sibyl.[1]

By the summer of 1861, Story was putting his Sibyl into marble, and feeling it was his best work. He already planned to send it to the World Exposition in London the next year, and threatened that if it did not get favorable attention he would give up sculpting.[2]

Truth herself did not know that Story was using her as an imaginary model for his statue. Story is not known ever to have seen Truth. It is even doubtful that Story had seen photographs of her, for Truth was not yet having photographs of herself taken to sell. An engraving of her was available in the frontispiece of her *Narrative,* which Story could have seen; but it was only a bust, while the statue he was making was a full figure. In any event, his calling the statue Libyan Sibyl, and not Sojourner Truth, meant that he was not necessarily portraying her directly at all. He was simply inspired by Truth as Stowe had described her to him.

Indeed, the Libyan Sibyl was a character from Greek and Roman mythology, having the god-given power to foretell the future. According to a Roman version, there were ten sibyls, all of them women, the Libyan Sibyl being the earliest of the ten, from before the Trojan War.

By using Truth as an inspiration for his Libyan Sibyl, Story was taking artistic liberty, as he knew. By ancestry Truth was not north African, not a Libyan who was likely to have relatively light skin and Caucasian features, but instead central African, dark skinned, with Negroid features.

Story wanted his Sibyl to be of the race of those who were often enslaved. Story wanted his Sibyl, he said, to be an "anti-slavery sermon in stone." Yet by producing his statue in white marble, he gave his Sibyl white skin. Moreover, he shied away from giving her black central-African features, although he seemed defensive about having done so: In 1861, Story wrote a friend that he had made his Sibyl "full lipped, long-eyed, low-browed and lowering," with the largely-developed limbs of the African. She sits on a rock, her legs crossed, leaning forward. . . . It is a very massive figure, big-shouldered, large-bosomed, with nothing of the Venus in it, but, as far as I could make it, luxuriant and heroic. She is looking out of her black eyes into futurity and sees the terrible fate of her race. This is the theme of the figure—Slavery on the horizon, and I made her head as melancholy and severe as possible, not at all shirking the real African type . . . —Libyan Africa of course, not Congo.[3]

Not only did Story present his Sibyl as unlike a central African black, but he also made her reflective, passive, brooding. Stowe had doubtless led Story to conceive of his Sibyl in this way.

As we have seen, Harriet Beecher Stowe first met Truth in 1853, when Truth made an uninvited visit to Stowe at her house in Andover, Massachusetts. Stowe found her so fascinating that she invited her to stay for several days. Not until ten years later, in 1863, did Stowe finally publish an account of Truth's visit in the *Atlantic Monthly*. In her article, Stowe followed Story's lead calling Truth the "Libyan Sibyl."

In her famous novel *Uncle Tom's Cabin,* Stowe had given a classic white expression to a "romantic" view of race, based on biological determinism. She had presented blacks as gentle, childlike, forgiving, and natural Christians, inherently different from Anglo-Saxons.

In keeping with this view, in her article on Truth, Stowe made Truth more of a preacher than a reformer, one who preached over and over on the same theme—"When I found Jesus"—and was given to singing about the "glory" that was to come in heaven. Stowe pictured her as inclined to "reverie," suggesting that there was a passive, inward aspect to her, and said that both her humor and her eyes were "gloomy"; it was especially Stowe's indication of these passive and gloomy qualities that Story had seized on for his purpose. Stowe also found Truth eccentric, but romanticized her eccentricity, portraying her as "warm," "droll," "shrewd," and having more "personal presence" than anyone she had ever come across before. Stowe emphasized her African origins (Stowe mistakenly said she was born in Africa), declaring that Truth stood among the company at Stowe's house, "calm and erect, as one of her own native palm-trees waving alone in the desert," when in fact Truth had probably never seen a palm tree or a desert in her life.[4]

It may help us to see Stowe's view of Truth in perspective if we compare it with Frederick Douglass's view of her. Both Douglass and

Stowe knew Truth from early in her public career. Douglass, like Truth, was an ex-slave and a radical advocate of black and women's rights. He worked with Truth as a colleague, although not a close one, sometimes speaking on the same platform with her. Stowe, from a substantial Yankee family, while a powerful opponent of slavery, was not a radical advocate of either black or women's rights, and scarcely worked with Truth as a colleague. Indeed, it is not certain whether Stowe ever heard her speak on a public platform.

Douglass first met Truth when she was at the Northampton utopian community. As he recalled later, she was respected there, for she was "honest, industrious, and amiable," thus portraying Truth as having down-to-earth qualities that Stowe skipped over lightly in her portrayal of Truth. Like Stowe, Douglass found Truth eccentric, but unlike Stowe, Douglass did not romanticize her eccentricity or relate it to Africa. Douglass, like Garrison and other radical abolitionists, was not so much a romantic or biological determinist on race as he was a a cultural determinist, holding that although all races have the same basic psychological and moral capabilities, the behavioral differences among them are due fundamentally to cultural differences.

Douglass found Truth "strange"—she was a "strange compound of wit and wisdom, of wild enthusiasm and flint-like common sense." He also found over the years as they worked together, that she differed from him and tried to change him: He found her seeming "to feel it her duty" to "trip" him in his speeches, and to "ridicule" his efforts to elevate his cultivation. Douglass, one senses, felt uncomfortable with Truth's illiteracy, and was embarrassed by her choosing to play the role of an ignorant, naive, amusing child of nature, whereas Stowe delighted in it, and played it up. But Douglass, unlike Stowe, emphasized Truth's contribution to the cause of freedom. When Truth died, Douglass commented that she was "remarkable" for her "independence and courageous self-assertion," characteristics that Stowe scarcely noticed.[5]

Other of Truth's abolitionist-feminist colleagues looked on Truth more as Douglass did than as Stowe and Story did. Garrison, Parker Pillsbury, Lucy Stone, and Elizabeth Cady Stanton did not see Truth as primarily passive, brooding, and reflective. They looked on Truth more nearly as sprightly, enthusiastic, optimistic, and sometimes even defiant.

• • •

In 1862, Pope Pius IX, as head of the Papal States, arranged to send Story's "Libyan Sibyl," along with other works of art produced in Rome, to London to be exhibited in the World Exposition in the Roman Pavilion. The statue became Story's first major triumph as a sculptor.

Story's Sibyl, said the London *Athenaeum,* is a "secret-keeping . . . dame," a characterization that might fit a sibyl better than Truth. To keep her secrets close, the *Athenaeum* continued, "she rests her shut mouth upon one closed palm, as if holding the African mystery deep in the brooding brain that looks out through mournful, warning eyes."[6]

In 1863, the year of the Emancipation Proclamation, *Harper's Magazine* declared that for Americans, Story's statue has become a national symbol: "It is our peculiar interest in the African race at this time which nationalizes Story's statue of The Libyan Sibyl." Soon afterward, James Jackson Jarves, an artist friend of Story who knew that Story had based his Sibyl on Truth, described it to be lofty, creative, and daring. Near the end of the Civil War, according to the urbane Massachusetts abolitionist Lydia Maria Child, the war had made concern about Africans so pervasive that even artists were "breathing" the concern: "Passing through the soul of Story, it came forth in the shape of an African Sibyl; and so strangely fascinating was the subject, that the statue attracted more attention than any other in the grand exhibition." Many years later, the novelist Henry James, writing on his friend Story, regarded the Libyan Sibyl as his best sculpture, and accounted for its great popularity by explaining that it told a rich, warm, dramatic tale in stone, which was what the public wanted.[7]

Even though many people did not at first know that Truth had inspired Story's statue, in time it contributed to Truth's being better known. More directly contributing to Truth's reputation, however, was Stowe's 1863 "Libyan Sibyl" article in the *Atlantic,* which told how Truth had inspired Story's statue.

Truth herself did not seem much interested in Stowe's article. She did not like having it read to her. According to a Detroit friend of hers, "She would never listen to Mrs. Stowe's Libyan Sibyl. Oh! She would say, 'I don't wan' to hear about that old symbol; read me something that is going on now.' "[8]

However, after the publication of Stowe's article, Truth was often called "the Libyan Sibyl." Elizabeth Cady Stanton called her that. Theodore Tilton called her just "Sibyl." Parker Pillsbury called her "Ethiopian

Sibyl." Newspapers often referred to her by such variations as "colored Sibyl," "sable Sibyl," "American Sibyl," or "ancient Sibyl." Once in a public announcement, Truth described herself as the "well known Mrs. Stowe's African Sybil [sic.]."[9]

The Springfield *Republican* insisted that "Libyan Sibyl" was not a suitable name for Truth because she was not a classical Sibyl but a Christian one, "and more devoted to good words and works than to obscure predictions." Indeed, if the word "Sibyl" suggested a person who made obscure predictions, it is a question how appropriate the name was for Truth. She only occasionally made predictions, and they were more likely to be down to earth than obscure. One of her characteristic predictions foreshadowed that the time would come when women would be legislators, along with men, and make their "power" felt. Another pointed out that the time would come when blacks would hold "prominent offices" in this country, and be God's "humble instruments" for "savin' dis nation from disgrace an' destruction."[10]

If the word "Sibyl" suggested a mysterious figure who brooded over ambiguous messages from Heaven, as some classical prophets were portrayed as doing, it seems only slightly appropriate for Truth. Most of the time she seemed to be less brooding and mysterious than forthright. She did not usually seem to feel that what God was saying to her was ambiguous. Although sometimes, when she was reporting what God was saying to her, Truth used parables and humor that could seem ambiguous to others, usually she spoke authoritatively, delivering bold messages from a God she was sure was compassionate and just.

Both Story and Stowe desired to portray Sojourner Truth as fascinating, deep, spiritual. Both artists were trying to reach educated, sensitive, middle- and upper-class Americans, and to awaken in them sympathy for blacks. In considerable degree both artists succeeded. They succeeded because the romantic, refined appeal they made was the kind to which many Americans were ready to respond. Many Americans were more willing to see Truth as passive than active, African rather than American, lofty rather than down to earth. Many were more willing to see her as brooding and secret rather than as aggressive and willing to threaten the established order. Story and Stowe, in the process of romanticizing Truth to suit American tastes, helped to arouse sympathy for Truth and blacks at large. Yet in retrospect, if they helped to cast light on some aspects of who Truth was, they helped to cloud others.

11

With President Lincoln and the Freedmen

"I felt that I was in the presence of a friend."

By early 1864, Truth had decided to visit Washington. As she put it in a letter at the time, she wanted to visit Washington "to see the freedmen of my people. This is a great and glorious day. It is good to live in it & behold the shackles fall from the manacled limbs."[1] The people she wished to see were blacks in the rebel states who had recently been freed by Lincoln's Emancipation Proclamation. Amid the chaos of the Civil War, many of them, especially from Virginia, were crowding in confusion into Washington, often hungry and lost, looking for refuge. As became apparent later, Truth also had been dreaming for a long time of visiting Washington to see President Lincoln.

At the beginning of the war, Truth had been disturbed by Lincoln's insistence that his purpose in the war was only to preserve the Union, not to free the slaves. Nevertheless she had supported him, hoping that he would change his view. By 1863, although Lincoln by his Emancipation Proclamation had freed the slaves only in the rebel states, not in the loyal slave states, according to a friend, Truth's "faith is strong that God's hand is in this war, and that it will end in the [complete] destruction of slavery."[2]

As it became clear at about this same time that the Lincoln administration was at last welcoming black troops to help fight for the Union, Truth perceived a sardonic aspect to this policy: "Just as it was when I was a slave—the niggers always have to clean up after the white folks." On the other hand, she welcomed the enlistment of blacks as "the most hopeful feature of the war." She was delighted that blacks would have this chance to fight "to redeem de white people from de curse dat God has sent upon them." When Massachusetts organized a Colored Regiment, she was proud that her grandson James Caldwell volunteered for it, saying to her, "Now is our time, Grandmother, to prove that we are men."[3]

In the fall of 1863, when Michigan also had organized a black regiment, and its volunteers were training in a camp in Detroit, she decided to collect contributions for a Thanksgiving dinner for them. Walking about Battle Creek asking for contributions, by chance she asked one man who refused, expressing his unhappiness with the war and "the nigger." Startled, she asked him who he was, and he replied: "I am the only son of my mother." "I am glad there are no more," she rejoined, and walked on.[4] She succeeded, however, in collecting substantial contributions, as from various merchants, from her long-time friends the Merritts, Willises, and Tituses, and from a Dutch Reformed pastor whom she often visited to express her anxieties about the war.

When Thanksgiving came, she herself took the food she had gathered to the black soldiers at their camp in Detroit, Camp Ward. The colonel in charge ordered them into line for her, and she gave them a patriotic speech. A few days later she went back to the camp again to speak to the soldiers, as had been arranged, but this time so many whites crowded about to hear her that she had to promise to come back yet again to speak to the black soldiers.[5]

By this time she had composed a song for black soldiers to sing. It was to the tune of "John Brown," a tune everybody knew, the same tune Julia Ward Howe used the year before to compose the "Battle Hymn of the Republic." Truth sang it to the soldiers at the camp:

> We are the valiant soldiers who've 'listed for the war;
> We are fighting for the Union, we are fighting for the law;
> We can shoot a rebel farther than a white man ever saw,
>   As we go marching on.
>   (Chorus:)
> Glory, glory, hallelujah! Glory, glory, hallelujah!
> Glory, glory, hallelujah, as we go marching on.
>
> Look there above the center, where the flag is waving bright;
> We are going out of slavery, we are bound for freedom's light;

We mean to show Jeff Davis how the Africans can fight,
  As we go marching on. (Chorus)

Father Abraham has spoken, and the message has been sent;
The prison doors have opened, and out the prisoners went
To join the sable army of African descent,
  As we go marching on. (Chorus)[6]

In this song, she included the phrase "fighting for the law," illustrating her characteristic respect for the law. She did not put into the song even a hint of her having any pacifist reservations about killing the enemy, such as she had once had. A historian in the 1890s claimed—a claim which has not been confirmed—that this song "became a favorite with all the colored soldiers" fighting for the Union, and that one veteran told him he had heard them sing it as they entered a battle.[7]

Truth remained in Detroit for several weeks, into February 1864, staying with friends. One of them reported at this time that "her whole soul is aglow" with the great issues raised by the war. When someone protested Lincoln's delay in freeing all the slaves, Truth replied: "Oh, wait, chile! have patience! It takes a great while to turn about this great ship of state." In two letters written at this time, she mentioned she wanted to visit Washington to see the recently freed slaves, without saying she also wanted to see Lincoln.[8]

After a few months at home, in the summer of 1864 Truth set out for Washington. She made a long, meandering trip, taking along her four-teen-year-old grandson Samuel Banks to help read and write for her. By July, she passed through Detroit. In August she was in Boston where she met Harriet Tubman, who had been in the South behind Confederate lines as a spy for the U.S. Army; Truth tried to persuade Tubman that Lincoln was a real friend to blacks, but Tubman insisted he was not because he allowed black soldiers to be paid less than white soldiers.[9] By September 25 Truth was in Orange, New Jersey, speaking for the reelec-tion of Lincoln, and expected to speak in Newark and Trenton as well. A few days later she was in Washington where, instead of merely seeing the freed slaves, as she had said she would, she began working with them.

On October 29, 1864, Truth visited Lincoln at the White House. At this time for any president to welcome black visitors, as Lincoln was occasionally doing, was new.

• • •

Much of what we know about both her early work with the freedmen and her visit to President Lincoln is from two of her letters, a private one of November 3, which still exists in its original form, and the other, a fuller letter, of November 17, which was intended for publication and was published at the time.

Truth's letter of November 3 was written from a government camp for freedmen, on an island in the Potomac River, opposite Washington. It was written to her friend Amy Post in Rochester, addressed to her affectionately as "daughter." In the letter Truth seemed exuberant:

Mason's Island, Virginia, November 3d, 1864

My Dear Daughter:

And here I am in the midst of the freedmen, women, and children—and I am in a comfortable place here at the house of Rev. D. B. Nichols, Superintendent of Freedmen [at the government camp for freedmen here] and am treated very kindly indeed. I do not know but what I shall stay here on the island all winter and go around among the freedmen's camps. They are all delighted to hear me talk. I think I am doing good. I am needed here. I see that the people here (white) [government employees] are only here for the loaves and fishes while the freedmen get the scales and crusts, and Mr. Nichols sees it too.

I have had ... opportunity to talk with Mr. Nichols and his wife and they have told me things that would render [rend] a heart of stone. And to hear what Mr. Nichols and wife have gone through in trying to elevate these folks, it is awful. These office seekers tries to root every one out that try to elevate these people and make them know they are free. . . .

I am going around among the colored folks and find out who it is sells the clothing to them that is sent to them [as free gifts] from the North. They will tell me for they think a good deal of me. . . .

Sammie and I are perfectly well and he is delighted with the place. He thinks he can be useful.

I don't calculate to ask the government for any thing, only what I have to eat, for the colored people must be raised out of bondage. . . .

I have been to see the President and was there three hours. Mrs. Coleman [Lucy Colman of Rochester] was with me [at the White House] all the forenoon from eight in the morning until twelve at noon. He put his name in my book and invited me to come again. . . . I calculate to go and see President Lincoln again. I hope all will do all they can in putting him in as President again. . . .

I have had two meetings in Wash. and two here at Mason's Island. Those in Wash. were for the benefit of the Freedmen's Aid Society. They took twenty-five cents at the door from everyone and gave me some of the money. . . .

Sojourner Truth[10]

Truth seemed especially exuberant because she felt that she could be useful to the freedmen. Though her visit to Lincoln pleased her, she did not particularly dwell on it, nor did she relate it to the work she was doing for the freedmen. In this letter, written only five days after she saw Lincoln, Truth indicates that she was already staying at the house of an official who was working with the freedmen, had twice spoken in Washington on behalf of the freedmen, had twice spoken to the freedmen themselves, and had decided that the freedmen needed her. Since all of this probably took more than five days to accomplish, it seems likely that she began to work with the freedmen before she met Lincoln.

Not long after writing this letter, Truth went to speak at another nearby government camp, this one in Arlington, Virginia, called Freedmen's Village, where about 1,600 freed slaves were being given temporary refuge. When the superintendent of the village, Capt. George B. Carse, a volunteer soldier from Pennsylvania, went to hear her, the first words he heard her say, he recalled, were "Be clean, be clean, for cleanliness is a part of godliness." Truth also told the freed people, Carse reported,

that they must learn to be independent—learn industry and economy—and above all strive to show the people that they could be something. She urged them to embrace for their children all opportunities of education and advancement. In fact she talked to them as a white person could not, for they would have been offended with such plain truths from any other source. I think she will do much good among them. She is one of them—she can call them her people—go into their houses and tell them much they should know. . . . She goes into their cabins with her knitting in her hand, and while she talks with them she knits. Few of them know how to knit, and but few how to make a loaf of bread, or anything of the kind. She wants to teach the old people how to knit, for they have no employment, and they will be much happier if usefully employed.

Carse arranged for Truth to live in a cabin at the village rent free, and also use another building, which could hold 200 people, for whatever she wished.[11] Carse made no mention of Lincoln's having placed her in this work, as he would have been likely to do if it had been true.

On November 17, Truth wrote from Freedmen's Village, reporting much more about her visit with Lincoln. This letter, composed with more care than her letter of November 3, Truth addressed to Rowland Johnson, a New Jersey Quaker and supporter of Lincoln whom she had visited on her way to Washington, and gave him permission to publish as much of it as he thought suitable. Johnson evidently sent the letter to both the *National Anti-Slavery Standard* in New York and the *Liberator* in Boston, both abolitionist weeklies which had long been printing news of Truth. The *Standard* published the letter on December 17, 1864, the *Liberator* on December 23. The *Standard* version, being fuller, is probably more authentic:

Freedmen's Village, Va., Nov. 17, 1864

Dear Friend:

... It was about 8 o'clock, a. m., when I called on the President. Upon entering his reception room we found about a dozen persons in waiting, among them two colored women. I had quite a pleasant time waiting until he was disengaged, and enjoyed his conversation with others; he showed as much kindness and consideration to the colored persons as to the whites—if there was any difference, more. . . .

The President was seated at his desk. Mrs. C[olman] said to him, "This is Sojourner Truth, who has come all the way from Michigan to see you." He then arose, gave me his hand, made a bow, and said, "I am pleased to see you."

I said to him, "Mr. President, when you first took your seat I feared you would be torn to pieces, for I likened you unto Daniel, who was thrown into the lions' den; and if the lions did not tear you into pieces, I knew that it would be God that had saved you; and I said if He spared me I would see you before the four years expired, and He has done so, and now I am here to see you for myself."

He then congratulated me on my having been spared. Then I said: "I appreciate you, for you are the best President who has ever taken the seat." He replied thus: "I expect you have reference to my having emancipated the slaves in my proclamation. But," said he, mentioning the names of several of his predecessors (and among them emphatically that of Washington), "they were all just as good, and would have done just as he had done if the time had come. If the people over the river (pointing across the Potomac) had behaved themselves, I could not have done what I have; but they did not, and I was compelled to these things." I then said: "I thank God that you were the instrument selected by him and the people to do it."

He then showed me the Bible presented to him by the colored people of Baltimore, of which you have no doubt seen a description. I have seen it for myself, and it is beautiful beyond description. After I had looked it over, I said to him: "This is beautiful indeed; the colored people have given this to the Head of the government, and that government once sanctioned laws that would not permit its people to learn enough to enable them to read this Book. And for what? Let them answer who can."

I must say, and I am proud to say, that I never was treated by any one with more kindness and cordiality than were shown to me by that great and good man,

Abraham Lincoln, by the grace of God President of the United States for four years more. He took my little book, and with the same hand that signed the death-warrant of slavery, he wrote as follows:

"For Aunty Sojourner Truth,
"Oct. 29, 1864 A. Lincoln."

As I was taking my leave, he arose and took my hand, and said he would be pleased to have me call again. I felt that I was in the presence of a friend, and I now thank God from the bottom of my heart that I always have advocated his cause, and have done it openly and boldly. I shall feel still more in duty bound to do so in time to come. May God assist me.

Now I must tell you something of this place. . . . I find many of the [freed] women very ignorant in relation to house-keeping, as most of them were instructed in field labor, but not in household duties. They all seem to think a great deal of me, and want to learn the way we live in the North. I am listened to with attention and respect, and from all things I judge it is the will of both God and the people that I should remain. . . .

Ask Mr. Oliver Johnson to please send me the *Standard* while I am here, as many of the colored people like to hear what is going on, and to know what is being done for them. Sammy, my grandson, reads for them. We are both well, and happy, and feel that we are in good employment. I find plenty of friends.

Your friend,
Sojourner Truth

In this letter, unlike the previous one, Truth emphasized her enthusiasm for Lincoln. Still she made no connection between her visit to Lincoln and her work with the freed slaves.

Many claims about Truth's association with Lincoln go beyond what she put in these two letters. The claims that have been most frequently repeated are those that most deeply fulfill the psychological and political needs of Truth, her friends, and the friends of Lincoln, desires that sometimes changed over the years and sometimes contradicted each other.

To many abolitionists, the image of Lincoln welcoming a poor, illiterate, black grandmother to the White House was appealing. In the 1870s, Truth's old friend Oliver Johnson, the wartime editor of the *National Anti-Slavery Standard,* asserted that Lincoln had "treated her with the utmost respect, and even reverence." However, more recently in the activist 1960s, when sit-ins were a powerful weapon against segregation, an article in a historical journal claimed that when Truth went to see Lincoln, she sat in his office "quietly and resolutely" as if she were unwelcome there, until he was willing to see her, and that thus Truth staged "the first Sit-In."[12]

What really happened, as far as we can tell from the most authentic early sources available, is this: Soon after Truth arrived in Washington, she attempted to secure an appointment with Lincoln, but found that she was unable to do so on her own. Truth then asked Lucy Colman—a white, Massachusetts-born abolitionist, whose permanent home was in Rochester, and who at the time was teaching freed slaves in Washington —to arrange an appointment for her. Colman admired Truth, once saying that Truth had never "disgraced" her name,[13] and was willing to help her. After some time, Colman, using Mrs. Lincoln's black dressmaker, Elizabeth Keckley, as a go-between, succeeded in arranging an appointment. When Colman finally took Truth to the White House on October 29, the two women had to wait several hours until it was their turn to see the busy president. Having every expectation of being welcomed, they were not "sitting-in" in protest.

When the president was finally able to see Truth and Colman, as Colman recalled in a letter shortly afterward on November 1, Lincoln received Truth with "pleasing cordiality." However, Colman, in her 1891 memoirs, written when she was free of any compulsion to make Lincoln look better, gave a less favorable impression of Lincoln's attitude toward Truth. Colman reported that Lincoln did not believe in the equality of the races, and "Mr. Lincoln was not himself with this colored woman: he had no funny story for her, he called her Aunty, as he would his washerwoman."[14]

In 1940 an article in *Opportunity* magazine made the large claim that Lincoln "always welcomed" Truth at the White House. However, while Lincoln was president, blacks were sometimes excluded from the White House on racial grounds, and on at least one occasion, Truth herself was barred from a public reception there, according to both Colman and Fred Tomkins. A British journalist, Tomkins happened to be present at the reception on February 25, 1865, when he saw Truth being refused admission because she was black. Two days later, when Tomkins interviewed Lincoln, Tomkins expressed his regret that Truth was "the only person I saw who had been refused admission." In reply, Lincoln "expressed his sorrow, and said that he had often seen her, [and] that it should not occur again." In fact, Tomkins said, Lincoln sent "for her a few days afterwards."[15]

Despite this report by Tomkins, Truth probably visited Lincoln only once, at least in a formal, prearranged interview, though she may have seen him casually at other times, as at public receptions. Truth herself often referred to her October 29 visit with Lincoln as if it was the only time she had talked with him, at least significantly. Frances Titus, who was as close to Truth as anyone in Battle Creek, wrote long afterward that Truth's first meeting with Lincoln was the "only meeting" she had with him, and quoted Truth as explaining that after her visit to Lincoln she became "deeply interested" in her work with the freedmen, and "never repeated my visit."[16] Altogether, available evidence indicates that although Truth was not "always welcomed" at Lincoln's White House, nor necessarily welcomed with "reverence," she was clearly welcomed— even if with some discomfort on Lincoln's part—for at least one formal interview.

Some reports of Truth's interview with Lincoln may have been affected by the desire of abolitionists to champion Lincoln as the Great Emancipator. As we have seen, according to what Truth stated soon after her interview in her letter in the *Standard,* when she complemented Lincoln for his Emancipation Proclamation, Lincoln responded that if the Southerners "had behaved themselves, I could not have done what I have." Lincoln concluded, "But they did not, and I was compelled to do these things," as if circumstances "compelled" him against his will to free the slaves. However, according to the version of Truth's letter published eleven years later, in Frances Titus's 1875 edition of Truth's *Narrative,* Lincoln instead concluded, "But they did not, which gave me the opportunity to do these things," as if he had been looking for an opportunity to free the slaves all along.[17] One cannot help but wonder whether Titus deliberately altered Truth's letter to make Lincoln look more like a friend to the slaves.

There are other claims that Truth significantly influenced Lincoln on behalf of blacks. One such claim, by Truth's friend, antislavery editor Oliver Johnson, can be easily dismissed. In 1876 he noted, "When the war broke out she went to Washington, to urge the President to free the slaves," and Lincoln was "deeply moved by her appeals."[18] However, Truth did not meet Lincoln until October, 1864, more than three years after the war broke out, by which time he not only had issued the Emancipation Proclamation, abolishing slavery in the rebel states as a temporary war measure, but also, as part of his presidential reelection campaign, had called for a constitutional amendment that would abolish slavery permanently in the whole United States.

Another such overstatement, more widespread, has Truth influencing Lincoln to allow blacks to enlist as volunteer soldiers. In the early 1940s, a textbook for black children asserted that Truth urged Lincoln to arm free blacks to fight for the Union. In the late 1940s, executive secretary Walter White of the National Association for the Advancement of Colored People (NAACP) insisted extravagantly that Truth returned to the White House "time and time again" to urge Lincoln to enlist free blacks and that "her arguments, combined with the manpower needs of the Union Army, eventually won over Lincoln and Congress." Since then many writers, including, alas, the present writer, have made similar, if less extreme, claims.[19]

It is true that early in the Civil War, Lincoln, along with most Northerners, opposed enlisting blacks. By the summer of 1863, however, Lincoln was praising the performance of black soldiers and encouraging more blacks, both the already free and the newly freed, to enlist, and they were enlisting in considerable numbers. When Truth first met Lincoln in October, 1864, his policy to support the enlistment of blacks was well established, so it seems unlikely that Truth would have felt it necessary to urge the cause further. Moreover, Truth's predominant goal in visiting Lincoln, according to both Colman in her letter of November 1 and Truth herself in her letter of November 17, seems to have been not to push Lincoln to grant any further rights to blacks but to thank him for what he had already done.

There are two intriguing stories about Truth that portray her as an old, uneducated, ex-slave woman who was cleverly brash to President Lincoln, manipulating him, and getting away with it. The first story has Truth telling Lincoln that she had never heard of him until he was proposed as a candidate for president. This tale was not mentioned in Truth's 1864 letters describing her visit to the president, but Truth recounted it in an 1869 speech in Detroit. When Frances Titus prepared the 1875 edition of Truth's *Narrative*, however, without acknowledging what she was doing, Titus apparently inserted this tale into Truth's letter of November 17, 1864, as if it had been there in the first place. According to this inserted passage, Truth said, "I told him [Lincoln] that I had never heard of him before he was talked of for president. He smilingly replied, 'I had heard of you many times before that.' " Hertha Pauli was so impressed with this story that she began her fictionalized biography of Truth with it.[20]

This story tends to suggest that Truth was well known and had long influenced Lincoln. It has an obvious appeal to those who would enjoy seeing a poor, uneducated, black woman unafraid of, if not impudent to, a white person of power. The remark attributed to Truth is in accord with the pert remarks she was fond of making. Still, if this story is even partially true, we must ask—because it is so striking an example of the tales Truth relished about herself—why did it not appear in Truth's letter as originally published?

The other story portrays Truth as trying to sell Lincoln her photograph for a "greenback" that bore a picture of Lincoln. This story was published in abbreviated form in 1880. It was published in detail in 1890, twenty-five years after it supposedly occurred, in a version offered by Calvin Fairbank, an antislavery hero whose health had been broken by his long imprisonment in Kentucky for helping slaves escape and who, of particular relevance here, had a reputation for being inaccurate. Fairbank said he had been at a huge public reception at the White House celebrating Lincoln's second inaugural on March 4, 1865, when Truth came in and asked to see the president. When she saw him, she handed him a copy of her photograph (which by this time she often sold to help support herself, normally for about 35 to 50 cents). She said, "It's got a black face but a white back; an' I'd like one o'yourn wid a green back." According to Fairbank, the president "laughed heartily" at her request and then drew a ten-dollar greenback out of his pocket for her, saying, "There is my face with a green back."[21] Because ten-dollar "greenback" bills carrying Lincoln's picture were in circulation at the time, the story does wear a face of plausibility.

However, Truth told a similar story about herself and President Grant, saying that when she gave Grant a copy of her photograph he gave her a five-dollar bill. Truth told this Grant story soon after it was supposed to have happened, and retold it in her 1875 Narrative, but it is doubtful that she ever told the Lincoln story. Moreover, contrary to the Lincoln story, the Grant story does not portray her as boldly requesting money for herself from a president.[22] It seems possible that some wag picked up the inert Grant story, embellished it, and gave it panache by attaching it to Lincoln.

Truth and her friends seemed to seek to project an image of her as having been appointed by Lincoln to work with the freedmen, or at least as having received Lincoln's encouragement for her work, as if this would enhance her effectiveness and prestige. As we have seen, Truth's letters of November 3 and 17 give us no evidence that Lincoln appointed her to any work or encouraged her to do any particular kind of work, or that she asked his guidance about it. Nor did Colman at the time or afterward say that Lincoln led her in any way in this work. In 1869, however, Truth recalled in an antislavery meeting, as reported in the minutes of the meeting, that her course in "denouncing slavery" and in working "for her race" had been "recognized as the proper course by Abraham Lincoln." Also in 1869 and 1871, friends of Truth, after listening to her, reported that Lincoln had put her to work with the freedmen. In 1871, a Topeka reporter, after talking with her, went so far as to claim that she had said that Lincoln "placed in her hands the important trust of organizing and carrying out a system for the care and management of contrabands [freedmen]." In editing the 1878 version of Truth's *Narrative,* Frances Titus claimed, perhaps on the basis of what Truth had said to her, that Lincoln gave Truth a "commission" to work among the freedmen in the Washington area. In 1879 Truth herself, in an interview with a Chicago journalist, said that when she met Lincoln, he "wanted me to see to the colored people at Arlington Heights and Mason's Island."[23] Many later writers have repeated such claims.

It is possible—perhaps even likely—that Lincoln encouraged her in working with the freedmen, if only incidentally. But no direct evidence is available—either in her own letters or in comment by others at the time —that Lincoln encouraged, much less authorized or guided Truth's work with the freedmen.

Because of her eccentricity and inability to read and write, Truth's activities were prime material for mythmakers and sometimes Truth herself appeared to encourage them. As an activist who felt a mission to speak out for God, Truth did not customarily focus on the objective truth about her own past. She interpreted her own life and the world at large more in terms of images and parables which could be used to convey symbolic truth.

Truth felt at ease with Lincoln in the White House. She felt at ease with white and black, rich and poor, powerful and weak. But she sometimes chose to identify with the black, poor, and unfortunate, such as the freedmen. She is all the more impressive in this identification because, according to the available evidence, she did not depend on Lincoln to guide her to work with the freedmen, but instead sought out the opportunity to work with them essentially by herself.

12

Riding Washington's Horse Cars

"Dere's nothin' like standin' up for yer rights!"

By 1865, when Truth was working with the freed slaves in Washington, she already had long experience with discrimination in public transportation. New York City horse cars had often been segregated, with blacks allowed to ride only on the outside platform, or only in certain infrequent cars reserved for blacks. Across the North on stage coaches, blacks had often been forced to ride on top, in the open, if they were allowed to ride at all. On trains, Truth as a black had often been sent into smoking cars, whether or not she wanted to "swallow" the smoke.[1] Now in Washington she found that sometimes when she signalled for a horse-drawn streetcar to stop, the drivers would turn their heads the other way, as if they had not seen her.

Before 1865 Truth is not known to have participated in ride-ins to desegregate transportation. However, anyone like Truth who had been familiar with the abolitionist movement over the years would be likely to know that a few abolitionists had already occasionally been conducting such ride-ins, often deliberately nonviolent ones. In 1841 the black David Ruggles, not long before he had joined the Northampton community, stepped onto a train in New Bedford, intending to go to Boston, and took a seat. But when conductors asked him to move to a Jim Crow car—as segregated cars for blacks were already called—he refused, and conductors dragged him out, tearing his clothes. Ruggles brought action against the railroad in a New Bedford court, but lost, the judge ruling that the railroad had the right to seat blacks as it wished.

Soon afterward, Frederick Douglass also insisted on riding in Massachusetts train cars reserved for whites. He too was asked by conductors to move to the Jim Crow car, refused, and was dragged out. According to Douglass, the ride-ins in which he, Ruggles, and others had participated, by heightening public awareness of discrimination, helped to make the railroad companies "ashamed" to discriminate, and by 1843 all the Massachusetts railroads had been desegregated. In the 1850s several New York City blacks, led by the black Presbyterian pastor J. W. C. Pennington, organized a campaign against streetcar segregation through ride-ins. Pennington himself rode in a Sixth Avenue car reserved for whites. When asked to leave, he refused and was censured by a court for breach of the peace.[2]

By early 1865, such efforts had helped to reduce segregation in transportation, so that blacks in Boston, New York, Chicago, and Baltimore generally rode as equals in the street horse cars. But in Philadelphia and Washington, streetcar segregation was still common.

In early 1865, Senator Charles Sumner of Massachusetts succeeded, after several years of struggle, in pushing through Congress a law forbidding all District of Columbia streetcar companies to exclude anyone on account of color, under the threat that they might lose their charters to operate. On March 3, 1865, President Lincoln signed the law.[3]

According to her *Narrative,* when Jim Crow cars had been legal in Washington, Truth had found that there were not enough Jim Crow cars, so that if she was able to get onto one of these cars at all, she usually had to stand, and she had complained about that to the streetcar company. It is not known whether Truth had tried, as a protest against segregation, to ride the cars legally reserved for whites. Other blacks, however, had. On a rainy day, Dr. A. T. Augusta, a black army surgeon, had climbed into a white car. When the conductor asked him to ride up front with the driver in the rain, he had refused, and so found himself put out of the car. Dr. Augusta publicly complained, and Senator Sumner read his complaint into the Senate's records.[4]

After Senator Sumner's new law was passed, Washington newspapers publicized it, Jim Crow cars disappeared, and some blacks rode the cars with whites. But whites were often rude to them. For instance, when a white woman wearing furs and scented with lavender entered a car, and found the only seat available was next to blacks, she "put her cambric to her nose to the infinite amusement" of other passengers, and muttered that "things" were not "as they used to be in Washington."[5] In other instances, blacks were kept out of cars altogether, though such exclusion was now clearly against the law.

Many Washington blacks, having been only recently freed, were so accustomed to being looked down on as slaves that they did not dare ride the horse cars as the equals of whites. When Truth had first come out of slavery, feeling ignorant and inexperienced in the world, she too had found it difficult to act as an equal. But now when she knew that the law was supporting her, as she did on this issue, she had courage to spare. To assure that the new law would be observed, Truth felt that blacks needed to push to use the cars as equals, and she was delighted to push.

In Washington one day in 1865, Truth signalled a car to stop. When it did not, she ran after it, yelling. The conductor kept ringing his bell so that he could pretend he had not heard her. When at last the conductor had to stop the car to take on white passengers, Truth also climbed into the car, scolding the conductor: "It is a shame to make a lady run so." He replied that if she said another word he would put her off. She threatened him: "If you attempt that, it will cost you more than your car and horses are worth." When a "dignified" man in the uniform of a general interfered on her behalf, the conductor let her alone.[6]

In this incident she showed not only fierce determination to ride, but also keen awareness that the law was on her side. After all, Lincoln had signed the new law. In this, as in all her known ride-ins, she did not try to organize groups of blacks to join her, but when circumstances seemed to suggest it, she acted directly, essentially on her own.

In another incident in Washington, Truth again held up her hand to signal a horse car to stop. Two cars passed without stopping. When the third came in sight, according to her recollection, she gave tremendous yelps: "I want to ride! I want to ride! I WANT TO RIDE!" Her shouting, whether intended or not, startled enough nearby horses, drivers, pedestrians, and boys pushing carts, to block the traffic, which stopped the horse car. That gave her a chance to climb into the car, to the laughter of some of the passersby, who decided with relish that she had outwitted the conductor, some of them calling out, "She has beaten him."

The conductor was furious and told her to go up front, outside with the driver. But she sat down inside, with the other passengers. He told her to get up, or he would throw her out. She told the conductor "to fro me out if he dar," for "she was neither a Marylander nor a Virginian" but "from the Empire State of New York, and knew the laws as well as he did." At least one of the passengers in the car, a soldier, seemed to sympathize with her, for, as new passengers came in, he exclaimed to them delightedly, "You ought to have heard that old woman talk to the conductor." She herself felt so pleased to be riding in the car that she rode farther than she had intended, and when she left, said happily, "Bless God! I have had a ride."[7]

Another day, she was going about the city with Josephine Griffing, a white abolitionist friend who like Truth was devoted to the welfare of the freed slaves. Griffing signalled an approaching horse-drawn streetcar to stop. The car stopped for Griffing but did not wait long enough for Truth also to get into the car, but, as Truth wrote a friend afterward, she did succeed in "holding on to the iron rail. They dragged me a number of yards before she [Griffing] succeeded in stopping them. She reported the conductor to the president of the City Rail Way who dismissed him at once, and told me to take the number of the car wherever I was mistreated by a conductor or driver, and report to him and they should be dismissed."[8]

This and all her reports of her ride-ins reveal her easy confidence that she was doing right. There are no signs that she agonized over whether she should insist on riding as an equal in the cars, or how she should do it.

On another occasion, when Truth was bringing a black nurse from Georgetown to the Freedmen's Hospital, Truth found that the nurse was uneasy about riding the horse cars with whites. Nevertheless, at a horse car station Truth led her into an empty horse car that was preparing to leave, and they seated themselves. After the car proceeded on its way, it stopped for two white women, who came in, sat opposite the two black women, and began to whisper about them. According to Truth's recollection:

The nurse, for the first time in her life finding herself in one sense on a level with white folks and being much abashed, hung her poor old head nearly down to her lap; but Sojourner, nothing daunted, looked fearlessly about. At length one of the ladies called out, in a weak, faint voice, "Conductor, conductor, does niggers ride in these cars?"

He hesitatingly answered, "Ye yea-yes," to which she responded, " 'Tis a shame and a disgrace. They ought to have a nigger car on the track."

Sojourner remarked, "Of course colored people ride in the cars. Street cars are designed for poor white and colored folks. Carriages are for ladies and gentlemen. There are carriages (pointing out of the window), standing ready to take you three or four miles for sixpence, and then you talk of a nigger car!!!" Promptly acting upon this hint, they arose to leave.

"Ah!" said Sojourner, "now they are going to take a carriage. Good by, ladies."[9]

Truth seemed to revel in her ability to manipulate the two white women into leaving the horse car.

In another incident Truth sought to ride a horse car in the company of the white Laura Haviland, a well-known Michigan abolitionist who was temporarily working along with Truth in the Freedmen's Hospital. As Truth recalled it afterward, Haviland, not Truth, signalled for the car to stop. At the same time, Truth, to trick the conductor, made it appear that only Haviland was getting on the car, by stepping to "one side as if to continue my walk." But when the car stopped, Truth ran ahead of Haviland, and, as Truth recalled it, "jumped aboard."[10]

Truth was again with Haviland in another incident, on September 13. When Truth climbed onto the platform of a car, with Haviland some distance behind her, as Truth reported it in a letter written soon after, a man just leaving the car called out:

"Have you got room for niggers here?" As the conductor then noticed my black face, [he] pushed me, saying "Go back — get off here."

I told [him] I was not going off. "Then I'll put you off," said he furiously . . . clenching my right arm with both hands, using such violence that he seemed about to succeed, when Mrs. Haviland reached us, and told him, he was not going to put me off, placing her hands upon both of us.

"Does she belong to you? if she does, take her in out of the way," said he, in a hurried angry tone.

She replied, "She does not belong to me, but she belongs to Humanity, and she would have been out of the way long ago, if you had have [sic.] let her alone."

The conductor pushed Truth hard, she recalled, slamming her against a door and bruising her right shoulder. But after Truth asked Haviland to note down the number of the car, the conductor left them alone. "It is hard for the old slaveholding spirit to die," Truth reflected, "But die it must." [11]

Back at the hospital, when Truth and Haviland asked a surgeon to examine Truth's shoulder, he found it swollen. Truth and Haviland then reported the incident to the president of the streetcar company. He promptly dismissed the conductor, the second conductor Truth had caused to be dismissed.

The company president also advised Truth to have the conductor arrested for assault, which she did, with the Freedmen's Bureau furnishing her a lawyer. A few days later, Justice William Thompson held a hearing for the conductor, as reported in a curious article published in at least four Washington papers:

Alleged Assault Upon Sojourner Truth.—John C. Weeden, a conductor on the Seventh street railroad, had a hearing yesterday before Justice Thompson, at the Park station, charged with assault and battery, on the 13th instant, on Sojourner Truth, a colored woman, eighty years of age [actually about sixty-eight]. Mrs. Laura S. Haviland, of the Freedman's Hospital, testified that when Sojourner was attempting to get in the car at the Seventh street junction, Weeden seized her with such violence as to injure her shoulder, and that it was done with unusual and unnecessary violence. Dr. W. B. Ellis, of the Freedman's Hospital, testified that the old woman's shoulder was very much swollen, and he had applied liniment, &c. In answer to a question from the justice, he replied that it was not from rheumatic affection, but from the wrenching of her shoulder.

On the other hand, William Kannough, H. McAllister, and two other witnesses state that the conductor held the woman back to prevent her from getting into the car, until the passengers, who were to get out at the junction had left the car. After a full hearing of the testimony, Justice Thompson decided to hold Weeden to bail for his appearance at court to answer the charge of assault and battery upon Sojourner Truth. Witnesses also testified to the general good character of Weeden. [12]

The only information available on the outcome of the case comes from a British journalist who wrote simply, Truth "has been rudely dragged from a street car, but she brought an action for trespass to her person, and obtained a verdict." [13] This was the third known time that Truth had taken a case to court, the first having been to recover her son Peter, the second having been to charge Benjamin Folger with slander against her. She apparently won all three cases.

Truth herself claimed that her taking a conductor to trial "created a great sensation." The fact that four Washington newspapers printed the story of the hearing in the case lends credence to her claim. Also according to Truth before the trial was over, so many blacks were now daring to ride in the cars that "the inside of the cars looked like pepper and salt," implying that she was responsible for the change. Soon conductors who before had "cursed me for wanting to ride," she said, "could stop for black as well as white, and could even condescend to say, 'Walk in, ladies.' " More directly Truth later claimed that by her Washington ride-ins—she had taken part in at least six of them, all in 1865—she had effected a "reformation" in the Washington horse cars.[14] However, the claims that she was responsible for the change have not been corroborated in abolitionist or Washington newspapers, or in any authoritative source from the time.

Other blacks insisted on riding the Washington streetcars at about the same time that Truth did, whether stimulated by what they heard she had done or on their own initiative; sometimes they too braved hostility. In March, 1865, when a black woman got into a car in Georgetown, a soldier asked her to get out, and when she refused, he struck her. She had him arrested. In June, according to the pro-segregationist Washington *Daily Times,* blacks kept insisting on riding the cars with whites, and when white soldiers "daily" protested against riding with them, "blows follow, and, finally, the blacks are ejected from the cars." In July, an "immense" black woman entered a car, could not find a seat, and no one offered her one. When a white woman entered, and a white man got up to offer his seat to the white woman, the black woman took it. When the white man protested, "But I gave it up to a lady," the black woman replied, "The lady has got it," and refused to move. At the end of 1865, three months after Truth had taken a conductor to court, a white passenger, who said he did not "associate with niggers," ordered a black man to get off a car, and when he refused, threatened him with a revolver.[15]

Nearly a year later, however, in November, 1866, Truth's old friend Giles B. Stebbins was reported as saying that he had seen whites riding in Washington cars beside blacks with "never a frown. . . . Because the equality of the black man in the cars there is an accomplished fact." But Stebbins was not reported as identifying this achievement with Truth.[16]

Certainly some twentieth-century commentators have given too much credit to Truth for her ride-ins. Popular journalist Bruce Bliven claimed that Truth "was the first Freedom Rider," which we have seen was far from true. Joanne Grant, in her *Black Protest,* claimed that Truth was "the most famous of battlers" against segregated transportation in the abolitionist period. But if David Ruggles and J. W. C. Pennington were less famous battlers than she, Frederick Douglass was probably more famous. The Detroit *Free Press* claimed extravagantly that Truth "single-handedly integrated the trolleys in Washington."[17] But surely many others contributed to the desegregation, including army surgeon Augusta and other blacks who defied white opposition to ride in the cars, as well as President Lincoln, Senator Sumner, Congress at large, the courts, the railway companies that responded to Truth's complaints, the Freedmen's Bureau that supplied her a lawyer, her friends Laura Haviland and Josephine Griffing who accompanied her, and Washington newspapers like the *Chronicle* and *Republican* that advocated equal rights for blacks in the cars.

When Truth confronted Douglass with her "Is God gone?" question in 1852, she was committed to nonviolence and, according to Douglass, even committed to the very idealistic form of nonviolence known as Garrisonian nonresistance. To what extent was she nonviolent in her ride-ins? According to the available reports on these six incidents, she herself used no direct violence. Although two conductors used violence against her, pushing her, and at least one other threatened to put her off a car, she herself did not shove or strike anyone.

But probing further, to what extent was she nonviolent in accordance with the principles of the Garrisonians' Nonresistance Society, the society to which she had been exposed through the Northampton Association and such friends as George Benson, Henry C. Wright, Lucretia Mott, and Garrison? The Nonresistance Society was more concerned with appealing to people's consciences than changing outward situations. It recommended individual non-cooperation with evil as more likely to reach consciences than action through government, including bringing actions in court. Idealistically, the society asked its members, who were virtually all abolitionists, to resist evil with good; to disobey unjust laws with meek acceptance of any resulting punishment; and not so much to inflict suffering on others as to take suffering on themselves.

In keeping with these principles, during the Civil War, the elderly Quaker Lucretia Mott, riding a Philadelphia streetcar one cold rainy day, deliberately rode with a black woman on the outside platform where blacks were supposed to ride, until a conductor, begged by white passengers inside, invited both Mott and the black woman to come inside. Also in keeping with these principles, Garrison once berated Douglass for using trickery as a means for getting a sleeping room on a Hudson River steamer. To avoid staying all night on deck as blacks were expected to do, Douglass had asked a white friend to rent a room and then turn it over to him. Garrison scolded Douglass: Unjust rules cannot be conquered "by stealth, which only irritates and hardens the spirit which framed them. They must be conquered openly, and through much suffering." [18]

In her ride-ins, Truth seemed to be comfortable with tricking conductors in order to ride, and with playing on white prejudice in order to get two white women to leave a car. Also, while she did not show signs of being vengeful, she seemed comfortable with causing the firing of two conductors and taking one conductor to court, thus inflicting pain on them. In these ride-ins she put her emphasis not on redeeming those who were unjust, as the Nonresistance Society recommended, and as she once had done when she had emphasized redeeming slave owners, but on abolishing the outward injustice.

Truth had already put the early Garrisonian scruples against war behind her when she frankly endorsed black participation in fighting for the Union cause in the war. Now by her style of ride-ins she was further putting the Garrisonian brand of nonviolence behind her. She was adopting a less self-sacrificing, more assertive brand of nonviolence of her own. She was becoming more independent of Garrison and his friends.

In perspective, the passage of Sumner's new antisegregation law for the District of Columbia created an opportunity for Truth, and she seized it. She initiated her ride-ins apparently without plan. If she scarcely seemed to think about possible theoretical inconsistencies in what she did, or any incidental pain she caused others, her timing was right. She acted boldly, with flair. She knew that because her name was known, she could focus attention on the illegality and injustice of segregation. She repeated her ride-ins often enough and over a long enough period of time to drive home her point.

She forced the streetcar companies to pay attention to the new desegregation law, and raised awareness among both blacks and whites about the evolving concept of equal rights for blacks. By not retaliating violently even when she was roughly pushed, she invited sympathy with her plight and the plight of all blacks discriminated against in the cars. Getting two conductors fired, and taking one to court, if not calculated to change their motivation, dramatized her struggle for equal rights, as well as the power of the law to reduce discrimination.

At a time when large numbers of blacks, accustomed to the degradation of slavery, were too fearful to assert their rights, Truth acted courageously for equal rights. She risked being humiliated. She risked her physical safety. By her forthright example, she encouraged other blacks to ride the horse cars, and helped to bring about a significant step toward equality.

In her ride-ins, far from being the brooding, passive, secret-keeping Libyan Sibyl of Stowe's and Story's creation, she revelled in being assertive. Recounting her ride-ins several years later, she told an audience, "I tell yer, dere's nothin' like standin' up for yer rights!"[19]

13

Moving Freed Slaves to the North

"They have all to learn."

Soon after Sojourner Truth arrived in Washington in 1864, she talked to the freed slaves in one of the temporary camps provided for them by the federal government. According to her recollection, she told them they were "in disgrace" living as they were "off the government." She told them to "get off the government and take care of themselves." They grew angry at her and turned her out of the building where she was speaking to them. But she followed them to their barracks, and continued to berate them. She told them "to hold up their heads and be men." Then they began to understand her, and they sang:

> Free, free, free indeed,
> Free, free, my people are free,
> Sound the loud cymbals,
> My people are free.[1]

Truth, having herself had cruel experiences growing up as a slave, felt that slavery had left scars on these blacks which made her "heart bleed." She also perceived, as she recalled it, that the government hired people to help these blacks who were not fit to do so, including "ministers that never preached a sermon in their life, doctors who feel the pulse with gloves on." When she tried to teach some of the freed women to sew— particularly some who had been field hands—she decided it would be "quicker to learn a hog to dance." Truth believed that giving them handouts was making them "lazy." When she herself handed out relief clothes to them, clothes such as Northern people sent down to Washington in boxes, some of them wore the clothes a week, she said, and then instead of washing them, threw them away, and came back to "grab" more relief clothes. Many were developing into thieves, she declared, filling the jails "as full as a beehive." And their numbers were increasing; they breed, she protested, "like hogs."[2]

In January, 1865, when two of her Harmonia neighbors, the Spiritualist lecturer Warren Chase and a Harmonia Seminary teacher, were visiting Washington, they came to see her at the camp called Freedmen's Village. When she recognized them, she "blessed the Lord long and loud," Chase reported. Then she poured out to them her fury at the condition of the freed slaves. Many of them were idle, she said, and "are worse off" here "than in slavery, and some even voluntarily return to it." Chase continued, "She was most scathingly severe on *some* of the officers connected with the freedmen's care." They neglect, she said, to inform the freed people of their rights; also the surgeons who are supposed to be caring for them, often "hasten" their deaths, "and sell the bodies of the poor victims." Chase was impressed that Truth felt so free to complain. "She holds some position there," he wrote, "that enables her to talk freely, as she should, for she is a power anywhere, as all know who have seen her in public or private life."[3] Chase thus implied that her position at Freedmen's Village was not likely to be that of a government employee, but he did not explain what her position was.

When a sympathetic lady visited Truth at the village, she found her "tall, dark, very homely," living in a little frame house provided by the village authorities, "with the American flag over the door." When the lady asked what Truth was doing there, Truth answered "Fighting the devil." What devil? "An unfaithful man," Truth explained, holds a government office in which he is supposed to be helping the freedmen, but he is only doing it "as a matter of business," not, as he should be, "from love"; he should be removed. The lady asked, why don't you go to the president with such complaints? Truth replied: "Don't you see the president has a big job on hand? Any little matter Sojourner can do for herself she ain't going to bother him with."[4]

At the camps, Truth tried to teach the freed slaves to know and defend their rights. At a time when slavery still legally existed in Maryland, some

Maryland thugs were raiding the camps, seizing some of the freed slaves' children and selling them off into slavery again. This may have been done with the acquiescence of some of the camp guards, for, Truth recalled, mothers who objected were thrown into a guard house, cowing them into silence. Truth became the mothers' champion, screaming at the thugs in protest. "Didn't I scare those Marylands, didn't I just scream out 'til I frightened them fellows," Truth remembered. "I told 'em I was a free agent, and the government had sent me to do this work." She also told them, she recalled, that if they "put me in the guard house" too, "I'd make the United States rock like a cradle." When the freed people understood that she was not afraid of the thugs, she said, they "began to lift up their heads at last . . . and you never heard such singing as those poor critters did sing."[5]

At about the same time, in February, 1865, journalist Tomkins found her one day in Washington in the basement of Calvary Baptist Church, which the National Freedmen's Relief Association, of New York, used for clothing distribution. Among several hundred black women who were pushing forward to pick up clothing, Tomkins found Truth in charge, "an erect, tall aged black woman, neatly clad, wearing a pair of gold spectacles." "She was reproving her dark-skinned sisters for their eager haste to obtain relief," Tomkins wrote. " 'You have your liberty,' exclaimed the good old woman; 'but what's your liberty worth without regulation; by your thoughtless eagerness you hinder your friends relieving you as quickly as they would." She scolded the women severely: "I have spoken to some of you before about this foolish haste, and now say to you in the words of the fable, that having tried what turf will do, if that fail, the next time I shall try stones." The journalist asked her if she found these people difficult to manage. She answered, "Lor' bless you, chile, no —they are as gentle as lambs, but they must be brought under rule and regulation. Ah! poor things, they have all to learn."[6]

Truth's outspokenness stirred up considerable hostility from those around her, not only from Maryland kidnappers and some of the government workers supposed to be caring for the freed slaves, but also from some of the freed slaves themselves. She had standards of behavior for herself and everyone else that were demanding, and she felt she had to live up to these standards herself no matter where she was. As she wrote her friend Amy Post: "You know I must be faithful Sojourner everywhere."[7]

However, Sojourner found some support from high officials in the Freedmen's Bureau, an agency created by Congress near the end of the war to help the freed slaves. By the fall of 1865, General John Eaton, the officer in charge of the bureau's District of Columbia region, had recommended her as having "good ideas about the industry and virtue of the colored people," and she was working at least part of the time in Washington at the bureau's Freedmen's Hospital.[8] She served primarily as a counsellor to the hospital patients, who included both black soldiers and destitute freed slaves.

At times government officials provided meals for her, and at least at Mason's Island and Freedmen's Village, they provided housing for her too. But it is doubtful that Truth, while she was working for the freedmen, ever became directly a paid government employee. In 1867 when Truth asked the Freedmen's Bureau to compensate her for some travel she had done for the bureau, her Battle Creek friend Richard B. Merritt wrote to the bureau: "I believe she has never received anything from the government in any shape while, on the other hand, she thinks she has given her time and considerable money, for the benefit of the freedpeople, and for the relief of the government."[9]

Even if she wanted to be, Truth could hardly expect to be hired by government in any very responsible position. After all, she was nearly seventy, still illiterate, and scarcely refined in her language or manners; while she sometimes seemed warm and gentle, she could also be volatile, with an explosive temper. She seemed directed from within, by what she considered to be the voice of God speaking to her, which might lead her in unexpected, unconventional directions. Moreover, soon after she had begun working with the freed slaves, she wrote her friend Amy Post, as we have seen, that she did not expect "to ask the government for anything, only what I have to eat, for the colored people must be raised out of bondage." She seemed to intend to be an example to the freed slaves of avoiding dependence on government, even in the form of employment by government.

In fact, as has not been generally understood, Truth, in most of her work with the freed slaves in the Washington region from 1864 through 1866, was employed by the National Freedmen's Relief Association, of New York, a private, nonsectarian agency. The association, one of several such philanthropic, paternalistic freedmen's aid societies based in the North, worked in cooperation with the Freedmen's Bureau and other agencies of the government. The association employed her, but by agreement with the bureau, lent her at various times to be a counsellor at Freedmen's Village, later at Freedmen's Hospital. Also the association gave her the status of "teacher" (the association employed 250 teachers, most of them whites, for their schools for the children of freed slaves in Washington and elsewhere in the South), with the responsibility of being a "visitor" and "distributor" of relief supplies.[10] Thus although Truth could reasonably say she was sent to work among the freed slaves with the approval of the government, the fact that she was not a government employee enhanced her freedom to criticize the government employees among whom she worked.

The National Freedmen's Relief Association paid Truth and other "teachers" in Washington on a subsistence level, far less than public school teachers generally received in the North. Nevertheless, the association took pride that Truth worked for them. Soon after President Lincoln was assassinated, when two officers of the association—one of them Truth's friend Lucy N. Colman—called on the new President Andrew Johnson, they asked him if he would like to see Truth. They reported happily in the association's journal that he said he "would be much pleased to see her . . . at any time," and Colman took her to the White House to visit Johnson, the second president Truth had visited there.[11]

In 1865 the Freedmen's Bureau began to move able-bodied but idle Washington freed slaves off government support by resettling them in jobs elsewhere. Truth, believing dependence on government to be degrading, felt called to help carry out this plan.

The Freedmen's Bureau, an agency of the War Department, was headed by Gen. O. O. Howard, after whom Howard University was soon to be named. By at least Christmas, 1865, Truth had become aware of Howard personally when they both had spoken at a dinner for the patients at Freedmen's Hospital,[12] and she came to admire him as desiring to be just to blacks. On the other hand, many top bureau officials were conservative army officers, not likely to be sensitive to blacks. Hardly any of them were outright abolitionists such as those with whom Truth had often associated. Moreover, Truth, an individualist, was not used to working with such a bureaucratic organization as the Freedmen's Bureau. Nevertheless, Truth could bring her own experience as a freed slave to this resettlement program. She had personal connections in both Michigan and New York State where there was a demand for black workers. Also Truth had faith, perhaps naive faith, that with God's help the lives of these freed slaves could be dramatically improved.

By the summer of 1866, for more than a year the Freedmen's Bureau had already been moving freedmen out of idleness in Washington to jobs in the North. At that time, Truth wrote Amy Post in Rochester, New York, proposing to resettle some of the freedmen there. Truth asked Post whether she or her friends could find "good" jobs for freedwomen, some with children, if Truth herself brought them to Rochester. But nothing seems to have come of Truth's proposal immediately.[13]

By fall, Truth was pushing more directly to resettle freed people out of Washington. She was doing so especially by working with Josephine Griffing, who had recently accompanied Truth in one of her ride-ins in the Washington streetcars. From 1864 Griffing had been the general agent of a private freedmen's relief agency similar to the one for which Truth worked. Griffing had also been at times a paid agent of the Freedmen's Bureau, which she herself by her strenuous lobbying in Congress had significantly helped to create; by this time Griffing was often goading the bureau to be more responsive to the freed slaves' needs. Truth arranged with Griffing that Truth, in working to move freed slaves out of Washington, would not be an official Freedmen's Bureau agent, but would work in cooperation with Griffing and the bureau. The bureau would pay transportation expenses for Truth and any freed slaves she transported.

In November, 1866, Josephine Griffing for the Freedmen's Bureau telegraphed Henry Willis, Truth's friend in Battle Creek, that twenty-eight freed people were soon to arrive from Washington for him in Battle Creek. As Griffing explained to other bureau officials, Willis "receives & provides temporary rest" for the freedmen in Battle Creek.[14]

Henry Willis had grown up as a Quaker in Baltimore, where he became conscious of the cruelty of the slavery around him. Garrison, visiting Willis in Battle Creek, had found Willis to be an active abolitionist and "a rough, energetic, enterprising farmer," as Garrison wrote to his family in Boston, but added that Willis was so "injudicious" (an ironic term to come from Garrison as he was widely believed to be injudicious himself) that he does "a great deal more harm than good to any cause" he espouses. However, in Washington, Josephine Griffing's daughter, herself a bureau agent, described Willis to a Freedmen's Bureau official as "an old resident of Battle Creek" who is "responsible."[15]

Josephine Griffing told bureau officials that she herself hoped to bring these twenty-eight freed people to Willis in Battle Creek, and along the way, drop off still other freed people at several sites in Ohio: Youngstown, Cleveland, Elyria, and Oberlin. Although Griffing did not say she planned to bring Truth with her, it is possible that Truth herself was on the train which brought these freed people to Battle Creek.

Long afterward, the black Payton Grayson recalled that in November, 1866, when he was only a boy of seven years, "Aunt Sojourner" brought him and his family from Washington by train to Battle Creek. "Aunt Sojourner wanted to help us help ourselves," Grayson recalled. "That's the reason she had us come to Battle Creek and small towns, instead of the big cities, so we could find work."

According to Grayson, Truth had visited the Grayson family—a mother and three children—where they were living in a temporary camp for freedmen, probably Freedmen's Village, outside of Washington. Blacks like the Graysons, he explained, freed from slavery in Virginia, had fled to Washington, looking for a better life, but when they got there, found no better place to go than such a camp.

Truth told the Graysons that there was no future for them there, Grayson recalled. "We were too thick there," she told us, "and she told us we wanted to go out west where we could get work." Truth was an authority figure to the Graysons. "Whatever she said we did," Grayson remembered.

According to Grayson, Truth arranged with Mrs. Griffing for the Graysons and others to go by train to the Midwest. Truth accompanied them on the train, which included four or five cars of freed people. Truth told the freed people at which place it was arranged that they were to get off to find new homes, he recalled. She directed the Graysons to get off at Battle Creek, where by Truth's arrangement, they stayed at first for a few days with a black family, the Frank Snodgrasses. Soon Mrs. Grayson found work with Henry Willis, and took her children with her to live at Willis's. After about a year, Grayson recalled, his mother married a freedman who had come out to Battle Creek on another of Truth's trains.[16]

Other blacks in Battle Creek recalled long afterward that Truth and Griffing had arranged for sixteen or seventeen of them to come from

Washington to settle in Battle Creek. While they said that Truth met them in Washington before they came and again in Battle Creek after they came, they did not say that she accompanied them on the train.[17]

Truth's Battle Creek friend Frances Titus, writing in 1875 that Truth found places for freedmen in the North, mentioned her doing so in Rochester but not in Battle Creek.[18] Moreover, Truth's name does not appear in the available Freedmen's Bureau records as taking freedmen to Battle Creek, but it does as taking them to Rochester. It is possible that Grayson was confused in his recollections, so that although Truth may have met the Graysons in their camp in Virginia and arranged for them to move to Battle Creek, she did not accompany them on the train.

In the fall of 1867, another Battle Creek friend of Truth's, Mrs. E. M. Rhoades, explaining in the *National Anti-Slavery Standard* why Truth was poor, wrote that she had been spending her money in "getting places" for the freed people. Rhoades did not mention that Truth brought any freed people to Battle Creek, but she did say Truth had been "carrying them from Washington to different parts of the country," which interpreted literally would mean that she took them to more places than Rochester. Also in 1879 a newspaper published in Kalamazoo, near Battle Creek, describing Truth's effort to move freedmen out of Washington, stated, "some of her wards were brought to Michigan and others to New York state."[19]

Could Titus and Rhoades have deliberately omitted to mention Truth's help in bringing freedmen to Battle Creek because this was a painful subject there? Everywhere in the North that the freedmen settled there were likely to be some whites who opposed their coming, claiming they would take jobs away from whites, or become public dependents. When Truth's friend Laura Haviland brought freed people to settle in Adrian, Michigan, the county superintendent of the poor accused her of bringing blacks who soon became public charges.[20] But certainly Titus herself favored bringing freed people to Battle Creek.

A month after the bureau in Washington had informed Willis that it was sending freedmen to him, in December, 1866, the bureau telegraphed Titus in Battle Creek that it was sending freed people also to her: "A party of eight (8) freed people will arrive Friday morning." Apparently Titus was receiving these freedmen, much as Willis had received others, on the understanding she would look after them until they could find jobs.[21]

Frances Walling Titus, who was to become Truth's most conspicuous long-term supporter in Battle Creek, had been born and raised, like her husband Richard Titus, as a Quaker, she in Vermont and he in New Rochelle, New York. Richard as a youth had gone to sea, and by the age of eighteen had become a sea captain, sailing to the West Indies and South America. After settling in Battle Creek, he became a flour miller, and when he died in 1868, his son Samuel Titus, about twenty-two, succeeded him in the mill, and continued to live with his mother in the family house. Frances Titus, while contemplative in style, became radical enough in her point of view so that she often entertained at her house the strident antislavery speaker Parker Pillsbury when he visited Battle Creek, even though Pillsbury attacked the church for its support of slavery so fiercely that he was widely considered to be an "infidel." By late 1867 in Battle Creek, Frances Titus had organized a class of adult blacks, most of them freed slaves, doubtless including some whom she and Truth had helped to bring to Battle Creek. Twice a week in the city hall, Titus and other volunteers taught them to read, write, and use simple numbers.[22]

Other Battle Creek friends of Truth, the Merritt family, were also supportive of freed people. Joseph Merritt had brought his family from Saratoga County, New York, to Battle Creek in about 1836 to clear land for a farm. He had helped to found the Friends meeting in Battle Creek. In the 1850s he had been president of the Michigan Anti-Slavery Society, and had frequently opened his house to visiting antislavery lecturers, including Garrison. Truth had worked for the Merritts as a domestic, had lived with them, and had helped to raise their children and grandchildren. In 1865, one of Joseph's sons, Charles Merritt, a grower of berries and peaches, was the head of a Spiritualist group which organized a block-by-block collection of clothes for needy freedmen.[23]

In April, 1867, Charles' younger sister Phoebe Merritt, by this time married to Frank Stickney and living in Painesville, Ohio, wrote Truth, asking her help in finding blacks to work for them. Phoebe Merritt Stickney, evidently having heard from her mother in Battle Creek that Truth was in Rochester trying to arrange to send freedmen there, wrote to Truth in Rochester. Addressing her as "Dear Old Sojourner," Stickney invited Truth to come to her house to see her two small children, and continued:

But Sojourner let me tell you what we want so bad and that is some one to help us indoors & out. You can well understand Sojourner (that with my little ones & slender health, and Frank the same, yet crammed full of business) how badly we need a good man & woman, that would be faithful & trusty. . . . An excellent home we would give if such could be found. With my little ones it would be bad to have other children. If it could be otherwise would greatly prefer even though it were only the woman. Will you let us know what you can do for us in this direction?[24]

Phoebe Stickney, like many Northerners who were requesting freed people to work for them, asked for adults without children. This was understandable from a prospective employer's point of view, but disturbing to Truth and Griffing. They did not want to see freed people of working age move out of Washington and elsewhere in the South without their children and old people, because it would separate families and deepen the problems of those left behind. But how Truth responded to Stickney's request available records do not say.

By early March, 1867, Truth was in Rochester with Amy and Isaac Post, working out with them her plan to bring freed slaves to Rochester. The Posts had long been active in such unpopular causes as the Underground Railroad, Progressive Friends, spiritualism, and women's rights. Isaac Post was a druggist, with Post and Bruff's drugstore. Amy Post was shy, not a public speaker like Truth, but often served as a major officer of reform conventions.

Undoubtedly the Posts helped Truth write out the following advertisement, which she published, beginning March 13, 1867, in two Rochester Republican newspapers:

To the Public.—Sojourner Truth, the well known Mrs. Stowe's African Sybil [spelling sic.], is now in Rochester, endeavoring to find employment for some of the Southern freed people, who are in Washington, several thousands of them supported by the Government and philanthropists, in idleness. They are willing and able to work, but there is none for them there.

It is therefore proposed to establish a depot for some of them in Rochester, where the farmers and citizens can supply their great need of such help. They will be transported here without expense to the employer [the bureau would pay for the transportation], but to pay expenses while in the city, fifty cents or a dollar may be required.

We therefore solicit all who need help, and are willing to pay them such wages as they may earn, to immediately avail themselves of this opportunity, by writing to or informing Sojourner Truth, care of Isaac Post, Rochester; of what number and kind; whether men, women or families, they desire.

On or before the arrival of these people, notice will be given in the city papers, that applicants may come and select for themselves.

Sojourner Truth, who is the life and soul of this movement, intends holding meetings in adjoining towns, in aid of this effort.[25]

Truth's advertisement appeared at a time when many residents of western New York were having difficulty finding enough help. So according to Truth, within four or five hours of the publication of her advertisement, many prospective employers "came rushing in" to Rochester to see her.[26] Other prospective employers wrote her from a nine-county area surrounding Rochester. More of them asked for women than men. Those who asked for women usually specified houseworkers; those who asked for men usually specified farm workers.

Some prospective employers requested that the workers should be strong, honest, temperate, experienced, or the like. Many asked for women only up to 30 years of age, men only up to 35. They asked for adults without small children. (From Washington, Griffing wrote Truth bitterly that nearly all applicants for freed slaves indicated they wanted "no young children, as though black babies were 12 years old when they were born.") One wrote that his family and two or three neighboring families would like black girls to do housework, and that because these families all attend the same church, the black girls could see each other occasionally at church. Another reported that several families would be glad to secure freed slaves "instead of depending upon foreign Romish help." (Irish help was common in the region at the time.) Another wrote, "I am ready to believe that justice will be the rule in any undertaking which bears the signatures of Sojourner Truth & Isaac Post." One promised to send a girl part-time to school, and keep her for several years, while another promised that if she liked a girl, she would provide her "a home as long as she shall live."[27]

Truth's advertisement also got a response from James O. Bloss, a Rochester businessman of an abolitionist family, who had already been doing what Truth was now also doing, acting in cooperation with the Freedmen's Bureau as a voluntary, unpaid agent in bringing freed slaves to Rochester. Besides Bloss and Truth there were at least nine other similar bureau agents operating at about this time in New York State.

Bloss was angry. In a public letter to one of the Republican papers in which Truth's advertisement had appeared, Bloss complained that, although so many employers in the Rochester area had asked for freedmen that he could have placed a thousand a week at good wages, Griffing and the bureau in Washington had only sent him ten freedmen. He suspected that bureau officers avoided sending freedmen away from Washington lest they have too few freedmen left to justify their bureau jobs. Bloss also blamed the freedmen themselves, "poor, ignorant, besotted" as they were, for enjoying being "fed and clothed" by the bureau in Washington, so that they did not want to leave there. Bloss declared that he had decided to give up on Griffing and the bureau, and predicted that Truth would have similar difficulty in getting them to send her enough freed people.[28]

The Rochester *Daily Union,* a Democratic paper that Truth castigated as "Copperhead," gleefully reprinted both Truth's advertisement and Bloss's letter. In doing so, the *Union* poured out its hostility to Truth, "an old negress who was once a slave in this state," and to Bloss, "a real simon pure negro lover," and to the Freedmen's Bureau, a "Radical" Republican creation, for trying to bring freedmen into the Rochester area to get jobs. The freedmen, the *Union* warned, would work for lower wages than whites and so take jobs away from whites, and besides would steal from whites—if they come, you whites had better "look to your chicken-coops."[29]

Meanwhile, despite Bloss's warning, Truth seemed ready to believe that a large number of freed slaves would be sent to her in Rochester. For on behalf of Truth, Amy Post wrote the bureau on March 18 asking for $100 to help Truth put up a "board shanty" in Rochester, near the railroad depot, to serve as a reception center for arriving freedmen, a building apparently simpler than the reception buildings the Freedmen's Bureau provided in some other Northern cities. Post explained that there are several persons in Rochester "who will assist" Truth, "without money or price . . . to make judicious distribution of these poorest of God's poor"; also that Truth "has given the freedmen all her earnings," and is now living in Rochester in the Posts' house, "supported by the Rochester friends of the needy." Post enclosed a newspaper clipping of Bloss's complaint, adding: "Sojourner wishes to prove to the people his [Bloss's] mistake—that there are agents there in the Bureau who are true to both government and the freedmen."[30]

Truth herself sent Griffing a copy of Bloss's letter of complaint. On March 26 Griffing replied, regretting that Bloss "cannot see our difficulties." "We have three thousand applications" for freedmen, and can send "only a few" to each place. "We are moving heaven and earth . . . to inspire the people to go," Griffing explained. "But all the causes that you remember to have existed last year, Sojourner, are still keeping them here. Then the Southern agents have been here for men, and have said so much against the climate and character of the North, that that also helps to indecision. The Bureau is now giving us all facilities for getting them where they can support themselves. . . . We do send some almost every day, but cannot get the women to go without the men & indeed cannot get many just now of any kind."[31]

On March 30 Truth explained in a letter to Griffing that many people who responded to her advertisement believed she "was doing a great work more than had ever been done before," but she was now finding herself uneasy whether she could supply half of the freed slaves whom employers wanted. Moreover, Truth wrote, she was annoyed that Julia A. Wilbur of Rochester, who had been sent by the Rochester Ladies Anti-Slavery Society to the Washington area to teach freed slaves, had written Truth that by announcing that she was charging fees, Truth was playing into the hands of Copperhead Democrats: She was giving the appearance of trying to make money out of resettling freed slaves. Truth protested: "The people all know I am not doing it for my benefit or profit. And then for Mrs. Wilbur to think that the Copperheads think that I am doing it for speculating!"[32]

More than a month after Truth published her advertisement, Griffing wrote Truth from Washington that she still could not promise to send any freed slaves to Truth, even though "they stand idle everywhere." One reason the men hesitated to go North, Griffing explained, was that they treasured their newly acquired right to vote in the District of Columbia, a right they would lose if they moved to New York State or certain other Northern states that had not yet granted blacks the equal right to vote.[33] The freed slaves were evidently taking Griffing's and Truth's advice to stand up for their rights in ways that thwarted what Griffing and Truth wanted to do for them.

Later in April, however, Truth returned to Washington, and herself helped to recruit some freed slaves. On April 25 she wrote back to Amy Post in Rochester exultantly:

I shall I think reach Rochester Wednesday or Thursday night next week with ten or twelve freedpeople men & women, & few children. Please put up the building without a fail. For in May I shall get a large company. I think by the 16th of May they will be there sure.

I am coming with them & shall come back for the rest. Shall have some first rate folks next time. We are working with all our might, Mrs. Griffing & I, and certain [to] accomplish something. . . .

Be at the Depot Wednesday night. If I don't come be there Thursday night. I shall be there if transportation is ready.

Bureau helps me with all their might.[34]

At least by May, Truth had brought freed slaves to Rochester. The difficulties one of them encountered was indicated by a letter to Truth from a Quaker woman in nearby Union Springs, on Cayuga Lake:

The man whom thou sent to us we liked very much. But as we were just papering, painting and varnishing all through the house, we had no place to put him, and so we told him if he would go to the school, and work for his board a few days till we could make the arrangement, then he could come here and work for wages all the season.

But when we inquired for him we found he was gone back to Rochester without letting us know anything about it.

We are really disappointed for they tell us he worked very smart at the school and seems just such a one as we wanted. I hope as soon as his wife comes he will return here—we have a vacant house they can occupy—but unless she comes soon it may be rented to some one else.

I enclose a dollar as requested in Amy Post's letter if he did not remain here.[35]

This freedman was making decisions for himself. Indeed, among the freed slaves who had been sent by the bureau to jobs in the North, significant numbers decided to quit their jobs, some of them returning to Washington. To the disturbance of some bureau officials, Griffing insisted on telling freed slaves that they had a right to do this if they wished.

In July the bureau approved transportation orders for Truth and seven freed slaves to go from Washington to Rochester. This may be the group of seven with whom Truth later reported she ran into complications. When it was time for them to take the train from the Baltimore and Ohio depot in Washington, Truth recalled, the bureau's transportation officer had not, as he had promised, sent the necessary transportation order to her at the depot. But Truth, exhibiting her considerable independence, herself paid the fare for the whole group as far as Baltimore. On arrival there, she also paid for feeding the group, as well as $3.50 for carting their "trunks," and $2.50 for overnight lodging for the five women, evidently leaving the two men to their own devices. Then Truth went back to Washington to pick up the missing transportation order, and returned to Baltimore to continue on with her group to Rochester. Truth afterward asked the bureau to recompense her for these extra expenses, and after delay, they evidently did so.[36]

It is possible that Truth, unable to find enough freed slaves in Washington willing to go to Rochester, brought most of those whom she brought to Rochester from farther south, from southern Virginia or even North Carolina. Afterward one of her friends recalled that she had met Truth in New York City, in May, 1867, when Truth "was returning from Rochester, to which place she had taken 12 of her people and found employment for them." She "was on her way to a town 200 miles south of Richmond to meet others for whom she was to perform like service. Three such trips she made in the following six weeks."[37]

On June 7, a Rochester Republican paper announced that Truth was expected to arrive in Rochester that evening, with "a dozen or more athletic colored men from Virginia," all farm hands, and that jobs on farms were wanted for them at once. It was evident that no such "board shanty" as Truth had wanted for their reception had been built, as the announcement said "there are no means of providing for them in the city. Those who desire to employ help of this kind should call at No. 4 Exchange Street (Post and Bruff's) [drug store] immediately. About one hundred persons have made application to have southern colored laborers sent to them, and it is hoped that they will make their appearance at once." In fact Truth reached Rochester one day late and with only seven men. But within half an hour of their arrival at Post and Bruff's drug store, a newspaper reported, "Most of them had found employers, and there were several parties on hand negotiating for the rest."[38]

By August, 1867, five months after her advertisement had appeared in Rochester papers, Truth had become considerably frustrated. Her motives had been questioned. She had awakened expectations in the Rochester area that she had not been able to fulfill. The bureau, short of money, was reducing its support for resettling freed people. Truth had decided to give up trying to move them to the North, and had returned to Battle Creek.

Truth, in her early seventies now, had been giving what little money she had to the freed slaves, and had come home with almost no funds accumulated for her old age. Nevertheless, she bought a lot with a barn on College Street in Battle Creek proper, and was trying to convert the barn into a house in which to live. She did some of the work herself—she helped to excavate the cellar by carrying earth in her apron. She took out a mortgage on her new property. She also appealed to friends to assist her with donations.[39] It was ironic that Truth was so insistent on blacks becoming self-supporting while she herself at this and many other occasions, was considerably dependent on private charity. She seemed to make a sharp distinction between dependence on government charity as disgraceful and dependence on private charity as acceptable, at least if the reason she needed it was that she had been devoting herself to the cause of God's poor.

However, when private donations proved inadequate to finish converting her barn, Truth eventually relaxed her effort to be totally independent of government. She evidently asked the Freedmen's Bureau for compensation for help she had donated to the bureau while receiving only subsistence wages from the private Freedmen's Relief Association or receiving no wages at all. She probably thought of this as asking the government for unpaid wages rather than charity. In 1870, a friend reported that she "has received from the government, through the influence of Gen. Howard, three hundred and ninety dollars, being fifteen dollars per month for twenty-six months." She applied this sum to her mortgage.[40]

It seems clear that Truth, despite her frequent anger and frustration, on the whole maintained good relations with Josephine Griffing, General Howard, and other Freedmen's Bureau officials, and believed, unlike Bloss, that many of them did what they could to send unemployed freed slaves to jobs in the North.

In helping to bring destitute freed slaves to the North, Truth's primary concern, like Griffing's, was simply moving freed slaves away from dependence on government, in Washington or elsewhere in the South, into jobs in the North. According to available evidence, Truth was not particularly concerned with such immediate details as what their pay would be or how their exploitation could be prevented.

Although Truth often spoke proudly about her work caring for the freed slaves in the Washington area, she seldom did so about her moving freed slaves to jobs in the North. Once she said she had arranged for "a hundred" to move. Another time she said she felt "satisfaction" in seeing those she had helped to move "amount to something."[41] However, neither Josephine Griffing, the Posts, Lucy Colman, nor her other friends involved in caring for the freed slaves are known to have written public letters celebrating Truth's work moving freed slaves to jobs in the North, while they did so celebrate her lecturing against slavery, her caring for the freed slaves in Washington, her visiting Lincoln at the White House, her campaigning for Republican candidates, and her ride-ins to desegregate the Washington horse cars.

By the summer of 1867, the Freedmen's Bureau was being starved for funds by its conservative critics in Congress and in President Johnson's White House. By the next year, the bureau had ceased to support even Griffing as an employment agent, and the bureau itself was well on its way to extinction.

In 1870 Truth returned to Washington to visit. Once again she found large numbers of freed slaves in Washington idle and dependent on charity, governmental or private, which "degrades" them, she said, "wuss an' wuss."[42]

Soon afterward, at a time when Radical Republicans were weakening in Congress, so that any new program for significant aid to blacks was not likely to be adopted, the indomitable optimist Sojourner Truth nevertheless began to advocate a new federal program of aid to the freed slaves in Washington. Ironically, despite her uneasiness with dependence on government, she found herself proposing even more temporary government assistance for the freed slaves, with the hope that it would get them permanently "off the government," a strategy that, in varied forms, was to become a controversial social policy question for the nation far into the future.

14

Western Land

*"God still lives and means to see the black people
in full possession of all their rights."*

For several years Sojourner Truth devoted herself to a plan of her own to
move freed slaves on a large scale from Washington to the West. Describing her plan in hazy terms, she called it variously a plan for a "home" or
"homes" for freedmen in the West, or "a grant of land," or a black
"colony" like Liberia, or a black "reservation" like an Indian reservation.
Some commentators have interpreted her plan as being for a separate
black "state."

By the time of the Civil War, the idea of sending freed slaves out of the
South to make a fresh start elsewhere on land of their own had a long
history, reaching back at least to Thomas Jefferson. During the war,
however, elements in the U.S. Army moved toward giving freed slaves
land in the South, land which had been confiscated from the rebels. But
there was a limited amount of confiscated land, and soon after the war,
President Andrew Johnson restored the rebels' right to this land. By the
end of the 1860s, Southern whites were making it almost impossible for
blacks to acquire land in the South. In November, 1869, Truth attended
a meeting where her friend, Editor Aaron Powell of the *National Anti-
Slavery Standard,* advocated that Congress help freedmen buy land on
easy terms in the South.[1]

In Washington in early 1870, Truth found that freed blacks were still
pouring into the capital region—the proportion of blacks in the popula-

tion of the District of Columbia went over 32 percent that year—and she found many of them in miserable condition. It was in Washington at this time, as she recalled later, that "I made up my mind . . . when I saw able [black] men and women taking dry bread from the government to keep from starving, that I would devote myself to the cause of getting land for these people, where they can work and earn their own living in the West, where the land is so plenty."[2]

At this time, Truth visited the benevolent General O. O. Howard, the head of the now weakened Freedmen's Bureau, who believed that Southern blacks, to become independent, needed to acquire land. With a letter of recommendation from Howard to President Grant, and the help of her Detroit abolitionist friend Giles B. Stebbins, she was able to get an appointment to see President Grant in the White House. In 1868 she had campaigned for Grant, even threatening to move to Canada if he were not elected. But there is no available evidence that Truth now tried to lobby President Grant, as has been claimed, for western land for freedmen, or for any other particular cause.[3]

Truth later recalled that when she began to work on her proposal for land for freedmen, "she applied to Congress . . . and was told that she would have to get the people to petition Congress" for her plan. One occasion when she may have "applied to Congress" was in April at a reception in the Senate's "marble room," when according to a Washington newspaper, many Senators extended "the hand of welcome" to her. About the same time, according to a note in her autograph book, she met Senator Charles Sumner of Massachusetts, an outstanding Radical Republican who had promoted a bill of his own for land for freedmen in the South, and who was the senator to whom Aaron Powell recommended that petitions for his campaign for land for blacks in the South be sent. But there is no evidence available that she discussed her proposal with Sumner or any of the other senators she met. Also in April she spoke at a meeting, held in front of the Washington city hall, celebrating the ratification of the Fifteenth Amendment that gave black males the right to vote nationwide. But the only available report of her speech does not indicate that she used the opportunity to advocate land for freedmen or any other particular cause.[4]

According to Truth's recollection, it was not until later in 1870, when she was lecturing in Massachusetts and Rhode Island, that she began her public campaign for Congress to give western land to freedmen. In

October, Fall River and Providence newspapers reported that she was speaking there for giving land to the poor Washington freedmen to help them become "self-supporting." In December when she attended a woman's suffrage bazaar in Boston, a newspaper reported that she was intending to "get up petitions," asking for western land for freedmen, to send to congressmen "for them spouters to chaw on." By January 1, 1871, when she spoke at a giant Emancipation Proclamation anniversary in Boston, she had asked someone to help her write out a petition—perhaps it was her friend, the radical Methodist editor Gilbert Haven, for she was staying in Boston under his aegis, and he was the one who introduced her on this occasion. She asked the audience to sign copies of her petition, and with her ringing voice and earthy language she won a warm response.[5]

The wording of her petition was vague, perhaps purposely so:

To the Senate and House of Representatives, in Congress assembled:

Whereas, through the faithful and earnest representations of Sojourner Truth (who has personally investigated the matter), we believe that the freed colored people in and about Washington, dependent upon Government for support, would be greatly benefited and might become useful citizens by being placed in a position to support themselves:

We, the undersigned, therefore earnestly request your honorable body to set apart for them a portion of the public land in the West, and erect buildings thereon for the aged and infirm, and otherwise so to legislate as to secure the desired results.

Gilbert Haven's Methodist weekly, the Boston *Zion's Herald,* published the petition in February, 1871, saying that its office would forward signed copies of it to Washington, and that Truth "ought to win this battle." Aaron Powell's weekly *National Anti-Slavery Standard,* which had been promoting Powell's own plan to secure Southern land for freedmen, published Truth's petition early in March, saying, "We hope it may receive many signatures, and be favorably considered at an early day by Congress." Later in March, Horace Greeley's New York *Tribune* published the petition without endorsing it, but along with a supporting letter from Truth. In June the Detroit *Daily Post* published the petition twice, along with sympathetic reports of an interview with Truth and a speech by her advocating the cause. Also in June, after Truth explained her plan to a Michigan state convention of Spiritualists, the convention appointed a committee to circulate her petitions.[6]

In speeches across the North she kept pounding away at her basic arguments. Whites owe blacks help, she declared, because by enslaving them, whites "took away from dem all dey earned." If the government can give western land to the railroads, she said, it can give western land to "these poor creters." Giving land to poor blacks would cost taxpayers less in the long run than having the government support them as at present, she insisted; now they are "costin' you so much." Giving land to poor blacks would help prevent them from continuing to be degraded by being dependent on government assistance, and would help them learn to support themselves instead. In any case, blacks need to get away from the South, she explained, because in the South unrepentant rebels will not let even "good" whites treat blacks justly.[7]

Meantime she had received a letter from Byron M. Smith, a white land agent in Kansas whom she had never met, inviting her to Kansas. Smith wrote without making clear whether he knew of her western lands proposal, but saying he venerated her, offering to pay her rail fare to Kansas, and inviting her to stay at his house as long as she was contented. Smith's being a land agent might suggest he had a self-serving purpose in inviting her. But Truth decided that his invitation meant that God had called her to Kansas to look for suitable land for blacks.[8] Kansas was eagerly seeking settlers. Also many blacks—especially because of John Brown's heroic struggle to make Kansas a free rather than a slave territory—considered Kansas a symbol of freedom.

After a visit home in Battle Creek, Truth left for Kansas in September, 1871. She took along her grandson Samuel Banks as a companion who could read and write for her.

In Kansas she stayed in the homes of various well-wishers such as the Smiths in Iola, an editor in Wyandotte, and a family of bankers in Lawrence. She found herself not especially seeking out suitable lands for settlement, as she had intended, but rather, as she said herself, trying "to interest the people" in her project.[9] She spoke in the Topeka Opera House, as well as in churches, black and white.

She visited neighboring states too. In Iowa she stayed with an old Quaker friend from Pennsylvania who found her "bowed" with age. He told her, "Sojourner, thou are not so tall as when I first saw thee a quarter of a century ago," and she replied: "No, dear child, I have been built so long I have settled."[10]

She ran into some unpleasantness. In Kansas City, Missouri, where she paid to stay with blacks, she scolded them publicly for overcharging her. When she took a train in Wyandotte, Kansas, a conductor at first would not allow her, because of her color, to enter the "best" car. However, continuing her "ride-in" tradition from Washington, she insisted on her "right" to enter that car. With the help of her white Wyandotte editor friend, who had walked with her to the station (a hostile newspaper reported that they had together "lovingly strolled toward the depot"), she succeeded in getting into the car. The conductor, however, took his resentment out on the editor by locking the doors to the car while the editor was still inside, so that he was forced to ride to the next station.[11] But Truth did not allow any such incidents to deter her from her mission.

In promoting her proposal, Truth often mixed it with other causes to which she had long been committed, such as Christian evangelism, temperance, black self-improvement, and women's rights. Her Wyandotte editor friend wrote of her that there are few Americans "who are possessed of greater ability, and none, we believe, who, considering their opportunities, have done more good in the world." A Lawrence newspaper, endorsing her land proposal, wrote of her that she "speaks so naturally and with such directness and wit, and impresses you so with her sterling earnestness and sense, that you almost forget her utter illiterateness." After hearing her speak in Topeka, the more than 200 attending all reportedly agreed to add their names to her petition.[12] By the summer of 1872, however, she had returned home to Michigan, scarcely any closer to putting her plan into effect.

Nevertheless, believing that God was with her, Truth persisted. Partly as a means of promoting her proposal, she campaigned in the fall of 1872 to reelect President Grant. Women, of course, could not yet vote, but because black males had recently acquired the vote nationwide through constitutional amendment, Truth often spoke to them. Her boisterous participation in this campaign was in contrast to her aloofness from politics in her early speaking for reform, when she had said she "did not know anything about politics."

President Grant was scarcely enthusiastic about helping blacks acquire land, but he was, as Truth said, the leader of the Republican party "which had freed the negro." On the other hand, the once regular Republican editor, Horace Greeley, now the liberal Republican and Democratic candidate for president, despite having over many years given a friendly hearing in his New York *Tribune* to Truth and other advocates for blacks, directly opposed any special help to blacks now that they were freed, including help to secure them land. Truth explained in a speech to Detroit blacks that she regarded Greeley, now that he was allied with Democrats, as a fallen angel, and insisted that Grant's reelection was "vital" to government approval of her project.[13] However, after Grant was reelected, her project continued to languish.

Truth seemed to explain her proposal vaguely, using a variety of expressions that led to differing interpretations of what she meant. The Boston *Zion's Herald* interpreted her plan to mean that freedmen would be given as a "homestead" a "large tract" of land, perhaps in Michigan or Indiana, from which they would fan out to "work all over the West," as if they would do seasonal farm work as migrants, returning periodically to their "homestead." But others, also sympathetic, emphasized that her plan would provide freed people not only land but also tools, livestock, schools, and teachers, which would enable them to get started and learn to support themselves on their own land. A Michigan writer endorsed her plan as calling for "a Government poor farm" in which Truth wanted Quakers to teach the freed people virtue and how to support themselves; Truth avers, he reported, that Quakers are "holding themselves in readiness to respond to the call." The Topeka *State Record* said that her plan meant that a "tract" of land would be divided into "small" parcels of which the deed would be given "to each freedman and freedwoman."[14]

In an 1871 letter that has been used by later commentators to interpret her plan as racially separatist, Truth wrote to editor Horace Greeley: "Instead of sending these [freed] people to Liberia, why can't they have a Colony in the West? This is why I am contending so in my old age. It is to teach the people that this Colony can just as well be in this country as in Liberia." Soon afterward, she was reported as saying that blacks were "destined to be a great nation out West."[15] Liberia, founded in the 1820s on the West coast of Africa as a haven for American blacks, had become by the 1870s, at least ostensibly, a self-governing, independent black nation. Was she intending her "colony" to become a self-governing, independent black "nation" like Liberia?

Truth is known to have described her plan as for a "colony" only once, and as for a "nation" also only once, but in several instances she compared her proposed black settlement to an Indian reservation, which further suggests her plan might have been racially separatist. A Kansas City newspaper reported her as advocating that the government stop feeding the freedmen, and instead "put them on land of their own, as it does the Indians, and teach them to work for themselves." In a letter to Gen. O. O. Howard, Truth explained that her plan was for freed people who "have been living on the government. . . . to have a place where they could earn their own bread and have Quakers to see to it as they did to the Indians."[16] Quakers at the time were taking considerable responsibility for Indian reservations. In 1869 President Grant, impressed that the federal government's reliance on force in dealing with the Indians was not working well, had invited Quakers to help make Indian policy and serve as agents on reservations.

While she was advocating her plan, it encountered some direct opposition. A Democratic paper in Saginaw, Michigan doubted its "practicability." A Republican paper in Niles, Michigan, opposed federal donations of public land to any one class in preference to others. However, some newspapers focused not on the substance of her plan, but, to Truth's dismay, on her, as when a Detroit Democratic paper charged she had allowed the attention she received to give her an undue "importance in her own estimation"; or when others speculated that she was over 100 years old, or maybe even about 200, helping to make her more than ever into a mythological character. Like many newspapers, the *New National Era,* edited by Frederick Douglass and his family, though it favored black land ownership, virtually ignored her campaign.[17]

In the spring of 1874, Truth, accompanied by her grandson Samuel, went to Washington again, intending, as she wrote General Howard, the former head of the now defunct Freedmen's Bureau, to "carry" her project "in effect." Although Howard advocated black land ownership, he was wary of advocating government aid to blacks to help them secure it. However, he lent her money. He may have helped to arrange for her to speak in Washington's First Congregational Church, the church he had recently led, overcoming fierce opposition, to welcome black members. For in April she spoke in this church, insisting that if blacks settled on public lands in the West they would learn regular habits and economy and eventually gain political power. In June, Howard wrote on her behalf to one of his fellow Civil War generals, the aggressive Benjamin F. Butler, who as a Radical Republican congressman from Massachusetts had been advocating that the government should assist blacks to own land in the South. Howard, naturally cautious, expressed himself to Butler gingerly, but he asked Butler to help the freedmen by trying "an experiment in the direction that Truth indicates," using the same government income Butler was already using as administrator of the federal system of homes for disabled soldiers.[18] Perhaps Howard meant that Butler might establish, as part of his federal system of homes for disabled soldiers, a home for the war-disabled freedmen on public land in the West.

Even though Howard's letter was by no means an outright endorsement of her proposal, Truth printed it, showed it, and asked her grandson Samuel to read it aloud to her audiences. She recalled several years later, with some exaggeration, that both Howard and Butler "approved of my general recommendation."[19]

When at last she presented her petitions to congressmen, there was hardly any reaction. She and Samuel returned home to Battle Creek in December, 1874, without having come close to putting any aspect of her project into effect.

Soon afterward, her grandson Samuel, who had been a great comfort to her, developed an aneurism in his neck and early in 1875 died, leaving her shaken. About then she became immobilized by an ulcer on her leg, becoming partially paralyzed. Weighed down by Samuel's death, her own illness, and her discouragement with her campaign, she felt low. In Washington, the Radical Republicans, her natural allies, were declining in power. For several years she virtually abandoned her land campaign.

Looking back at her campaign, Truth came to believe it had failed especially because blacks and others who otherwise would have supported her plan were concentrating on Senator Sumner's civil rights bill—the bill Senator Sumner first began to promote in 1870 that barred segregation in such public facilities as schools, transportation, and amusements. It turned out, however, that in 1875, when the Republicans finally pushed the civil rights bill through Congress into law, it was only in a watered down form, and according to Truth, in practice it "did the black man no good," perhaps even hurt him. As she saw it, her plan would promote civil rights more effectively than the civil rights law did. She wanted to move blacks out of the South, she said, to "where they could get civil rights for themselves."[20]

It is hardly surprising that Truth's campaign failed. Other campaigns to help freedmen secure land also failed, such as those led by Senator Sumner and editor Powell, both of whom had positions of more leverage than Truth. By this time the public was tired of the Civil War and the social issues it raised, preferring to concentrate on building up the nation again. As General Howard explained, many people believed that government had already done enough for the victims of slavery. Moreover, there was as yet almost no American tradition of government aid to the disadvantaged. Even such generally pro-black figures as Brooklyn preacher Henry Ward Beecher, New York editor Horace Greeley, and Massachusetts abolitionist Col. Thomas W. Higginson argued that homestead land was already available equally to everyone, and that any special aid to blacks for land or anything else would be likely to pauperize them. Although Frederick Douglass favored helping blacks secure land, he argued that blacks should stay in the South and fight for their rights there. There is no sign that any major black leader gave Truth significant direct help in her campaign. Truth herself, although effective in appealing to individual consciences, lacked any organized political constituency, black or white, and was too free wheeling, and too unworldly, to know how to organize one. While her many friends provided a loose network of support, she lacked strong ties to any organizations that could provide fund-raising, advice to shape her proposal to make it more practical, or sustained support in promoting it.

In early 1879, blacks began moving out of the South in what came to be known as the Exodus. Fed up with what seemed to them continuing white oppression, thousands of them felt an impulse to move North and West, especially to Kansas. Often carrying little more than a few clothes in a bundle, they went by foot, by wagon, by train, by steamboat up the Mississippi and Missouri Rivers.

Truth, in Battle Creek at the time, heard of this Exodus with delight. She felt that God, by leading blacks to Kansas, was rescuing her plan from failure. By summer, her health having been partially restored, Truth decided to go to Kansas, and persuaded her Battle Creek friend, Frances Titus, to go with her.

On the way in Chicago, Truth explained to journalists that she was going to see for herself the blacks arriving in Kansas where "I have prayed so long that my people would go." She was as sure that it was right for blacks to leave the South to go to Kansas, she said, as it was for the children of Israel to leave Egypt to go to Canaan. "The blacks can never be much in the South. They cannot get up. As long as the whites have the reins in their hands, how can the colored people get up there?" The

migration to Kansas exhilarated her. "The movement means the regeneration, temporally and spiritually, of the American colored race, and I
always knew the Lord would find some way. . . . There will be, chile, a
great glory come out of that. . . . The colored people is going to be a
people. Do you think God has had them robbed and scourged all the days
of their life for nothing?"[21]

By September, 1879, Truth and Titus reached Kansas. They only
expected to stay a month. But as they watched the freed people arriving,
often poor, hungry, and unfamiliar with the Kansas way of life, they
became so engrossed in helping them that they stayed into December.

In Kansas, Truth and Titus worked in association with two well-
known benevolent Quaker women from Michigan, Laura Haviland, of
Adrian, who had accompanied Truth in her ride-ins in Washington, and
the English-born Elizabeth Comstock, of Rollin. All four of them became
in effect unpaid volunteers working in cooperation with the private Kansas Freedmen's Relief Association.

Kansas Governor John P. St. John, a Republican, welcomed the black
refugees to Kansas, just as he welcomed at the same time the much larger
number of whites—from the East Coast and from Europe—who were
settling on the still thinly populated prairies of the state. But he worried
that while the whites usually arrived with resources, the blacks did not.
The state itself did not offer relief assistance to any immigrants, white or
black, but Governor St. John led in organizing a private agency, the
Kansas Freedmen's Relief Association, to provide relief to the blacks.

Comstock and Haviland came to have major responsibility for running
the Relief Association. Comstock widely reported the needs of the refugees, eliciting contributions for them from across the North and in Britain. Haviland became the Relief Association's secretary. Comstock and
Haviland were so well known for their long record of reliable humanitar-
ian service that the governor proudly broadcast the idea that the Relief
Association was under their management.

It has been claimed that refugee relief "programs" in Kansas were
"under the direction" of Truth, along with Comstock. It has also been
claimed that Truth, still "firm" of step, worked for the refugees "preparing food" and "tending the sick." But such claims are doubtful. Truth's
leg ulcer made it difficult for her to walk. She was about eighty-two, the
oldest of the four women, and scarcely strong enough to take any major
day-to-day responsibilities. Truth's primary function in Kansas, accord-

ing to one of her Kansas friends at the time, was "giving counsel to the refugees themselves, and awakening an interest in them among the white people." She spoke to the refugees in the "barracks" near Topeka where relief workers placed them until they could find jobs. She also spoke in both black and white churches. Comstock, in a report on Kansas relief activities, wrote that Truth "is doing a good work here."[22]

Some Kansans worried whether giving the freedmen food, clothing, and temporary housing when they arrived in Kansas—even if these were provided by private rather than public benevolence—would encourage more blacks to come to Kansas than the state could handle. A Topeka newspaper bristled at what it called Truth's "enthusiasm" for "the idea that the colored of the South should all come to Kansas," and warned against assisting them because it might attract those who want to escape work.[23]

At a crowded meeting of blacks at a Topeka black Baptist church, as a black paper reported it, Truth said that the Exodus from the South was "God directed," and that Governor St. John, in welcoming freed people to Kansas, "was God's chosen instrument to help the down trodden people to rise up to the level of the most favored people of earth." In an unusually fierce statement, she declared, "God still lives and means to see the black people in full possession of all their rights, even if the entire white population of the South has to be annihilated in the accomplishment of His purpose."[24]

Saying she needed to "recruit her health," by mid-January 1880, Truth had returned home to Battle Creek. She remained hopeful about the migrants, believing they were happy to be "in a state where they can enjoy the fruits of their toil."[25]

Was Truth herself a significant factor in causing blacks to migrate to Kansas or elsewhere in the West about this time, as various writers long afterward claimed? It may reasonably be argued that many freedmen fled the South not so much because of the influence of any particular individual as because the federal government was relaxing its protection of blacks in the South, allowing unrepentant rebels more opportunity to use fraud and violence to deny blacks the vote, education, land, and a decent return for their labor. Truth herself, after talking with migrants in Kansas, explained that blacks fled the South because the federal government was not protecting them from "persecution and butchery."[26]

At the time, however, both those who favored and those who opposed the Exodus pointed out particular persons who they claimed significantly helped to promote it. They pointed, for example, as Truth did, to Governor St. John. They also pointed to several Southern blacks, among them Benjamin Singleton of Tennessee, who was sometimes called the Moses of this Exodus. Though illiterate like Truth, Singleton had already been promoting the migration of blacks out of the South for several years before 1879, distributing flyers, hunting for suitable lands in the West, and establishing black colonies on those lands, as in Kansas. In October, 1879, when Truth was speaking in Topeka, the Republican Topeka *Commonwealth* urged "everybody" to hear her, but soon afterward it said that it was Singleton who, "if anybody, is justly entitled to the credit of having started the exodus movement," and the *Commonwealth* failed to mention Truth in this connection at all. Truth herself, according to a sympathetic reporter who interviewed her in Topeka, "disclaims having any hand" in getting blacks "to come to this state, but believes they were brought here to Kansas by Providence." Although certainly Truth had been one of the many voices preparing the way over many years for the Exodus, and she was considerably known in the North, she was not well known in the South, and particularly not in the deep South where this migration largely originated. Nevertheless, in 1881 the Chicago *Inter-Ocean* called Truth the Miriam of this Exodus, honoring her for helping to keep the idea of a black Exodus to the West alive through long, discouraging years.[27]

Several twentieth-century writers have claimed that Truth, in promoting the settlement of blacks in the West, asked for the creation of a black "state." The earliest of these writers, according to available evidence, was Herbert Aptheker, a radical historian, who in his 1951 "documentary" history of American blacks wrote, ironically without documentation, that by 1890 "the concept of a Negro state had been projected by Negroes, including leaders like Martin Delany and Sojourner Truth, for many years." After Aptheker, several writers also claimed that Truth advocated a black "state."[28]

Other twentieth-century writers, while not saying her plan was for a black "state," nevertheless claimed that her plan called for racial separation. Her biographer Arthur Fauset suggested in 1938 that she envisioned blacks as "set apart" in the West. Walter White of the NAACP, writing in 1948, declared that Truth proposed to have the freed slaves "take themselves out" of the "main stream of life" and settle in the West in "a segregated and remote bayou," which he considered "impractical and even dangerous." In 1962 another of Truth's biographers, Hertha Pauli, explained that Truth's plan would give blacks a chance to "escape from slavery's backwash without being scattered all over." Recently a black scholar claimed that Truth "clearly enunciated" her plan as being for a "separate homeland," an idea, he said, that Marcus Garvey and Malcolm X also favored.[29]

Truth herself is not known to have said her plan was for a black state. When she wrote that her plan was for a "colony" in the West, like the colony of Liberia, it seems likely that what was most important to her in this statement was not that blacks should settle separately from whites, but that blacks should settle in the American West rather than in Liberia. When Truth compared her plan to an Indian reservation, she may have done so—according to a Battle Creek newspaper at the time—because she hoped President Grant would see that her proposal was similar to the Grant administration's aid to Indians through reservations, and become convinced that her plan was similarly justified.[30] Thus what she seemed to see in a reservation as useful for her plan for blacks was not so much that it would separate blacks from whites, or that it would give blacks an opportunity to govern themselves, as that it would be a politically feasible way of getting government help for blacks to settle in the West and to secure white guidance to help them become self-supporting.

While Truth was in Kansas during the Exodus, was she concerned about whether the black refugees settled separately or scattered among whites? Groups of white migrants arriving in Kansas, such as Scandinavians, French, Mennonites, and Mormons, had sometimes settled in "colonies," and sometimes blacks, arriving in Kansas before the Exodus began, had done so too. During the Exodus, however, only a few new black colonies were created. The Kansas Freedmen's Relief Association, with which Truth and Titus worked, itself established one small new black colony in 1879, at Waubaunsee. But in general colonies required capital that neither the black migrants nor the relief workers could easily marshal, and on the whole the Exodus, instead of building up the movement for black colonies, weakened it. The Relief Association believed that if blacks arrived in Kansas with scarcely any resources, they should be placed near established whites to secure employment from them. The association helped a few blacks to take up homestead land and build the customary sod or dug out houses, but helped far more to hire out to whites as farm hands, railroad hands, miners, or domestics. As Laura Haviland wrote, the association's policy was for "scattering" the migrants through the state.[31] Truth is not known to have opposed this scattering policy. Nor during the Exodus is she known to have pressed for the creation of any black "colony," "reservation," or "state," or any significant separation of blacks and whites at all.

If Truth were seriously advocating separatism, it seems unlikely that over the years she would have so forcefully fought segregation in public transportation, or so often lived among whites and associated with white reformers. If Truth were seriously advocating separatism, it is likely that she would have found black churches to be a natural base from which to operate, as did such leading advocates of separatism in her time as Henry Highland Garnet and Henry M. Turner. However, once she moved away from New York City, Truth is not known to have become close to any black church. Also if Truth were seriously advocating separatism, it is likely that when she was campaigning for her plan she would have especially addressed blacks. But she more often addressed whites, which was her usual practice throughout her public life as a reformer. Also if Truth were seriously advocating separatism, one might expect her to associate with or especially admire some leading advocates of black separatism, such as Garnet, Turner, or Martin Delany, but she is not known to have done so. In fact, in the 1870s, from the limited information available, far more whites than blacks publicly endorsed her plan, arranged for her to speak on it, and housed her while she promoted it. Moreover, among these associates of hers, General Howard questioned the wisdom of separate black colonies as in Liberia or Florida, and struggled to desegregate his church in Washington. Gilbert Haven, after becoming a Methodist bishop, dared to work for racially mixed congregations in the deep South. It seems unlikely that such antisegregationists would associate easily with her in her campaign for land for freedmen if they understood that her intention was sharply to separate blacks from whites.

In fact, during the Exodus, both while she was in Kansas and after she left, Truth did not focus on either separatism or integration. That issue was not her predominant concern. Rather, she emphasized the refugees' need for immediate relief and her hope that they would become self-supporting.

According to one of her Kansas friends, Truth said God was doing in the Exodus "just what I have been praying for these eight years."[32] She said this despite the fact that many aspects of the Exodus did not turn out as she had originally intended. She had originally had a vague notion that blacks should go to the West to settle in some degree separately from whites, but most did not settle separately. She had advocated her plan especially as a means of removing destitute, idle blacks from dependence on government welfare in the Washington area. But most blacks migrating to Kansas came not from Washington but from the deep South—from such states as Mississippi, Louisiana, and Texas—and had not been idle but employed as field hands. She had hoped the federal government would give blacks special financial help to acquire land, tools, and buildings, but no governments on any level—federal, state, or local—are known to have given the blacks migrating to Kansas any such aid. She had hoped blacks would take up land, but in fact, as we have seen, most of them did not do so. Truth simply swept aside such differences in detail, in the invigorating belief that God was acting to help her downtrodden people by leading them away from the stifling, cruel South to tolerant Kansas, where they would find it easier to learn to support themselves, much as she had prayed.

During the Exodus, Truth had two contradictory visions for America, indicating that she could look to the future with both despair and hope. In a speech at a predominantly white Topeka church, as reported in a Topeka newspaper, Truth had a sardonic vision: She foresaw "all the colored people" leaving the South, and God, to "avenge their wrongs," turning the Southern whites against each other, so that they would then "kill each other" off, leaving the colored people free to return to the South by themselves to "dwell in peace and safety." In this vision there was no hope for peaceful coexistence between the races. In a more generous vision, which she described to a Chicago newspaper reporter in an interview, she foresaw that blacks, by migrating to Kansas and elsewhere in the North, will learn from Northern whites. They will "get the Northern spirit in them," she said. Then "they will prosper." Then, and this is the most intriguing part of this vision, some of them will return to the South to "teach these poor whites. . . . These colored people will bring them out of Egyptian darkness into marvellous light. The white people cannot do it, but these [colored] will . . . teach the slaveholders the truth that they never had and never knew of."[33] This was not a vision that Americans were so inevitably racist that separation was the only way out. In this vision, in keeping with her more characteristic optimism, she saw blacks continuing what she herself had long been doing: associating with whites, learning from whites, and teaching whites.

15

Women's Rights

"We have many booby men in de land, and they came
from weak women, who say, 'I've got all de rights I want.'"

As Truth grew up, she experienced the degradation of slave women. After she was freed, she knew the demoralization of poor women who worked for other families to the neglect of their own. After she had already begun to develop her talents as a preacher, she fell under the spell of an authoritarian cult leader who would not allow women to preach.

She eventually emerged from slavery, poverty, scandal, and a sense of failure, as a survivor, strengthened by faith, determined to improve herself and the world. By the time she joined the Northampton Association, her deep voice and strong frame, her having worked in the fields and wandered alone as an evangelist, had already set her in opposition to the Victorian ideal of a delicate, submissive woman whose place was in the home. In the association she found that her own unique experience resonated with what she heard there of progressive reform, including the movement for women's rights. Within the next few years, continuing to believe that it was God who had called her to speak and told her what to say, she became a formidable advocate for women.

She remembered later that the early opposition to women's rights scared some women. The "simple announcement" that a women's rights meeting was to be held, she recalled, "was notice for all the ministers, lawyers, and doctors to commence to whine, bark, and growl," so that the women who came to the meeting "were so frightened that they wanted to go home." But she felt, as she looked back on it, that she faced the opposition forthrightly. She "never got frightened at any face of clay, and gave it back to dem better dan dey sent." [1]

In New York City, at a women's rights convention in 1853, crude young men invaded the convention in order to disrupt it. According to the New York *Times,* when Truth rose to speak at the convention, the invaders greeted her with "a perfect storm" of "hisses, groans and undignified ejaculations." In response, when she reached the speaker's desk, she "rolled up her eye-balls in scorn," and "frowned indignantly." She said, "I know it feels funny, kinder funny and tickling to see a colored woman get up and tell you about things and woman's rights, when we've all been trampled down so't nobody thought we'd ever git up agin. But we have come up, and I'm here." As she spoke, the invaders continued to hiss and call for her to serve them "stew" as if they considered her proper place to be that of a servant, not that of a speaker. She spoke angrily, said the *Times,* like "the roar of the cataract." Or like the Trinity Church organ with its "bass and trumpet stops pulled out, all the keys down, and two men and a boy working for dear life at the bellows." "You may hiss as much as you please," she shouted, but women will get their rights anyway. "You can't stop us, neither." [2]

As Truth told Harriet Beecher Stowe in 1853, when she first attended women's rights meetings, and women asked her to speak, she said, "Sisters, I a'n't clear what you'd be after. Ef women want any rights more'n dey's got, why don't dey jes' take 'em, an' not be talkin' about it?" This might seem to be ironical advice for Truth to give, being such a talker herself; however, she persisted in encouraging women to seize their rights, by varied means. In a speech at an 1866 equal rights convention, she advised women not "to beg for their rights," but "to rise up and take them." At a women's rights meeting in 1869, she was uneasy that the women there did not speak up enough for their rights, leaving too much of that to the friendly men present. "Dat will never do," she advised. "If you want any ting, ask for it. If it ain't worth asking for, it ain't worth having." At an 1878 convention, she was still suggesting a similar theme: "If women would live as they ought to, they would get their rights as they went along." [3] Throughout her life Truth often secured rights for herself essentially by asserting them, as when she escaped from her slavemaster Dumont, sued for the recovery of her son, moved to New York, quit her job as a domestic to become a wandering evangelist, and rode on the Washington horse cars.

As both a Christian and an advocate for women, Truth faced the problem of contending with parts of the Bible which opponents often cited, with devastating impact, as teaching against rights for women. Opponents often referred, for example, to Genesis as saying that it was Eve who first brought sorrow into the world, which led God to declare that Adam should rule over Eve. Truth repeatedly replied that if it was woman who first "upset the world, do give her a chance to set it right side up again." Opponents also often cited Paul's first letter to the Corinthians, which said that women should "keep silence in the churches," and if they wish to "learn any thing, let them ask their husbands at home." In defense of women, Truth pointed out that Jesus "never used a harsh word in speaking to them, but called men 'a generation of vipers.' " As for the argument that Jesus was a man, thus properly giving predominance to men, at the Akron women's convention Truth asked, "How came Jesus into the world? Through God who created him and woman who bore him. Man, where is your part?"[4]

Truth expressed many opinions on the appropriate roles for men and women, sometimes in delightfully provocative ways. If women had equal rights, she said, they "would be capable of standing without being propped up." Insisting that women "should be something better than mere toys," she scolded them for too often being given to "vanity and love of dress," and to choosing "small" subjects to think about. Opposing the exclusion of women from juries, she said that "men had no right to be in places where women could not be properly admitted." In New York, she said that women talk better than men, so "men should no longer unsex themselves by leaving the plow . . . for the pulpit," but let women do the preaching instead. Speaking to women in Michigan, she told them they were like lions who, if they only knew their own power, "could not be caged." She insisted that women, by "bringing the children into the ranks of reform," had the power to usher in the millennium "with this generation." Meantime, however, she felt obliged to scold women for not taking care of children well, and said, "It's because women don't take care of this kind of work that we have so many boobies among men." Similarly, speaking in Iowa, she said, "We have many booby men in de land, and they came from weak women, who say, 'I've got all de rights I want.' I tell you if you want great men, you must have great mothers." On the other hand she also said that the kind of men who teach their children to question whether their mothers, because they are women, know anything, should look after the children themselves. "Some of 'em," she said, "ain't good for nothing else!"[5]

In Truth's time, middle-class women were largely excluded from holding jobs outside the home, so that for them the issue of equal pay was often not as pressing as opening up jobs to women. However, Truth, with her experience as a farm and domestic worker, was conscious of the inequality of pay for working-class women. At the 1851 Akron women's rights convention, Truth said, I "can do as much work as any man," and "can eat as much too, if I can get it," but she did not go on to say explicitly that she therefore deserved to be paid as much as a man. In 1867 at an equal rights convention in New York, however, when the concept of equal pay was still way ahead of general public opinion, Truth used some of the same phrasing she had used in 1851, but went on to make it more explicit: "I used to work in the field and bind grain, keeping up with the cradler; but men never doing no more, got twice as much pay. So with the German women. They work in the field and do as much work, but do not get the pay. We do as much, we eat as much, we want as much. . . . What we want is a little money. You men know that you get as much again as women when you write, or for what[ever] you do. When we get our rights, we shall not have to come to you for money, for then we shall have money enough of our own."[6]

Asking for women's right to vote was one of the many concerns of the women's rights movement in the 1850s, along with asking for equal rights at home, at work, and at school. During the 1850s and 1860s, women made progress in securing some rights, such as to enter occupations, inherit property on their own, and share in controlling their own children, but scarcely in the right to vote. However, from about the end of the Civil War, when the question of giving the vote to blacks became a big issue, giving the vote also to women became central in the women's rights movement. From that time it became central for Truth too. By 1867 she was saying that she would not let herself "get out of this world" until women could vote.[7]

Truth maintained that men in government positions—all too often drinkers, with "a nose red like a cigar"—treated women disdainfully, "for their amusement." If women could vote, she argued, they could put women in government positions where they could at least look after the interests of women. We need, she said, women lawyers, women judges, women on juries, women in Congress—she did not herself want to serve in Congress, she explained, but she wanted women to have the right to do so.[8]

Like many advocates of women in her time, Truth held out great hope for what women in government could accomplish. Arguing that men were not capable of cleaning up government, she queried, "Who ever saw a man clean up a house? Men can make dirt, but can't clean it up. It will never be done till women get into government." Furthermore, "As men have been endeavoring for years to govern alone," she said, "and have not yet succeeded in perfecting any system, it is about time the women should take the matter in hand." She also believed women would secure peace. "I want to see women have their rights, and then there will be no more war. All the fighting has been for selfishness. They [Confederates] wanted . . . to hold something that was not their own; but when we have woman's rights, there is nothing to fight for. I have got all I want, and you have got all you want, and what do you fight for? All the battles that have ever been was for selfishness."[9]

By late 1865, only a few months after the end of the Civil War, it began to seem likely that women would not get the right to vote but that black men would. It seemed apparent that black men would get it not because most Americans favored it in itself (they did not), but primarily because many Republican leaders thought giving black men the vote was the only politically feasible way to make reconstruction work in the South. From about this time, many of the leading abolitionist-feminist men, such as Garrison, Wendell Phillips, Gerrit Smith, and Giles B. Stebbins, argued that feminists should temporarily put aside their demand for the vote for women, to concentrate instead on helping black men get their vote. They believed that if reformers mixed their campaign for the vote for black men with the even less popular campaign for the vote for women, the blacks' cause would be hurt. Moreover, they believed that blacks as blacks were far more threatened in their personal safety and in their rights to housing and jobs and education than women as women were, and therefore blacks deserved preference. Most black supporters of women's rights including

Douglass and Frances Harper came to embrace this view. But Truth did not.

In early 1866, when Truth was working with the freedmen in Washington, many congressional Republicans were supporting the Fourteenth Amendment, which was intended to insure that Southern states, as they were readmitted to the Union, could not deprive blacks of their civil liberties. At that time, Susan B. Anthony, the Quaker abolitionist-feminist whom Truth had long known, wrote Truth, asking her "to put her mark" on a petition to Congress to make sure that the amendment was not worded to exclude women from voting. Anthony also asked her to circulate the petition for signatures. Some congressmen, Anthony wrote her, want this amendment to shut "all women out," and to that "I know Sojourner Truth will say, No." [10]

In late 1866, Truth journeyed from Washington to Rochester to attend a New York State equal rights convention. Among the speakers, Elizabeth Cady Stanton, advocating that both blacks and women be given the vote now, was adamant that black women deserved the vote more than black men did—to give the vote to black men before giving it to women, she said, would mean increasing the number of voters who opposed giving the vote to women. Similarly, Truth spoke for the equal right to vote for both blacks and women, putting her emphasis on women. Walking vigorously about the platform and chuckling to herself from time to time, she said, it was women's "own fault if they were deprived of their rights. God is willing that they should have them." According to one newspaper report, Truth was the only one among the many speakers at the convention "who elicited hearty applause." [11]

In early 1867, Stanton, angry that, as she saw it, many long-time abolitionist-feminists were deserting the women's suffrage cause, wrote Truth, inviting her to come to an equal rights convention to be held in New York to help secure for both blacks and women the full rights of a citizen. As Stanton, using one of her latest slogans, put it to Truth: "Help us to bury the woman & the negro in the citizen." [12]

In May, Truth came to New York for the convention, staying for about a week in Stanton's house. At the convention Truth spoke several times, sang at least twice, and sometimes sat on the platform where, one reporter said, she was treated by all the others there with "the greatest attention, deference, and homage." In this situation she was so uninhibited that she felt free to interrupt the proceedings several times. When her old friend Rev. Samuel J. May was presiding, he asked the women in the audience to indicate by show of hands whether, if they had the right to vote, they would in fact exercise that right. Truth "held up both hands." She explained that she did so because the result would be clearer if Mr. May, instead of calling for a show of hands, called for a show by standing, to which the patient May then agreed. On another occasion when her old friend Frances Gage told the convention that she had found in the South, that the black man had learned from his slavemaster how to be "as bad a tyrant" to his black woman as his master had been, Truth cried out, "That's a fact, child; that is a fact." Gage responded: "Yes, Sojourner knows that."[13]

In a speech to the convention, Truth argued that black women needed the vote in order to protect themselves from black men. As reported by the New York *Tribune,* she was hard on blacks, both men and women:

White women are a great deal smarter, and know more than colored women, while colored women do not know scarcely anything. They go out washing, which is about as high as a colored woman gets, and their men go about idle, strutting up and down; and when the women come home, they ask for their money and take it all, and then scold because there is no food. I want you to consider on that, chil'n. I want women to have their rights.[14]

Illustrating the difficulty of knowing what Truth really said, the New York *World* reported part of this same passage in a different, more earthy style:

I want the colored women to understand that if she earns anything it is her own. But if a colored wife goes out to do a little washing—that is about as high as black folks get—(laughter), when she comes back with a little money the husband comes in, "Where have you been?" "To work." "Well, you got paid?" "Yes." "Then let me have it." "But I want to buy so and so for the children." "Well, I don't want words about it. So hand it over." (Laughter.) So he takes it and walks away, nobody knows where. . . . The man claims her money, body, and everything for himself. (Laughter and applause.)

It's not right. Now's the time to make a strong appeal for women's rights.[15]

In the same speech, according to the New York *Evening Post,* Truth sided with Stanton and Anthony, insisting that suffragists should work for the vote for both blacks and women together, now:

There is a great stir about colored men getting their rights, but not a word about the colored women; and if colored men get their rights, and not colored women get theirs, there will be a bad time about it. So I am for keeping the thing going while things are stirring; because if we wait till it is still, it will take a great while to get it going again. . . .

I suppose I am about the only colored woman that goes about to speak for the rights of the colored woman. I want to keep the thing stirring, now that the ice is broke. . . . [16]

You [men] have been having our right[s] so long, that you think, like a slaveholder, that you own us. I know that it is hard for one who has held the reins for so long to give up; it cuts like a knife. It will feel all the better when it closes up again. [17]

The *Tribune* declared this speech was "one of the most pointed, clear, chiseled arguments we have ever heard in favor of equality, without regard to race or sex." [18] It was especially because of this speech that Truth became a symbol of the effort to combine the struggles for black and female rights. Since then she has often been celebrated as such a symbol.

Truth's warning that if American women did not get the vote now along with black men, it would be hard to raise the issue of the vote for women later, proved to be prescient, for it was not until 1920 that women finally got the vote nationwide.

Meantime it was becoming painfully apparent to Stanton and Anthony that many leaders who had supported suffrage for both blacks and women had decided, as a matter of strategy, to push at present only for suffrage for black men, as in the proposed Fifteenth Amendment. Stanton and Anthony, reacting furiously, refused to support the Fifteenth Amendment. The fiery Stanton declared that giving suffrage to the crude, uneducated, recently freed black males without giving it also to educated females would increase prejudice against blacks. In 1869 at a meeting of the American Equal Rights Association, which had supported both blacks' and women's right to vote, Stanton, Anthony, and their friends helped to break up the association over this issue, forming the new National Women's Suffrage Association that was dedicated to working for women's suffrage only.

In response, late in 1869 Lucy Stone led in forming another new women's group, called the American Woman Suffrage Association, of a more moderate nature, which favored giving the vote not only to black men, through the Fifteenth Amendment, but also to women, through another amendment. Despite efforts to reunite the two groups, their leaders bitterly attacked each other. They were divided also by other issues that underlined the greater radicalism of Stanton's group (which was more suspicious of Republicans) and the greater conservatism of Stone's (which was more willing to work with Republicans). The two groups remained split for twenty years.

A recent woman's historian has claimed that Truth, like Anthony and Stanton, "took the position of not supporting" the Fifteenth Amendment because it would not give women the vote.[19] How justified is this claim?

Truth was not present at the equal rights association meeting in New York in May, 1869, where the open split between the Stanton and Stone forces finally occurred. Late in 1869, however, Truth was in Philadelphia at a meeting of the Pennsylvania Anti-Slavery Society when it adopted "without dissent" a resolution urging passage of the Fifteenth Amendment. Although Truth spoke at the meeting, she was not reported as opposing the resolution. About a month later, Truth participated in the formation of a new Pennsylvania state women's suffrage association that affiliated with Lucy Stone's new organization, not with Stanton's, and Truth gave it "a few words of encouragement."[20]

Moreover, soon after the Fifteenth Amendment went into effect giving black males the right to vote, Truth, in Washington in April, 1870, spoke at a celebration of its adoption.[21] We lack a report of what she said on this occasion, but it is unlikely that she would speak in a celebration of the Fifteenth Amendment unless she favored it.

Accordingly, while Truth can reasonably be called radical in 1867 for insisting like Stanton and Anthony that suffragists should push for the vote for both blacks and women together, by 1869 and 1870 she was not as adamantly radical as Stanton and Anthony had become on this issue, because she did not join them in resisting the Fifteenth Amendment. She had become more moderate and conciliatory, more like Lucy Stone and most other feminists, including the blacks Douglass, Charles Remond, Robert Purvis, and Frances Harper, who supported the Fifteenth Amendment even though it did not give women the vote.

However, Truth became militant in another aspect of suffrage activity. By 1868 the Fourteenth Amendment had been adopted with the intention of protecting the civil liberties of blacks. Although this amendment was not intended to give women the right to vote, some woman's suffrage leaders claimed that the amendment permitted women to vote because a part of it defined what a citizen is without mentioning gender.

In the presidential election of 1868, the suffrage leader Portia Gage, in her home town of Vineland, New Jersey, led a group of women to the polls to vote, but they were not allowed to do so. In 1870 Truth visited Gage in her home in Vineland, and doubtless heard Gage tell the story of her attempt to vote.[22]

In 1871 several Michigan women suffragists, asserting their rights under the Fourteenth Amendment, attempted to vote in a state election. Among these were two Detroit friends of Truth's, Catharine A. F. Stebbins, the wife of Giles B. Stebbins, and Nanette B. Gardner, a widow and big taxpayer who therefore had a special claim on the right to vote. Mrs. Stebbins did not succeed in voting, but Mrs. Gardner did. Soon afterward, Truth visited Detroit and stayed with Gardner. Impressed with Gardner's success in voting, Truth persuaded her to write out for her an account of her voting. Gardner wrote that her voting was "the first vote for a state officer deposited in an American ballot-box by a woman for the last half century."[23]

During the presidential campaign of 1872, because black men now could vote, Truth often made campaign speeches to them. The Republicans had helped to give black men the vote, and their national platform that year could be interpreted as friendly to giving women the vote also. Large numbers of both blacks and women suffragists, including Truth, supported the reelection of Republican President Grant. Truth was so fervent for Grant's reelection that she threatened again, as she had when Grant first ran for president, that if he were not elected, she would move to Canada.[24]

Shortly before the 1872 election, Susan B. Anthony, in her home city of Rochester, led about a dozen women into a registration office, and asked that they be registered as voters. Anthony read to registration officials the part of the Fourteenth Amendment that forbade states to abridge the privileges of citizens, which she interpreted as including women, and threatened to arrest the registration officials if they did not allow these women to register. The officials decided to allow them to register, and on voting day permitted them to vote. Afterward, however, Anthony was arrested for having voted.

Similarly Truth, shortly before the election, tried to register to vote in her home town of Battle Creek. As the Battle Creek *Journal* reported it:

Sojourner Truth, on the Saturday before the recent election, appeared before the Board of Registration, in the third ward where she resides, and claimed the right to have her name entered upon the list of electors. Upon being refused, she repaired to the polls on election day in the same ward and again asserted her right to the ballot. She was politely received by the authorities in both instances, but did not succeed in her effort, though she sustained her claim by many original and quaintly put arguments.

Sojourner states that she learned one thing by her visit to the polls on the 5th inst. She verily thought before that day that a literal pole was erected to designate the voting place, and she asked the bystanders to point it out. Her astonishment upon being undeceived, as described to us by her own lips and in her characteristic style, is peculiarly amusing. It is Sojourner's determination to continue the assertion of her right, until she gains it.[25]

When Anthony went to vote in Rochester, she took a group of women with her. Anthony was an organization woman. However, when Truth went to vote in Battle Creek, she went alone. Truth was not an organization woman.

Claims about Truth's role as a feminist have often been exaggerated. In 1870 the Washington weekly with which Douglass was associated claimed that she "has always been as ardent" for "the rights of women as she was of anti-slavery." A scholar has recently even claimed that she was "much more active for women's rights" than for the abolition of slavery. However, the years in which it would be most meaningful to make such comparisons would be the years in which she was a reformist speaker before the abolition of Southern slavery, that is, 1850–64, and in those years available records indicate that when she spoke, she included appeals for slaves' rights in 63 speeches, but for women's rights in only 9. In regard to the years after emancipation, a historian has claimed that she "made the rights of women a special feature of all her talks," but this is far from true.[26] During all the years she spoke publicly as a reformer, from 1850 on, she advocated improving the condition of blacks in 136 speeches, but advocated improving the condition of women in only 28.

Nevertheless, Truth played a conspicuous role among feminists because she was one of the few black women who were active feminists. Moreover, she was conspicuous in opening up public activities to women. While her role as a relief worker for freed slaves might be said to be within the traditional realm of women's care-giving, much of the range of her public activities was not. Beginning in 1827, when few black women took cases to court, she took three cases to court. Beginning about 1830, when few women, black or white, spoke in public, she began to preach, and eventually as a public speaker, she spoke from Maine to Kansas. At a time when few women were so aggressive, she insisted on entering where it was doubtful that she as a black was welcome, as in Washington streetcars, a Washington church, and a Kansas train. At a time when it was not expected that women would march in the streets, in 1868 in Geneva, New York, she marched at the head of a procession celebrating black emancipation.[27] At a time when few women were active in politics, she petitioned Congress, lobbied Congress, campaigned in presidential elections, tried to vote, spoke to the Michigan legislature, and visited three presidents in the White House.

Considering that most feminists were white, middle class, educated, and often anxious to prove to the world that they were respectable despite their feminism, it is remarkable how well they accepted the black, uncultivated, bumptious Truth. According to the New York *Times,* at the 1867 equal rights convention in New York, when Truth took a seat on the platform, "her independent demeanor was the cause of some merriment and much evident satisfaction to the audience." The New York *Herald,* which was often nasty toward both feminists and blacks, described Truth as "among the more prominent persons" at an 1870 women's rights convention in New York, and said she "has so long been petted by the woman suffragists that she is 'jest as good as eny on 'em now.' "[28] In fact, suffragists sometimes did seem to treat her as their darling, perhaps at times condescendingly, as a black token, or in more favorable terms, as a symbol of the unity of the cause of freedom for both blacks and women. She herself, with her belief that God had given her a special mission, sometimes seemed to feel that she was just as good as any of them, if not better.

Indeed, feminist leaders often felt Truth's strength. Stanton and her friends claimed, in their *History of Woman Suffrage,* that for the crude mob of men who invaded the 1853 woman's rights convention in New York, Truth "combined in herself, as an individual, the two most hated elements of humanity. She was black, and she was a woman, and all the insults that could be cast upon color and sex were together hurled at her," but she withstood such insults, remaining "dignified." Susan B. Anthony, in introducing Truth at the 1866 Rochester equal rights convention when about 500 persons including Stanton were attending, said that Truth "had done more than any other in the room for the cause of freedom."

Portia Gage, after Truth had visited her in Vineland, New Jersey, wrote she was a "wonderful teacher." Parker Pillsbury, at a New York State equal rights convention, called Truth "probably the ablest mind which New York ever produced." Wendell Phillips said that her speech was "rich, quaint, poetic and often profound."[29]

Truth, by her compelling presence among the relatively well-off, educated, white feminists, pressed them to take a wider view of womanhood. She pressed them to include in their conception of womanhood—difficult though it was likely to be—slave women, black women, poor women, uneducated women. And she challenged both feminists and their opponents to consider that these less favored women could shed their accustomed passivity, rise up to take their rights, and join more favored women to become a power in the land.

16

Goose Wings and High Heels

"Oh mothers, I'm ashamed of ye!
What will such lives you live do for humanity?"

Exuberant as Truth sometimes was, and certain that God was guiding her, she could not easily be contained within set bounds. She did not fit neatly into the patterns of behavior expected of blacks, or of women, or of women reformers. This was true of her behavior in various aspects of her life, including dress.

As a young slave, she dressed in homespun cloth that did not always reach long enough for a fast-growing girl. As she explained it once, slaveowners "used to weave what dey called nigger-cloth," a coarse cloth such as whites would not wear. Masters gave the cloth out to the female slaves in "a strip," Truth recalled, and we "had to wear it width-wise." If you were short, it was tolerable, but if you were tall like Truth, it was embarrassing.[1]

While living with the Van Wagenens, she acquired clothes of better cloth. "Oh, didn't I swing myself in my homespun clothes," she recalled. Once she felt a wild impulse to go back to the Dumonts' to show off these new clothes. "When I had got fixed up, and had new clothes," she explained in a speech, "I thought I'd like to go back, and let my old associates see how fine I looked. I guess some of you ladies know what that feeling is."[2]

While she was living in New York City, for some time her religious mentor was Elijah Pierson, who emphasized the virtue of simple living, including simple dress. As a wandering evangelist in New England, she met an Adventist who recalled later that she and her friends responded warmly to Truth. They admired "her commanding figure" in front of an audience, "her unwavering faith in God," and "her contempt of what the world calls fashion."[3]

In the 1850s, women's fashions, in accordance with the Victorian ideal of delicate women, called for squeezing midriffs into hourglass shapes, and for long, puffed out skirts worn over mountains of petticoats. Some feminists felt that such fashions placed women under debilitating physical and psychological restraints. A few of these women, including Truth's friends Lucy Stone and Elizabeth Cady Stanton, tried wearing the bloomer costume, which was essentially a loose-fitting short dress, worn over pants. These women were pleased with the freer movement bloomers allowed, but found they could not continue to wear them very long because much of the public, reinforced by the web of commercial interests that profited from fashion, heaped scorn on them for dressing like men. When women asked Truth why she did not wear the new bloomers, Truth answered that what she had worn when she had been a slave was too much like bloomers: "Tell you, I had enough of bloomers in them days."[4]

There was considerable tension among feminists about how to dress. Some, like the intense, Quaker-raised Abby Kelley Foster of Massachusetts, dressed in a simple manner, in keeping with her belief that women should reduce their expenses to be better able to support social causes. Other feminists, reacting to the constant derision of feminists as making themselves unfeminine because they demanded the same rights as men, tried to appear especially demure, or dainty, or motherly—anything but masculine. Lucy Stone, of Massachusetts, after she gave up bloomers, dressed inconspicuously, and kept her voice quiet and low. However, Pauline Wright Davis, of Rhode Island, after giving up bloomers, chose to dress elegantly, in keeping with the height of fashion, saying she intended to do all she could to remove the idea that women who advocate women's rights were determined to seem like men. How women dressed became an issue in choosing presidents for women's rights conventions; one fashionable Boston woman was said to have been rejected because she dressed too extravagantly, with too low a neck line.

Once when Truth had a photograph taken of herself, perhaps to appear feminine she held knitting in her lap. She is not known ever to have had a photograph taken of herself while smoking her pipe.

It was sometimes said that Truth dressed like a black farm woman. According to a New York reporter in the 1860s, she dressed with "a white kerchief around her head a la mamma all over the South." In 1871, a Rochester newspaper reported that "her dress is a mixture" of what "used to be worn by the female slaves of the South" with the dress of the Quakers. Although Truth never became a Quaker, in the 1870s it was often said that she dressed like one. A Chicago newspaper reported her as wearing a "Quakerish livery," including a white cap, white neckcloth, and white cuffs, which was "exactly suited" to her "hard, practical sense."[5] While progressive Quakers by this time were turning away from traditional Quaker dress, Truth, by often selecting Quaker dress, was choosing a modest, simple, and relatively nonrestrictive dress, which may have been in keeping with her own inclination toward dress reform. One of the leading dress reformers in Truth's time, the physician Dr. Rachel Brooks Gleason, who recommended that dress should be comfortable and fit the form of the body, regarded Quaker women's dress as not perfect, but more favorable for health than customary forms of dress, and thus a point of departure for dress reform.

Truth usually dressed modestly. As an artist sketched her scrubbing laundry at a tub, her head was bare, her sleeves were pushed up high, but her skirt reached to the floor, hiding even her ankles. When she spoke, she was often described as dressing in a "plain," "simple," or "dignified" style. She sometimes wore a turban or Quaker bonnet on her head, and long, full dresses in dark colors—gray, blue, green, or black—but brightened by something light around her head and shoulders. Sometimes she wore shawls, though shawls could restrict walking, as one women's dress reformer protested, because the wearer was obliged to hold the shawl in place with her arms.

Truth's friend Parker Pillsbury recalled that the impression she made when speaking in Ashtabula County, Ohio, was less modest than fierce: "Her tall, erect form, dressed in dark green, a white handkerchief crossed over her breast, a white turban on her head, with white teeth and still whiter eyes, she stood, a spectacle weird, fearful as an avenger." The Detroit *Free Press* reported her on the platform as "inspiring a degree of respect that commands attention," but also as being "grotesque and ludicrous." When she spoke at a women's rights convention in Massilon, Ohio, a journalist reported that Truth's costume "was neither male nor female, nor yet a bloomer, making it somewhat difficult to determine to which of the sexes she belonged."[6]

In a bizarre incident in Indiana, some of her enemies said that she came across to them as masculine, and they harassed her about it. An abolitionist reported what happened in the form of a letter to the editor of a Republican newspaper published in Warsaw, Indiana, near where the incident occurred:

Silver Lake, Kosciusko Co., Ind.
October 4th, 1858

Editor of Northern Indianian
Sir:

Sojourner Truth, an elderly colored woman well known throughout the Eastern States, is now holding a series of Anti-Slavery meetings in Northern Indiana. Sojourner comes well recommended by Harriet Beecher Stowe and others, and was welcomed and received by the friends of the slave in this locality. Her progress in knowledge, truth, and righteousness is very remarkable, especially so, when we consider her former low condition as a slave. . . .

The Slave Democracy of Indiana, however, appear to be jealous and suspicious of every Anti-Slavery movement. A rumor was circulated that Sojourner was an impostor; that she was, indeed, a man disguised in woman's clothing. . . .

At her third appointed meeting in this vicinity, which was held in the meeting house of the United Brethren, a large number of Democrats and . . . pro-slavery persons were present, and at the close of the meeting Dr. T. W. Strain, the mouthpiece of the Slave Democracy, called upon the large congregation to "hold on," stating that a doubt existed in the minds of many persons present respecting the sex of the speaker, and that it was his impression that a majority believed the speaker to be a man, and [he] also proposed that Sojourner should show her breast to some of the ladies present, so that by their testimony the doubt might [be] solved.

A large number of ladies were present, who were ashamed and indignant at the Doctor's proposition.

Dr. Strain further said (which was not believed by the friends of the Slave) that it was particularly for the speaker's sake that he made this demand. . . .

Confusion and uproar ensued. A gun or pistol was fired near the door. However, the tumult was soon suppressed by Sojourner rising in all the dignity of womanhood, and demanded [demanding] why they suspected her "to be a man?" and was answered, "your voice is not the voice of a woman; it is the voice of a man."

Sojourner told them that her "breasts had suckled many a white babe; that some of those babies had grown to man's estate, and that they were far more manly than they (her persecutors) appeared to be."

In vindication of her truthfulness, she told them that she would show her breast to the whole congregation; that it was not to her shame but to their shame, that she uncovered her breast before them. Two young men, viz.: A. Badgely and J. Hamer voluntarily stepped forward to the examination. As Sojourner disrobed her bosom, she quietly asked them if they too "wished to suck." As she presented her naked breast to the gaze of the audience, a Democrat cried out, "Why, it is a sow, for I see the teat." . . .

As "the agitation of thought is the beginning of wisdom," we hope that Indiana will yet be redeemed.

Respectfully,
William Hayward

The editor of the *Indianian* not only chose to publish this astonishing letter, but also to comment on it. What interested him as a partisan Republican was not the rudeness to Truth or the means she used to vindicate herself, but that a Democrat defender of slavery, Dr. Strain, was put down by a black. Strain got "bored," the editor gloated, "by a 'cullud pusson.' Served him right!"[7]

Hayward also sent his letter to Garrison's *Liberator* in Boston. The *Liberator* also chose to publish it, but without comment, though apparently heavily editing it first. Later Frances Titus, in editing a revised version of Truth's *Narrative,* also chose to print the letter, and also without direct comment of her own. However, Titus omitted the crudest expression in the letter, the reference to the sow's teat. She also added a comment, written years later by Parker Pillsbury, in which he said that in this incident, as in all incidents in which Truth met hostility, she was able to "scatter" her enemies, in "dismay and confusion."[8]

Truth was not forced to respond to the rude challenge as she did. She could have refused to respond at all. She could have responded only verbally, or she could have consented to show her breasts only privately, to a few women.

Truth's showing her breasts to the whole audience is startling. Despite her general inclination to choose modest dress, when the occasion seemed to her to demand it, she was able quickly, apparently without hesitation, to abandon modesty about dress, to say the least. She could express her anger dramatically, seemingly without inhibitions. Evidently her experience of slavery and poverty, her feminist outlook, and her biblically based contempt for the world, had readied her to flout the stereotype of what modest femininity meant, and to do it with poise.

Although Truth had long opposed elaborate fashion for women, it was only in 1870 that she is known to have begun to speak out conspicuously against it. She seems to have begun to do this at about the same time that she also began to speak out freely against smoking and drinking, as if they were related in her mind. Perhaps the fact that she herself had finally been able to give up smoking helped to make her feel free to speak out on several kinds of what seemed to her frivolous and damaging behavior.

In July, 1870, speaking on woman's suffrage in Hopedale, Massachusetts, she included "criticisms of the fashion and extravagance of the people," which a newspaper writer conceded "are awkwardly severe," but added, her hearers "know that it is their friend who speaks."[9]

Then in October in Providence, she made a particularly vitriolic statement against fashion. She had recently attended a Rhode Island state women's suffrage society's convention in Providence, and as she observed the leaders of the convention sitting on the platform, she had become disturbed by their dress, particularly their hairstyles. It was a time when fashionable women dressed their hair elaborately, often with the aid of hair pieces. The president of this society was the fashion-advocate Paulina Wright Davis, and in fact it was Davis who had introduced Truth to speak at the convention.

Truth did not speak against fashion at this convention. But after the convention was over, Truth stayed on in Providence to speak at a meeting of her own, especially on western lands for freedmen. On this occasion, according to a Providence newspaper, Truth was herself dressed in "a very plain, Quaker-like garb, with a snowy white neckerchief folded across her breast, a close fitting white turban on her head, and silver-bowed spectacles, and was dignified and impressive in manner."

It was only in a digression that she spoke about women's dress. She began: "I'm awful hard on dress, you know," as if she felt she already had a reputation for denouncing fashion. She continued:

Women, you forget that you are the mothers of creation. You forget your sons were cut off like grass by the war and the land was covered with their blood. You rig yourselves up in panniers and Grecian bend-backs and flummeries; yes, and mothers and grey-haired grandmothers wear high heeled shoes and humps on their heads and put them on their babies, and stuff them out so that they keel over when the wind blows. Oh mothers, I'm ashamed of ye! What will such lives you live do for humanity?

When I see them women on the stage at the Women's Suffrage Convention the other day, I thought, what kind of reformers be you, with goose-wings on your heads, as if you were going to fly, and dressed in such ridiculous fashion, talking about reform and women's rights? 'Pears to me you had better reform yourselves first.

Here she caught herself, seeming to realize that she might irritate some of her friends. Half in apology, but half in forthright explanation of why she felt led into such bold criticism, she said:

But Sojourner is an old body, and will soon go out of this world into another, and wants to say when she gets there, "Lord, I have done my duty, I have told the whole truth and kept nothing back."

This attack on women's fashion, originally published in the Providence *Daily Journal,* was soon copied by other newspapers, as in New York, Washington, and Detroit. Neither the publication of the original attack nor these reprints of it were accompanied by any report of what the women of the suffrage convention—including Paulina Davis—thought of this criticism by one of their own, directed against their leaders on the platform. However, the New York *Tribune* editorialized that we would earnestly support Truth's protest "if we thought reform possible; but we don't. There has been no simplicity of womanly attire since our grand-mother Eve made her first apron of fig-leaves." Another commentator said, the clergy do not dare to bring out the truth of the gospel against "prided fashions," and so we leave Truth "to battle almost alone" against "these world-wide evils." [10]

Evidently Truth liked the fuss she stirred up by her bold attack on fashion in Providence, for she continued thereafter to attack fashion more conspicuously than she had ever been known to do before. The next year in Syracuse, she herself invited people to come to hear her speak for a temperance society at the city hall, saying, "Come up chillin'; I lecture on drinkin', on smokin', on chewin', on snuffin', and on dressin'," thus rolling several of her pet peeves together. People evidently liked her invitation, for a Syracuse newspaper reported that the hall was "filled to overflowing." [11]

In the mid-1850s the National Dress Reform Association had been organized, with abolitionist-feminists like Gerrit Smith among its leaders. It was still holding annual conventions in the 1870s. Meanwhile in Battle Creek, Ellen White, one of the principal founders of the Seventh Day Adventist movement, became a leading dress reformer among Adventists, urging healthier, more economical dress for women, including pants with short skirts. But Truth in regard to dress reform, as in regard to other areas of reform, often operated to a considerable degree independently. Truth is not known to have had connections with any dress reform organizations or with Ellen White's dress reform drive.

Truth's focus in regard to fashionable dress was not the same as that of many other feminist dress reformers at about the same time. Other reformers often focused on its unhealthy and restrictive qualities, while Truth focused on its frivolity and extravagance, and how it distracted women from the noble work they should be doing. In effect, Truth's attack on women's fashion was part of her larger attack, often expressed in a religious context, on the "vanity and pride" of women that she called "the great stumbling blocks" to their achieving their "rights."[12]

Speaking to women in a private home in Grand Haven, Michigan, Truth urged them "to ignore the absurd fashions, and lead more earnest lives." Speaking in a Chicago church, she warned mothers against the "worldly way" in which they "fixed up" their children for church; she asked everyone to "come out of this world" and "give up dress and frivolity." In a black church in Topeka, she was "terribly down on the foolish habits and fashions of the young people of our day." In a white church in Topeka, Truth "censured the ladies for being swallowed up in fashionable vanities, spending their time in primping instead of praying."[13]

17

Drink and Smoke

"Treat them as human beings should be treated,
and fewer temperance converts would backslide."

When Truth was young, she liked to dance with her fellow slaves. According to Gertrude, the daughter of her slavemaster Dumont, she was an "excellent" dancer, being "quick in her movements." She was also "fond of liquor and tobacco, and used both when she could get them, for years."[1]

After Truth had walked away from the Dumonts' and was living at the Van Wagenens', when she realized that it was nearly Pentecost, she longed to be back again at the Dumonts to join in the holiday fun. Pentecost—which Truth, like the slaves in the Hudson valley generally, called by the Dutch name Pinkster—was a slave holiday lasting several days. Though in the Hudson valley Pinkster was originally a Dutch Christian holiday which came seven weeks after Easter, some of the slaves had made it over for themselves into an African holiday. On these days off, they sang African songs, drank, decorated themselves, as with feathers, pounded out African rhythms, made grunts and grimaces, and danced African dances.

As Pinkster approached, Dumont made a visit to the Van Wagenens, and Isabella told him she wanted to return to his house with him. Though Dumont told her she could not, she did not believe he meant it, and got ready, bringing out her new clothes to show off to her old friends. As

Dumont was getting his wagon ready to drive off, she was about to climb in, she recalled, when God told her not to. Afterward she felt guilty that she had wanted to go, to drink, dance, and show off her clothes, and she associated her guilt with her feeling that she had been forgetting God.[2]

By the time Truth moved to New York City, her religious associations may have inhibited her drinking. The temperance movement was well advanced by this time, fired up to a large extent by its associations with evangelicals such as Methodists, and it was strong in New York State. Moreover, two of her religious mentors, Pierson and Matthias, both cautioned against drinking. But she continued to smoke, then and long afterward. In 1868 her friend Amy Post wrote that "all of her old friends know that she has been an inveterate smoker, she says from [a] very early age."[3]

Soon after leaving New York City and becoming a wandering evange- list, when she found that a temperance meeting was to be held in Cold Spring, Long Island, she joined in the preparations for it, as if she were quite comfortable with a temperance meeting.[4]

Once Truth settled in the Northampton Association, she was among reformers who were all said to be temperance advocates. In the 1850s, as a speaker for blacks' and women's rights, she continued to be surrounded by advocates of temperance. Her mentor, Garrison, was a temperance advocate—he had a special reason to be, for both his father and brother were alcoholics.

Americans probably drank more in the nineteenth century than they had in the preceding century, and drunkenness was widespread. In reac- tion, by midcentury the temperance movement had become strong, much more pervasive than the movements for either blacks' or women's rights. Many advocates of temperance did not support blacks' or women's rights, but both abolitionists and feminists usually supported temperance. Advo- cates of women's rights usually regarded drunkenness as a male practice which victimized women, subjecting them to cruel abuse. Because di- vorce was virtually impossible, a woman married to an abusive, alcoholic husband had little protection for herself or her children. Therefore, to advocates of women's rights, the temperance movement was another radical reform, like woman's suffrage and the abolition of slavery, for the protection and emancipation of women.

During the 1850s and 1860s, Truth's interest in temperance scarcely came to the surface, her primary interests being blacks' and women's rights. In 1853 in New York Truth attended a world temperance convention as a registered delegate,[5] but is not known to have spoken there or at any other temperance meetings in the 1850s or 1860s.

Although she continued to smoke, she was considerably exposed to reformist pressure against the use of tobacco. She was exposed to it from feminists such as Pauline W. Davis, who objected to women using tobacco because it made women seem like men. Truth was also exposed to it in reformist meetings, such as a Pennsylvania Yearly Meeting of Progressive Friends, which resolved that the use of tobacco is among the worst evils of our day: It injures the health of mind and body, and leads to "bondage" to tobacco.[6] Once she settled in Battle Creek, she was subject to pressure against both liquor and tobacco from the Quakers, Spiritualists, and Seventh Day Adventists with whom she mingled. Seventh Day Adventists, who had their national headquarters there, were developing a special emphasis on health, which they associated with their opposition to alcohol, tobacco, and fashionable dress.

When she was in Washington working with the freedmen, Truth found herself subject to a different kind of pressure against tobacco. One of her colleagues there, Lucy Colman, reported that until this time Truth had been "a great smoker." But when she tried to teach the freedmen "economy" in the use of what little money they had, she found that it was "not best to take with her such a useless habit as smoking." Truth may have tried to stop smoking at this time, for she said later that she had long wished to stop, but could not.[7]

Moreover, Truth was becoming conspicuous for her smoking, which was undoubtedly embarrassing both to herself and to her friends. In 1867 while Truth was staying in New York in Elizabeth Cady Stanton's home, according to Stanton's report to a newspaper at the time, Truth was still smoking and was giving as an excuse for doing so, that when she was travelling by train, to segregate her as a black she was often "sent into the smoking-car," so "she smoked in self-defense—she would rather swallow her own smoke than another's."[8]

The next year another newspaper report about her smoking appeared, this time in the form of a story. It appeared in March, 1868, in a newspaper published in Coldwater, Michigan, near Battle Creek. True or not, it became a popular story, often retold:

Sojourner Truth

This old colored woman, now living in Michigan, recently visited Milton, Wis., where she was the guest of a Mr. [Joseph] Goodrich,[9] who was an out-and-out temperance man, and a noted hater of tobacco. One morning she was puffing away with a long pipe in her mouth when her host, Mr. Goodrich, approached her, and commenced conversation with the following interrogatory.

"Aunt Sojourner, do you think you are a Christian?"

"Yes, Brudder Goodrich, I speck I am."

"Aunt Sojourner, do you believe in the Bible?"

Yes, Brudder Goodrich, I bleeve the scripters, though I can't read 'em, as you can."

"Aunt Sojourner, do you know that there is a passage in the scriptures which declares that nothing unclean shall inherit the kingdom of heaven?"

"Yes, Brudder Goodrich, I have heard tell of it."

"Aunt Sojourner, do you believe it?"

"Yes, Brudder Goodrich, I bleeve it."

"Well, Aunt Sojourner, you smoke, and you cannot enter the kingdom of heaven, because there is nothing so unclean as the breath of a smoker. What do you say to that?"

"Why, Brudder Goodrich, I speck to leave my breff behind me when I go to heaven."[10]

Although this story may have been told especially to illustrate how quick-witted Truth could be, nevertheless its circulation may have prodded her to try again to quit smoking. Goodrich's argument against tobacco may have impressed her, for later she employed it herself and even extended it: She said anyone whose breath smells of either tobacco or liquor cannot enter heaven.[11]

A few months after the Goodrich story appeared, in August 1868, she attended a national Spiritualist convention in Rochester that resolved to deplore the "alarming increase" in the use of tobacco.[12] During the rest of the summer and fall she remained in western New York on a speaking tour, circulating considerably among abolitionists, feminists, Progressive Friends, and Spiritualists, including her long-time friends Amy Post and Lucy Colman, all of whom were likely to be antitobacco.

By September, Truth tried again to quit smoking. In December, Amy Post, with whom she was staying at the time, wrote with "much joy" to the *National Anti-Slavery Standard* that Truth had "not smoked once in three months. I wish every smoker who reads this would take courage, and do likewise."[13]

When one of Truth's Quaker friends read Amy Post's announcement in the *Standard,* the friend wrote Truth that she was glad that Truth had been freed from slavery "to the filthy weed" and thus had "been freed twice from slavery."[14]

On January 18, 1869, Truth herself, increasingly certain that she had succeeded in quitting permanently, wrote Amy Post from Detroit:

I want you to let it be known that it was of my own will and desire to quit smoking. It was the Spirit that spoke to me to give up tobacco, and I long had been wishing to do so, but could not, and I prayed to God that he would make me feel the necessity to give it up, and he did and I have had no taste or appetite to take it again. Tell Miss Coleman [Lucy Colman] that [it] was all of my own power or the power that God gave me to give up tobacco, & the dear Lord has filled the part that longed with his own love and Spirit, & now my great prayer is that all who smoke may have the Spirit that spoke to me to work in them to destroy the desire for tobacco.[15]

Her Battle Creek friend Frances Titus explained that Truth gave up smoking in part because she did not have the "courage to chide people for using spirituous liquors while indulging in the use of tobacco herself."[16] Indeed, as far as can be judged, it was only in 1870, after she had given up smoking, that Truth began to speak openly against alcohol.

In the 1870s the temperance movement had a rebirth of energy, and this time it became, as it had not been before, largely a women's movement. Women employed the temperance movement, more than they employed either the abolitionist or feminist movements, as a vehicle by which they gradually progressed toward full participation in American public life. By moving from the home into what temperance leader Frances Willard called activities for the "protection of the home," they moved into public speaking, public demonstrations, and promoting the right of women to vote on local alcohol-related issues. From there they moved to promoting women's right to vote in general, and on to lobbying for broad social legislation.

From 1870 to the end of Truth's life, temperance, as measured by the number of known speeches in which she included advocacy of it, was a major concern for Truth, greater than her concern for women's rights, but less than her concern for blacks' rights. From 1870 on, reports of twenty-five of her speeches are available in which she included support for temperance. While she said that she lectured as much against tobacco as against alcohol, available newspapers reported her as lecturing more against alcohol. She spoke at least thirteen times for temperance organizations, including once at an Indiana temperance convention with such leading temperance advocates as Governor St. John of Kansas and national president Frances Willard of the Women's Christian Temperance Union. In 1881 the Union's Chicago paper claimed enthusiastically that Truth "has probably delivered more temperance addresses than any other person living." [17] But she is not known to have been a member or officer in any temperance organization, whether local or otherwise, again illustrating her propensity to act individually.

Although she sometimes spoke about temperance in regard to alcohol by itself, at other times she spoke of it along with temperance in regard to tobacco (it was not unusual in Truth's time to combine opposition to alcohol and tobacco), and sometimes along with temperance in dress. Speaking to a temperance group in Grand Haven, Michigan, she described any kind of excess as intemperance, including overeating.[18]

Truth argued that tobacco is a waste of money, is "filthy," and "destroys the health." Speaking to boys, she urged them not to pick up the stumps of cigars they found "thrown about," and thus learn to smoke, because then their bodies would not be clean. Against chewing tobacco, she said she knew ministers "who carried the nasty weed in their mouths," but asked, "what sort of a mouth was that to talk about Jesus?" Speaking in Kansas, she looked disgustedly at the tobacco juice being spit on the floor, and declared, "If Jesus was here, he would scourge you from this place." [19]

Against alcohol, she made fun of lawyers who drink, calling them "brandy-nosed pettifoggers." She laughed at the excuses drinkers often gave for drinking, saying once: "Some folks had a way of gettin' 'toxicated, and pretendin' they took the stuff coz they was sick!" She charged that drinking, particularly of whisky, "is at the bottom of a great many crimes." She argued that "not one cent" spent on tobacco or liquor "is spent for good." She appealed to fathers to set an example to their children, saying, you cannot expect children to be temperate, so long as their fathers are "a-smokin' an' a-chewin' an' a-slobberin' aroun'." She supported the prohibition of the manufacture of alcoholic beverages, as temperance workers at the time usually did, and said it was a "blessing" in 1880 when Kansas, with the overwhelming support of its black voters, became another prohibition state. One of her arguments for giving suffrage to women was that men, so long as they controlled government by themselves, would at best only "license" such evils as "drunkenness and houses of ill fame," but would never "destroy" them. "They will never be cleared out," she said, "till the women do it."[20]

She encouraged use of an already traditional temperance device, the pledge to stop drinking. She urged one of the young men in the Merritt family in Battle Creek to sign the pledge, and he did, and his sister recalled long afterward that he kept his pledge all his life. But Truth believed that the pledge was sometimes misused. She felt that it was a mistake to suppose that once a father whose drinking had brought his family to grief had signed a pledge to stop drinking, this was all that needed to be done. She sensed such a father would need substantial support, material and psychological. "You ought to get him work," she said, "and carry food and clothing to his poor starving wife and children. Treat them as human beings should be treated, and fewer temperance converts would backslide. God's law is the law of forgiveness."[21]

18

Friend Titus

"She is of the salt of the earth."

In Truth's time, close supportive relations between women reformers often developed, as between Elizabeth Cady Stanton and Susan B. Anthony, and between Frances Willard and Anna Gordon. But because such relations between black and white women were rare, Truth's relationship to Frances Walling Titus has special meaning.

Titus was a New England–born Quaker who had known Truth through the Progressive Friends before Truth settled in the Battle Creek area. Like many Quakers, Titus had drifted away from the Quakers somewhat —she and her husband had joined the Battle Creek Swedenborgian Church during its brief existence, and she felt the attraction of both spiritualism and "free thought." After the Civil War, as we have seen, Titus had helped to bring freedmen to Battle Creek. After the death of her husband in 1868, Titus was to become active in a larger arena, serving on the executive committees of both Michigan and national women's suffrage societies.

In the fall of 1867, shortly after Truth had returned from Washington to Battle Creek, Truth was working to remodel the small barn she had just bought in Battle Creek proper, on College Street, into a house. A little farther back from the street than most houses, it was a story-and-a-half house in a predominantly white neighborhood, on an unpaved, ungraded street. It was about a mile from Titus's fine house on Maple Street. Truth sometimes walked that mile to visit Titus.

In buying the lot and barn, Truth had been obliged to give William Merritt a mortgage on "everything I have," she said, "lacking my body and a few rags."[1] But she still did not have enough money to make her new house comfortable for the first winter. She asked Titus to appeal for help, as Titus did in this matter-of-fact letter to Eliza Leggett, a friend with whom Truth sometimes stayed when she was in Detroit:

Battle Creek, Nov. 13/67

Mrs. Leggett
Dear Madam:
Our friend Sojourner Truth desires me to thank you for the two kind letters she has recently received from you, one of which contained money ($6.56), & to tell you how grateful & thankful she is for your kind & encouraging attentions to her.

She is in much need of present assistance. Her house is progressing slowly & cannot be made comfortable for the winter unless she is assisted by her friends.

She expects to hold meetings in Kalamazoo next week where she will probably take up collections.

She wishes me to say to you if a loan or collections could be forwarded to her from Detroit, of $30, she will come out, hold meetings & sell her photographs & by such means refund the money after a few weeks. She cannot leave now as her presence is necessary here. Her stay in Kalamazoo will necessarily be short, a couple of days perhaps.

Mrs. Haviland owes her about $20, which would be very acceptable if convenient for Mrs. H. to pay. [Laura Haviland was visiting the Leggetts at this time]

She would like some of her friends to solicit a donation from Captn. [Jonathan] Walker.[2]

She is anxious to have a little home of her own where she can be comfortable & make her friends comfortable. We think with a little more assistance she will get a couple of rooms into suitable condition to live in—the other parts can be finished at another time.

She needs flannel clothing, also blankets for her bed.

Told me to tell you that Giles Stebbins called on her & gave her a donation. In haste,

Truly & respectfully yours,
F. W. Titus

[Postscript] Thursday
morning [Nov. 14]
Sojourner has just called. . . . She is cheerful & hopeful. . . . She is anxious to have all letters & contributions sent to my care.[3]

This letter suggests that Truth and Titus were part of a network of Michigan friends who informed and supported each other. In the letter

Titus does not hint at qualms on Truth's part in soliciting funds for herself, nor does Titus express qualms on her own part in soliciting funds for Truth. Titus keeps herself out of the letter as much as possible, but the final request that all letters and contributions be sent to Titus hints at the managerial role Titus could play in Truth's life.

During Truth's campaign for western land for freed people, Titus wrote some of Truth's correspondence, as she had before, including correspondence about trips to promote her campaign. Although Titus often held back her own opinions, in editing the expanded 1875 version of Truth's *Narrative,* she specifically endorsed one of the key ideas Truth used as a basis for her western land proposal, namely, the idea that the nation owed blacks a debt because it had profited for generations from blacks' unpaid labor.[4]

While Titus herself put up some of the money for the publication of the revised *Narrative,* she arranged for the proceeds to go to Truth. Certainly Truth needed more income. By 1871 Truth had paid off to William Merritt the original mortgage he had held on her house. But by 1874, when both she and her grandson had been seriously ill and she had incurred heavy doctors' bills, Truth was forced to take out another mortgage on her house, this time probably from Titus. Truth hoped to pay off this new mortgage by selling copies of her revised *Narrative.*

In this revised *Narrative,* Titus indicated she warmly admired Truth, as by writing: "For one who is nobody but a woman, an unlettered woman, a black woman, and an old woman, a woman born and bred a slave, nothing short of the Divine incarnated in the human, could have wrought out such grand results."[5]

To help Titus revise the *Narrative,* Truth provided clippings, letters, and the like. But the illiterate Truth could scarcely involve herself directly in Titus's writing. Titus reported that when she was selecting from Truth's papers what to publish, Truth "trusts her scribe to make the selections."[6] Truth relied on Titus, letting Titus mythologize her, as she had also let Stowe and Gage and others do, without, as far as we know, attempting significant correction.

Titus, if less self-effacing than Olive Gilbert who wrote the first version of Truth's *Narrative,* generally kept herself out of this new version; she seldom mentioned her own name, and, like Gilbert, kept her name off the title page. At the time, Titus, in her late fifties, lacked experience as a historian or biographer or serious writer of any kind, and modestly invited criticism of her work.[7] Like most American women of her time, Titus was little educated. Feeling a need to improve herself, in 1870 Titus had attended in Battle Creek a history class for women, led by Lucinda H. Stone, who had taught at Kalamazoo College and was an advocate of equal education for women. But Titus remained considerably unseasoned.

In revising Truth's *Narrative* three times (1875, 1878, 1884), Titus performed a service to posterity, particularly by preserving documents related to Truth. However, Titus's work, romanticized as it was, is of limited value to twentieth-century readers. In including Gilbert's original 1850 *Narrative* in the 1878 revision, Titus omitted Gilbert's passage that estimated sensibly when Truth was born, and inserted instead a dubious claim that Truth had been born twenty years earlier, thus contributing to the common legends about Truth's age.[8] Moreover, Titus seemed to tamper with documents to make Truth look better, as by improving the way Truth's pronunciation was reported, by omitting crude comment by others about Truth, and by altering a significant word that made a report about how the public responded to Truth seem much more favorable than it was. Titus also altered documents in more serious ways: She omitted key passages in Gage's report of Truth's Akron speech that would have warned readers that Gage's report might not be accurate. She inserted significant passages, not in the original as it was published, into Truth's letter about her interview with Lincoln. Also Titus mixed up essential dates, not only when Truth was born, but also when she was freed, and when she made various trips. She failed to identify the date and source of many clippings she used, and when she did attempt to identify them, she sometimes got them wrong.[9] She did not discuss several essential questions, such as why Truth chose to move to Michigan from Massachusetts, how she related to Battle Creek blacks, and what her connections were to various Battle Creek churches.

When Truth was younger, she often went on speaking trips alone. Even as late as 1873, when she was speaking in Grand Rapids, a newspaper there reported her to be travelling "everywhere without assistance."[10] On longer trips, however, she often travelled with her grandson Samuel Banks, until he died in 1875. By the later 1870s, as Truth grew older, she needed more than ever to have someone travel with her. By that time, Titus's husband having long since died, and her son being grown and operating the family's flour mill in Battle Creek, Titus felt free to travel. In 1876, when Truth hoped to visit Philadelphia, she expected Titus to be there too. In 1877 Titus accompanied Truth on a speaking trip of about a week in Michigan, to Grand Haven and Muskegon. In 1878–79, Titus accompanied Truth on a ten-month trip to New York State, first to attend a national women's rights convention in Rochester, then to tour upstate New York, and finally to visit New York City. Later in 1879, when crowds of poor Southern blacks began to migrate to Kansas, according to Titus, Truth "felt such a desire" to go to Kansas to see the Exodus in process "for herself," and was "so anxious to have me come with her," that she persuaded Titus to accompany her.[11]

When Truth and Titus, this unusual black–white pair, travelled together, how did they relate to each other? In 1876, when both Truth and Titus were planning to visit Philadelphia, Truth expected that she and Titus would stay there separately. In 1878–79, when they were travelling together in New York State, they often stayed together, as at Emily Howland's, although Titus for a time went off by herself to a Freethinkers' convention, suggesting that she could pursue her own interests apart from Truth. In later 1879 when they first arrived in Topeka, a newspaper announced that Truth and Titus were travelling together, that Titus was "wealthy" (somewhat of an exaggeration), and that they would probably stay together as guests in the home of one of the officers of the Freedmen's Relief Association. In December, when they were back again in Topeka, a newspaper announced that they were both staying at Mrs. Burt's boarding house.[12] Their staying together in Topeka and elsewhere, and doing so publicly, suggests their easy acceptance of each other. It might also reflect their desire for convenience, or for economy, or to make a statement against racial segregation.

They also stayed together in Osage City according to a letter which Titus wrote from there to Governor St. John's wife:

Osage City [Kansas], Oct. 29, 1879

Mrs. St. John
Topeka, Kansas
Dear Friend:

Did you not make a mistake about your husband's appointment at this place? The people here think the Gov. is to be here Monday next. If we could have an hour's conversation with Gov. St. John, we would remain here till he comes, otherwise we will go to Emporia on Saturday.

We are boarding with Mrs. Bryant on the corner of Lord & Sixth Sts.

It is important that we have an interview with Mr. St. John & we hope you [are] to be here also, for something must be done speedily. I would be very much obliged to you for a reply by tomorrow's mail.

Hastily, but very truly yours,
F. W. Titus [13]

This letter suggests that Titus had become bolder than the Titus of her 1875 version of Truth's *Narrative*. Titus seemed to address the governor's wife assertively, as if she and Truth knew her well. Titus sounded distinctly managerial, as if she felt free to speak for Truth, with authority, without even mentioning Truth's name. Is her failure to mention Truth's name essentially because Mrs. St. John already knew that Truth and Titus were travelling together? Is it a sign that Titus was becoming more of a figure in her own right, apart from Truth?

In the Kansas press, Truth was regularly presented as in charge of her own life, freely giving her judgments about the course of events, pleading, scolding, cajoling in accordance with her own very distinctive experience. Truth was often lionized, whereas Titus was not, and indeed Titus was not reported as making any speeches. However, a Topeka black meeting resolved: "We believe that Sojourner Truth and Mrs. Frances E.[sic.] Titus are Christian women whose life and conduct commands the confidence of the good people of the country," suggesting a regard for Titus beyond what a secretary or travel guide would elicit. [14]

Truth herself, while she and Titus were in Kansas together, said of Titus, "She is of the salt of the earth." [15] Trusting Titus, Truth let her manage her daily affairs.

Near the end of their trip, on December 3, Titus wrote from Topeka to a friend of Truth's in Massachusetts, a private letter which was nevertheless printed in a newspaper. The letter suggests that Titus was growing restless in her relation to Truth:

Sojourner Truth is here in Kansas, in very good health and spirits. . . . I brought her here last September. We did not expect to remain longer than a month, but became so much interested that we are still here. Sojourner has done good work since she came, and made her mark, which will be long remembered. . . .

Last week I went in company with [the Kansas Freedmen's Relief Association's General Superintendent] John [M.] Brown and Mrs. Dr. Green [probably a misprint for Mrs. Caroline De Greene, Comstock's daughter, who was not a doctor] to visit two colonies [of freed people], 75 miles distant, and disburse supplies to them. We went in an open wagon across the prairies, following the old Mormon trail for a guide. We . . . distributed clothing and bedding to over 300 people. . . .

A little more about Sojourner. She wants to travel and collect for this work, and wants me to take her. The officers of the society want me here. As the winter approaches, and Sojourner is very sensitive to the cold, I think I will take her to her home in Michigan and have her hold meetings on the way as she is able, then leave her there, and return. I have taken upon myself the whole responsibility of her support, else she would have been a public charge for the past five years. If people who are able would donate three or four hundred dollars for her support, and place it in the Battle Creek Bank, so that she could draw three or four dollars per week, I should feel free to engage in this work, which so greatly needs helpers. Perhaps the way will open when least expected.[16]

In this letter Titus indicated that she had done some travelling in Kansas without Truth, and that she did not wish to cooperate with Truth's continuing to travel on behalf of the refugees. Bearing the principal financial burden for Truth for five years seemed to have left Titus chafing and eager to strike out on her own, for a cause she valued, provided Truth's financial needs were otherwise met.

A few days later, on December 9, 1879, Truth, Titus, and Haviland left Topeka together, leaving Comstock behind to continue the work there. As one of their Topeka co-workers wrote, the three were expecting to carry on the work in Illinois, Michigan and "perhaps other states." The co-worker continued: "Very rarely will so many women of such advanced years be found at work so faithfully, and in a way that tasks so severely both physical and mental powers, as this noble band. Sojourner, one hundred and four years [really about eighty-two], Mrs. Haviland, seventy-two, Mrs. Comstock [sixty-four] and Mrs. Titus [sixty-three] long gray in the service, but vigorous, strong in the cause they serve, sparing no labors, shrinking from no toil, hardship or privation, that they may feed and clothe the hungry and naked."[17] This letter appears to give Titus the same status as Truth, Haviland, and Comstock, as a major figure in the relief work in her own right.

On the way home, Titus and Truth together stopped off in Streator, Illinois. From there, on December 15, the secretary of Streator's Kansas relief society, Mrs. J. J. Taylor, wrote Governor St. John about forwarding four barrels of secondhand clothing by train to Kansas. Taylor also reported to the Governor:

Sojourner and Mrs. Titus arrived safely on Wed. evening last, Sojourner suffering with a severe cold, and a slight malarial attack. Fortunately my husband is a physician and versed in matters pertaining to such conflicts.

Mrs. Titus is busy writing and meeting ladies to sew for refugee children. Today we finish twenty prs. mittens, for some school that Mrs. Titus is interested in.

Sojourner is waiting to gather strength for a lecture which we hope will do something to replenish her purse. They will go to Ottawa the last of the week if well enough.

We hope to have one or two more barrels of clothing to forward this week; and that after Sojourner's lecture on Wed. evening interest will increase. . . .

We will send freight hereafter according to Mrs. Titus' direction.[18]

On this trip to Kansas, as well as on the previous one, Truth had used a variety of methods at her lectures to raise money to pay for her trip, including charging ten or twenty-five cents for admission, taking up collections, selling photographs of herself, and selling her *Narrative*. As the letter implies, all these methods combined had proved insufficient. In fact, while Truth and Titus were in Streator, Titus announced she was soliciting nationwide to build up a $100 fund for Truth "as a recognition of Sojourner's valuable services for her race and country, and to afford present support to one who gives her all to others." So far Titus had collected seven dollars.[19]

As the year 1880 approached, Truth and Haviland were in Chicago, staying at the house of Haviland's daughter in suburban Englewood. As announced beforehand, they were "at home" on New Year's Day, a day traditional for receiving callers, and they received many callers. According to Chicago newspapers, "Sojourner Truth's" hair was becoming less gray and more black than it used to be, and her face fuller and smoother; she looked younger than "Mrs. Haviland." Although Truth was not called "Mrs." and Haviland was, Truth received more attention. Truth testified to the needs of the Kansas refugees, and "kept up a lively conversation with all who wished to converse with her."[20]

In the next few days, we lack evidence of any public activity by Truth; perhaps she was not strong enough. But both Haviland and Titus—

Titus seemed to be staying separately in Chicago—were busy on behalf of the refugees. Haviland announced that contributions for the Kansas refugees could be left at a downtown office, while Titus announced that they could be left at a Friends meeting house. Another day Titus begged all the ministers of the city to collect offerings for the refugees from their next Sunday's congregations, to be sent to Comstock in Kansas. Titus called on the editor of Chicago's weekly Spiritualist newspaper, asking his support, and in response he announced in his paper that Titus is "thoroughly trustworthy," and any donations made to her for the Kansas refugees "will be honestly and discreetly used." Another day Titus attended a meeting with Chicago politicians and industrialists, called to organize a Chicago society for the relief of the Kansas refugees, and this time Titus spoke.[21]

In the years that followed, despite signs that Titus was capable of acting independently from Truth and felt some urge to break free from her, Titus remained faithful to Truth, continuing to travel with her, as to Indiana and Chicago in 1881, and during her declining health, providing care for Truth at Truth's Battle Creek home. When Truth prepared her last will, Titus and William Merritt acted as witnesses for Truth's putting her "mark" on it. Just after Truth died in 1883, a Battle Creek Adventist paper reported that Titus had "managed" Truth's "correspondence, and seen to her physical wants with a faithfulness which challenges admiration." Truth's Detroit friend Giles B. Stebbins testified that Titus kept up her "constant and watchful care" of Truth "to the end," as she had "for years." The Kalamazoo women's advocate Lucinda Stone said Titus "always provided for Sojourner as for a sister," visited her in her last illness "daily," "buried her, and paid for her funeral expenses."[22]

In the years after Truth's death, Titus issued another revision of Truth's Narrative. She struggled to raise funds to erect a stone monument for Truth at her grave in Battle Creek, and finally succeeded. She also struggled to raise funds to keep Truth's daughter Diana from being sent to the county home, an endeavor that succeeded as long as Titus herself remained alive.[23]

19

Friends and Supporters

"I don't fritter my mind away in caring for trifles."

In addition to her close friends like Titus and Haviland, in her later years Truth had many other friends and supporters. Warren Chase, her neighbor in Michigan, wrote of her in 1863, she "has many friends in our state." A New York journalist, observing her make her way to the rostrum at a women's suffrage convention in 1870, and later being given an "ovation," reported that "her friends . . . seemed to be many." [1]

These friends were often co-workers with her in various causes, or supporters of those causes. They were often part of overlapping, informal networks, especially of abolitionists and feminists, but also of such others as temperance advocates, Progressive Friends, and Spiritualists.

From the limited information available, 155 friends and supporters of hers in Michigan can be named who corresponded with her, endorsed her ideas, helped her to speak, entertained her in their homes, or the like. Of these 155, 16 are identifiable as clergy, 57 as women, including some of her closest friends, but only 17 as blacks, and none of these blacks seem to have been close to her.

Perhaps she had few black friends and supporters because many blacks were too busy with survival to have much time for the public issues she cared about. Perhaps also the opportunity to have black friends in Michigan was relatively slight because the proportion of blacks in the population during the time she lived there remained at about 1 percent, smaller than in some other midwestern states. Perhaps also the proportion of blacks among her friends appears less than it actually was because records about blacks have not been preserved as well as records about whites. She herself, in explaining why her campaign for land for blacks in the West failed, said that a significant reason was that she lacked black support. She seldom brought blacks with her to conventions or otherwise travelled with blacks unless they were members of her own family. There is little evidence of significant connections between Truth and other black leaders in either the antislavery, women's rights, or temperance movements. There is also little evidence that she was close to black leaders in Battle Creek, even though Battle Creek had black churches, and was the site of two Michigan State Colored Conventions, one in the 1860s and one in the 1880s, which suggests that there was significant black leadership there.

Scanty though it is, the record of Truth's relation to the black William Still of Philadelphia may help to illuminate Truth's relation to black as well as white friends. Truth had known Still from as early as 1853, when Still, then a clerk in the Pennsylvania Anti-Slavery Society office in Philadelphia, and the dominant figure in running the Underground Railroad in that city, arranged speaking engagements for her in the area.[2] In 1874, when Truth had been travelling in support of her western lands proposal, she and her grandson Samuel had evidently visited Still. By that time Still had become a prosperous coal dealer, had published his impressive book telling the story of the Underground Railroad, and had been a leader in desegregating Philadelphia's streetcars.

In Battle Creek, in January, 1876, Truth wrote Still, asking him to help her plan another visit to Philadelphia. This time it was in connection with the city's great Exhibition in celebration of the centennial of the Declaration of Independence, to be held there later in the year. Truth explained to Still that her grandson Samuel had recently died, and she herself had been very sick for about a year with a gangrenous leg sore. She had not been able to walk for two months. "The doctors gave me up but I got a woman doctor[3] who got me so I could walk but . . . my leg swelled and then I got a horse doctor who took the swelling out . . . and I am fast improving. . . . It seems I am like a horse."

She explained that to help her financially, Frances Titus had just published an expanded edition of her *Narrative*. "My expenses in my sickness was heavy and I had to mortgage my little house and with the expenses of my sickness I am between 3[00] and 400 dollars in debt, and

the [book] was got up to pay my debts and to help me in my old age."
Besides, Truth explained, she owed Titus for the $350 that the printers
required before they would even start to print the book.

Truth continued:

If I should live I expect to come to Philadelphia to that great time [the Exhibi-
tion]. I want to come down there in April or May. . . . I will have an opportunity
to see all my old friends. And I can dispose of my books and can raise the
mortgage off my house and have it free from debt once more. I had it all paid for
but sickness brought me in debt. Samuel's funeral expenses costed me a great
[deal] and I did not want him buried by the town, and I have not paid them
all yet. . . .

Friend Still you have helped me years ago and maybe this is the last time I
shall need any help. . . . I want you to assist me in getting 2 rooms if it is in your
house, or any place about Philadelphia you think is as good place. And I will see
you paid for your trouble.

My friends has advised me to secure a place [because of] the great rush of
people. I have no one to send down to see about it. My grandson [Samuel] the
one I depended on is dead. I have got another grandson Willie who is 14 years
old, but he is too young to go down there to see about a place as he has never be
in a large city. He does my writing and wrote this letter, if there is any mistakes
please excuse them as I cannot read writing. He must come with me down there
to do my writing and reading, and his mother to see to me. . . .

I am very anxious to come down there for I think I can sell my books fast
and then I can pay my debts for I cannot do as I used to do for I cannot travel
and brouse about. I would like to see you very much and give you to understand
how all things is and I would like to see my old friends. It would be great joy
to me. . . .

The lady that wrote my book will be down there too but she will provide a
place for herself. She is a excellent woman.

I would send a book but it cost something more than my limited means can
afford. But I will send a circular. Write to me immediately. I have nothing more
to say. My love to you and family. I hope to see you soon.[4]

This and other of Truth's letters raise the question whether her preoc-
cupation with her financial problems could sometimes have been such an
overriding factor in her relations with her friends, black or white, that it
prevented her from developing more mutual, more intimate relations with
them.

As it turned out, Truth was not well enough to come to Philadelphia.
But in July, when a false rumor that Truth had died was circulating, the
Philadelphia *Bulletin* asked Still for his reminiscences of Truth. In reply,

Still's choice of words suggests he was ambivalent about her. Truth, Still wrote, was "a strangely-made creature with regard to physical structure, manner, language and thought, a wonder not easily described." As a slave she had been "under no improving influences," and as an antislavery speaker was regarded even by the sympathetic as "ignorant." Nevertheless, Still described her as Douglass did, as brave, saying, "She would dauntlessly face the most intelligent and cultivated audiences, or would individually approach the President of the United States as readily as she would one of the humblest citizens." He quoted the Detroit *Post* as saying she has been "one of the chief attractions" at antislavery and women's rights meetings, and was "very valuable" at the freedmen's camps in Washington. He explained sympathetically the financial pressure that drove Truth to wish to come to Philadelphia, emphasizing perhaps more than Truth's letter did that it was for Truth to raise money to repay Mrs. Titus: "As Mrs. Titus was obliged to make great sacrifices in getting out this last edition of her life, Sojourner was very anxious to come on to the Centennial Exhibition to help sell her book in order to repay her friend, and at the same time to secure something for her support in her last lingering days on earth."[5]

Still's comment may seem more clearly respectful of Truth than warm toward her. Still does not, as much as Stowe, emphasize her spirituality or romanticize her strangeness. Like Douglass he notes her "ignorance," underlining the possibility that at least some significant blacks who were struggling to lift the level of black education and culture were wary of Truth because of her "ignorance."

Reviewing the evolution of Truth's relationships with blacks, we recall that because she worked hard for her slavemaster Dumont, she was derided by her fellow slaves as a "white folks nigger." In turn, she had some contempt for her fellow slaves for having thoughts "no longer than her finger." Also we recall that after she was freed and went to New York City to work, she wanted to preach to blacks, but found that they rejected her because, she said, they preferred to listen to "great people." In her later speaking, Truth sometimes said what blacks might not like to hear, as when she scolded freed slaves for not supporting themselves, black men for "strutting," black women for not knowing "scarcely anything," and "young colored swells" for snickering at her." But she also made comments blacks were likely to welcome: Blacks are "a great deal better" than whites "had brought them up" to be; because blacks have suffered so, "the promises of Scripture were all for the black people, and God would recompense them for all their sufferings"; and the "time will come" in America when "to be black ... will be an honor." Speaking to a predominantly black audience, she recalled that when she was young she used to ask why she was not white so "I could have plenty of food and clothes? But now she gloried in her color. . . . that God had been pleased to give her."[6]

Truth herself once seemed to try to explain why, when her primary focus as a reformer was on improving the condition of blacks, she lived primarily among whites and spoke primarily to whites. She said that as a speaker she knew what she wanted to say to whites, but found she "had always felt this difficulty" that she did not know what to say to blacks because they were the "sufferers" in the matter of slavery, and had little "control."[7] Perhaps she gravitated toward whites partly because she perceived whites as having the power to improve the conditions of blacks, and because she felt she had learned how to use white prejudice, guilt, and idealism to motivate whites to move toward improving those conditions.

If Truth in approaching friends could sometimes seem preoccupied, and not encouraging intimate friendship, perhaps in turn some of her friends were attracted to her not so much for the sake of intimate friendship as for her romantic aura, her ability to inspire them, and her ability to promote causes. Although her white critics could say that she was "childish," or "despotic," or so crude that when she spoke "she moves her jaws as though she was chewing carpet tacks,"[8] her white friends often seemed to feel, like Stowe, that her peculiarities made her more intriguing. Perhaps some whites were more accepting of her because she often played the role—in some measure deliberately—of being naive and ignorant and amusing, so that she did not entirely upset the white stereotypes of blacks; thus, despite her frequent scolding of whites, they might be less likely to feel her as a threat.

There are signs that some of her white supporters genuinely welcomed her into their homes, and felt honored to entertain her or work with her. Eliza Leggett reported that when Truth stayed in her home in Detroit, her presence was a "comfort," and the family "all love her." Giles B. Stebbins of Detroit recalled that Truth could lift a sick man "to the best place on his bed as easily and tenderly as a mother would lift her baby," and "her word, 'There honey, you's easier now,' had a strange power to ease and calm." One of the Merritts recalled that they welcomed her to their table as an honored guest, even though they were criticized for doing so. The Merritt adults doted on her wit and wisdom and the news she gave them from her travels, and their children loved her warmth, her deep voice, and her songs. Amy Post reported that ever since knowing Truth she had "never ceased to feel myself stronger in spirit, and more earnest for justice." After Truth had visited the Brooklyn home of Theodore Tilton, the editor of the nation's leading religious weekly, the New York *Independent,* Tilton reported that her "conversation is witty, sarcastic, sensible, and oftentimes profound. Her varied experience during a long life gives her a rich and deep fountain to draw upon for the entertainment and instruction of her friends."[9]

On the other hand, it was possible even for whites who were seriously concerned for blacks to feel distanced from her. For example, the testy Quaker Emily Howland seemed uncomfortable with Truth when Truth visited her in 1878 at her rural home in Sherwood in the Finger Lakes region of New York. Howland, like Truth, had worked with freedmen in the Washington area for several years during and after the Civil War, especially as a teacher. But Howland was more of a doubter than a believer, more demanding than accepting of herself and others, including blacks. She was intellectually understanding of what seemed to her the frenzied black singing that she encountered, admitting that for blacks to be able to become absorbed in such singing lifted them above their degradation and helped them survive, but she remained uneasy with it.

When Truth, accompanied by Frances Titus, first came to Howland's home neighborhood to speak, and Howland heard her, Howland wrote that she considered her "witty & original." But after Howland invited Truth and Titus to stay with her a few days, Howland seemed more at ease with Titus than with Truth. Howland noted in her private journal that she had a "good talk" with Titus, but found Truth close to "vulgarity": When it came time for Howland to take Truth to a meeting where Truth was to speak, Howland wrote that she "dreaded it because only her earnestness & age redeem her effort from coarseness & vulgarity." At the meeting, however, Howland found Truth "impressive," and afterward admitted, "I came home relieved."[10]

Truth was considerably dependent on her friends because she was illiterate. Her daughters, who at times lived in the same house with her, were able to help with housekeeping, but they could not read and write for her since they were illiterate themselves. Of her grandchildren, Samuel Banks often read and wrote for her and travelled with her; after his death, Willie Boyd sometimes wrote for her, but he was perhaps too young or otherwise unsuitable, for he never became as useful to her as Samuel had been. From at least the 1860s Haviland, Titus, and the Merritts wrote letters for her, and kept financial records for her as well.

Truth was also considerably dependent on her friends because she was poor. When younger, Truth could support herself by doing domestic work as needed; as she grew older this became more difficult and eventually impossible. At times her only income seemed to be from collections taken at her lectures, or from selling copies of her songs, photos of herself, or the book on her life. Sometimes she was sick for long periods and unable to earn even this inadequate income. She lived simply. The abolitionist Parker Pillsbury, visiting her in Battle Creek at her house on College Street in 1875 when she was sick, reported she lived in a "miserable little house, of two rooms—the one contains her cot, also . . . the cook stove which, with a chair or two, took up all the space." About a year later she was so poor that for months she could not pay for her subscription to a Battle Creek newspaper, and asked the editor to continue sending her the paper anyway, promising to pay later after she had a better opportunity to sell her books.[11] It was at about this time that she felt obliged to take out a mortgage on her house again, and she probably had still not paid it off when she died.

There are signs that some of Truth's friends could be irritated with her dependence on them. Titus, while travelling with her in Kansas, became impatient to do relief work by herself. When Truth, touring in behalf of her western lands proposal, arrived unexpectedly in the New York City area at the home of Garrison's son Wendell, Garrison heard about it and wrote his son that Truth's turning up "must have been a surprise to you all. She is indeed a remarkable woman, and always deserving of considerate and kind treatment; but, at her extreme age . . . it is a pity that she cannot remain quiet at her home in Battle Creek, instead of perambulating about the country, compelling hospitality whether or no."[12]

However, Truth's friends often gave her donations, or appealed to others to do so, and they often did so graciously. In 1863 when Truth was ill and not expected to live long, Phoebe Merritt Stickney, at Truth's request, wrote from Battle Creek to one of Truth's friends, the progressive Quaker minister Joseph Dugdale in Iowa, saying Truth would be grateful for a contribution to "help her to live a little longer to praise God and speak to de people a few more times in this glorious day of emancipation." Dugdale not only sent a donation, saying "few if any in the land are more worthy," but also circulated the letter. Later Stickney acknowledged the receipt of donations for Truth from as far away as Harriet Beecher Stowe in Massachusetts and Gerrit Smith in New York.[13]

Truth's response to her financial dependency ranged from denial of it to apparent acceptance of it and to strenuous effort to overcome it. Because Truth pushed hard over many years to help the freedmen become self-supporting, she might be expected to be anxious to be self-supporting herself, and sometimes she clearly was, as in her letter to Still. She herself argued that when she sold her book or songs or photographs of herself, she was supporting herself. When she was selling her photograph, she often said neatly that she wanted to "sell the shadow in order to support the substance." Selling her photograph at a convention in New York, she said in a poignant expression, that she herself "used to be sold for other people's benefit, but now she sold herself for her own." More directly in a speech in Michigan, she claimed she was selling her photograph because she was "bound not to beg or receive charity." Yet Truth was also capable of appealing directly for charity for herself. At a meeting of the Pennsylvania Anti-Slavery Society in 1869, with the black Robert Purvis presiding, and the venerable Lucretia Mott present, Truth reviewed her life, her experience of slavery, the "good she had done for her race," and, according to the minutes, said "that now, being poor, she wanted something done for her." Whereupon "a subscription was raised for her."[14]

When her grandson Samuel died, Truth was determined, as she wrote Still, that he would not be "buried by the town." For her in this case, having friends contribute to paying her family's necessary expenses was acceptable, but having the town do so would have been a disgrace. She went to great trouble not to let that happen, borrowing money for the funeral.

Truth's frequent acceptance of her dependence on friends, reluctant though it may sometimes have been, may be understood in several ways. In her time, evangelists and reformers, as they moved about, often took up collections to pay their expenses and accepted the hospitality of friends they met along the way. Also, in the tradition of the biblical prophets, Truth believed that God had called her to help do His work, so that it was natural God would care for her, as through her friends. Once when she was sick and unable to raise money by her usual speaking, Truth prayed, "Lord, you sent de ravens to feed 'Lijah in de wilderness; now send de good angels to feed me while I live on thy footstool." [15]

Moreover, though significantly dependent on her friends, Truth chose to think of herself as independent. She revelled in being "a free agent, to go and come when I pleased," she recalled. She avoided organizational ties. She avoided lecture bureaus. She chose to interpret her lack of education as meaning that she was free from having been influenced by anyone but God, saying in 1851: "I'm fresh from the hand of the great Maker! Nobody's been modelling me after any of their patterns." She was still boasting similarly in 1874, that it was God, not any college, which "has brought me where I am." When she gave up smoking, she insisted that no one had influenced her to do so. When she felt the need to differ with valued co-workers, she could do so, loudly. She not only rebuked Frederick Douglass for saying that slavery could only be abolished by bloodshed, but also just after the Civil War, when Gerrit Smith wanted a quick reconciliation with the defeated Confederates, Truth protested vehemently in a public letter: it "makes all my nerves quiver," that Smith already wants to forgive the Southern "rebels, thieves, robbers, and murderers. . . . Couldn't he wait for them to repent?" [16]

Though sometimes she seemed preoccupied by her poverty, at other times she seemed to rise above such concerns. In Battle Creek, Phoebe Merritt Stickney was impressed that Truth was content to live simply, saying it would be "a much better world" if other people had the "goodness of heart" that Truth has "to extract happiness from material surroundings in proportion to their possessions." When people asked her how she came to live so long and keep her mind, she answered, "I think of the great things of God, not little things. I don't fritter my mind away in caring for trifles." When she visited a friend in New Jersey, the friend reported, she "is continually praising God for the blessings bestowed upon her, and never murmuring because of hardships endured." When she was on her way to Kansas, a Chicago newspaper reported, "There is in her manner a dignity of bearing, a consciousness of worth, a sense of equality, even if her skin is black as night, that commands respect." [17]

20

Singer

"If we can laugh and sing a little as we fight the
good fight of freedom, it makes it all go easier."

At its best, Truth's singing, warm and distinctively her own, powerfully conveyed her experience as a slave, a black, a woman, and a child of God struggling for justice. Truth's singing also reflected African influences more clearly than most aspects of her life.

When Truth was the slave of Martin Schryver, the innkeeper, he gave a dance. Just a child then, Truth watched the dancing, and became entranced. She heard the dancers sing what she recalled as "the then famous song, 'Washington's Ball,'" a song which proclaimed that Washington was a "brave Christian soldier who planted the tree of liberty, each verse ending with some advice to the dancers in some very spirited measures." She could still sing the song in her old age.[1]

Truth sang heartily from the time she was young. Gertrude, the daughter of her master Dumont, remembered her as having a "rich and powerful" voice.[2]

At the first religious meeting she recalled attending, a Methodist meeting held in a private home just after she was freed from slavery, she heard the little known hymn, "There Is a Holy City." As she recalled in her old age, she never heard anyone else sing it again, but from hearing it only that once, she was able to sing it the rest of her life.[3]

Singing became important to her. Although she found herself attracted to both Methodists and Quakers, she decided to join the Methodists, as she explained later, because the Methodists would let her sing, while the Quakers, in keeping with their tradition of silent worship, would not.[4]

Truth learned to sing in the North, not the South. She never even visited the South until she was in her sixties during the Civil War. However, her singing style was recognized as like that of Southern blacks: It was called "southern" or "true plantation style."[5] Since it was so recognized, it evidently had in it elements of black African style common to both Southern and Northern black singing, such as a rousing basic beat, guttural voice texture, slurs in tone, improvisation, and accompanying body movement.

What we know of the Hudson River slaves' celebration of Pinkster, and her own eagerness to participate in it, suggests that among the blacks she associated with in the region, the African tradition of song and dance persisted, and she felt its power.

While Truth was still a slave, Northern blacks, like Southern blacks, were creating their own religious songs, both words and music. Blacks often created such songs because they were isolated from churches, and because, being illiterate, they were unable to read hymns. In these songs they expressed both their feeling of being oppressed and their need for hope. They combined African and Christian traditions, including strong repetitive rhythms and, to match, strong repetitive phrases, often from the Bible.

Early in the 1800s, many educated whites took little interest in black singing, disdaining it as inferior, or at best merely amusing. Some whites, however, especially illiterate whites, found they liked the strong rhythm and repetitive phrases of black religious songs, and learned to sing them with delight. In 1819 a white Methodist reported that in northeastern churches and camp meetings, both white and black Methodists were singing hymns, not in hymn books, which had been improvised by illiterate blacks. He complained that these hymns were too much like dance music, that both blacks and whites sang them too loudly, too late into the night, and with too much "animal spirit," and that he sometimes found it difficult to make sense out of their words because they endlessly repeated "idle expletives" like "glory, glory, glory."[6]

Truth evidently participated in such singing. In New York City she took part in prayer meetings, she recalled, where the participants clapped and stamped until they became, she felt, too delirious with excitement.[7] But such meetings gave her experience in improvising songs.

When Truth visited Harriet Beecher Stowe in Andover, Massachusetts, in 1853, Stowe described her as given to talking and singing of "glory." She would sing songs whose burden was, "O glory, glory, glory, won't you come along with me?" And "when left to herself, she would often hum these with great delight, nodding her head."[8] Repetitions of such words as "glory, glory, glory" and such questions as "won't you come along with me?" were common in black songs, in camp meeting songs, and in Methodist songs.

By the time Truth left New York City and became a wandering evangelist in New England, it was clear that her singing had become a significant part of her appeal to audiences. As one of her Adventist friends of this period recalled, she was a "great favorite in our meetings, both on account of her remarkable gift in prayer, and still more remarkable talent for singing."[9]

She sang not only songs she learned from others but also songs she herself composed. She recalled, "I used to make many songs." Both the songs she composed and the way she sang them were very much her own. Her friend Olive Gilbert recalled that whoever heard Truth sing "It Was Early in the Morning," one of the hymns she herself composed, "will probably remember it as long as they remember her." The hymn, the tune, and her peculiar style were "each too closely associated" with her "to be easily separated from herself."[10]

Even when she sang songs she herself had not composed, she made them her own. When she visited Mrs. Stowe, Truth sang one hymn, according to Stowe, "in a strange, cracked voice . . . mispronouncing the English, but seeming to derive as much elevation and comfort from bad English as from good." She sang it, according to Stowe, "with a triumphant energy that held the whole circle around her intently listening. She sang with the strong barbaric accent of the native African, and with those indescribable upward turns and those deep gutturals which give such a wild, peculiar power to the negro singing—but above all, with such an overwhelming energy of personal appropriation that the hymn seemed to be fused in the furnace of her feelings and come out recrystallized as a production of her own." She also "seemed," Stowe wrote, "to impersonate the fervor of Ethiopia, wild, savage, hunted of all nations, but burning after God in her tropic heart, and stretching her scarred hands toward the glory to be revealed."[11]

Early in her antislavery career, Truth attended a huge antislavery meeting held in a grove near Boston. At the meeting, as she remembered afterward, she sold flyers of some of her "home-made" songs, with the words printed out, for five or ten cents a piece. "I always had something to pay my way with," she recalled. But some people hesitated to buy them, asking, "What tune do you sing it to?" and she had to admit that she "didn't know," apparently meaning that she did not know how to identify the tune by name.

William Lloyd Garrison noticed her difficulty. He spoke to her, as she remembered long afterward: " 'Now, Sojourner, you go on the platform and make a speech, and you will sell your songs like anything.' . . . So I went up there, and Garrison called for order. Said he, 'It is time to begin.' And the people came and sat down on the boards, and some stood. 'Now,' said he, 'Sojourner Truth will address you in her own peculiar way, and Wendell Phillips will follow.' "

Truth felt embarrassed to be speaking just before the illustrious Boston patrician Phillips. But, she recalled, "I thought, I can do one thing that he can't do. . . . So I said I had a home-made song that I wanted to sing. So I sung one; and if I skipped a part, nobody was the wiser."

She sang one of her favorite songs, which, she recalled, in those days she could make "roar," including these verses:

> I am pleading for my people,
> A poor, down-trodden race,
> Who dwell in freedom's boasted land,
> With no abiding place.
>
> I am pleading for the mothers
> Who gaze in wild despair
> Upon the hated auction-block,
> And see their children there.[12]

From this song it is apparent that by this time Truth had developed a taste not only for emotional songs with repetitive phrases in them, but also for songs of conceptual power.

Truth often sang at meetings just before or just after she spoke. She often seemed to sing with ease, fervently. She was described, whether as a speaker or singer, as having a voice that was, variously, "deep, powerful," "rich," "resonant," and "well modulated." A Providence newspaper called her voice "a clear, strong, but rather heavy voice for a woman."

Her old friend Joseph Dugdale recalled that it in her early years it had been a "clarion" voice. As late as 1877 a Michigan newspaper declared that it was "still like a trumpet." [13]

On occasion Truth slyly used her singing to introduce antislavery images into religious meetings that were not necessarily antislavery. As she explained it much later at a convention, eliciting "great laughter": "You see I have sung in the anti-slavery meetings and in the religious meetings. Well, they didn't call anti-slavery religious, and so I didn't call my song an anti-slavery song—called it religious, so I could make it answer for both." [14]

Although by the 1840s many American urban churches, including black churches, were beginning to have choirs, Truth is never known to have sung with a church choir. When she sang in front of audiences, she is never known to have sung with a group of any kind, not in a duet, or with a chorus, or even with instrumentalists accompanying her. She sang alone. In her public singing, as in much of the rest of her life, she seemed to be, conspicuously, an individualist.

Like many blues singers, however, Truth sang not only out of her own experience but out of the experience of blacks at large. She sang especially of the agony of herself and others as slaves. Not feeling the need to protect herself by masking her meaning as blacks who were still slaves often felt the need to do, she sang of the agony directly:

> Whilst I bear upon my body
> The scars of many a gash,
> I am pleading for my people
> Who groan beneath the lash. [15]

But she also held out hope, as in this song:

> O, slave mother, hope! see—the nation is shaking!
> The arm of the Lord is awake to thy wrong!
> The slaveholder's heart now with terror is quaking,
> Salvation and mercy to Heaven belong!
> Rejoice, O rejoice! for the child thou art rearing
> May one day lift up its unmanacled form,
> While hope, to thy heart, like the rainbow so cheering,
> Is born, like the rainbow, 'mid tempest and storm. [16]

She also held out a different kind of hope, in another song:

In every day of trouble
I'll raise my thoughts on high,
I'll think of that bright temple
And crowns above the sky.[17]

Her audiences, mostly white, often responded warmly to her singing. At a Progressive Friends meeting in Pennsylvania in 1853, she said she felt "deeply moved to sing," and sang the following song, which had appeared in an antislavery song book. It was particularly appropriate for her, as a former slave mother, to sing:

I pity the slave mother, careworn and weary,
Who sighs as she presses her babe to her breast;
I lament her sad fate, all so hopeless and dreary,
I lament for her woes, and her wrongs unredressed.
O who can imagine her heart's deep emotion,
As she thinks of her children about to be sold;
You may picture the bounds of the rock-girdled ocean,
But the grief of that mother can never be told.

By this song, one listener felt, Truth "reached the deep fount of parental tenderness."[18]

In Rochester at an equal rights convention in 1866, at the age of about 69 (but said to be nearly 100), according to one Republican newspaper, her singing "was received by the audience with every manifestation of delight." According to another Republican newspaper, however, she had some difficulty with a song:

Sojourner, who is a tall and somewhat remarkable looking negress, of very advanced age, came forward and proposed to sing for the delectation of the audience. The suggestion was received with decided manifestations of approval, and she immediately broke forth with a camp meeting hymn of most singular character. The old woman's voice while singing is quite masculine, and it occasionally "splits" at the close of a bar, and changes into something between a squeal and a whoop, producing a very ludicrous effect. From the laughter which found vent in every part of the hall, it might have been supposed that she was favoring the convention with a comic song. At the conclusion she good naturedly referred to the amusement she had created and apologized for the defects of her voice upon the ground of her age.

Another Rochester newspaper, a Democratic one and therefore likely to be more hostile to her as a black, interpreted her singing on this same occasion differently. It said that when she began to sing, she first made "several attempts," and then finally "got off in a hymn to the great amusement of the audience—the boys in particular. At the high notes in the tune she would break—her voice being inadequate to compass them." At the conclusion she apologized to her audience humorously, saying that even if the audience could not hear her high notes, at least she could hear these notes. She said: "Chilren—ye've hearn the ecker [echo], haven't yse? Well my voice has an ecker, but it's inside of me and ye don't hear it. Dat's de way of it."[19]

Whatever difficulties Truth had with her voice on some occasions, she kept on singing in public for many years. At an equal rights convention in New York in 1867, she said she had not heard any singing at the convention, but "there ought to be singing here." Though she admitted, I "can't sing as well as I used to," she proceeded to sing, to "hearty applause," what one newspaper called "a weird, wailing song, with a very queer tune, an odd though clear pronunciation of words, and her old head swaying to and fro in harmony." The song, which she sang twice to the same convention, she called one of her favorites:

> We are going home, we have visions bright
> Of that holy land, that world of light
> Where the long dark night is past,
> And the morning of eternity has come at last.
> Where the weary saints no more shall roam,
> But dwell in a sunny, and peaceful home.
> Where the brow, celestial gems shall crown
> And waves of bliss are dashing 'round.
>
> [Chorus] Oh! that beautiful home—oh! that beautiful world.[20]

The next year she sang the same song to some 600 listeners at a Progressive Friends meeting in Erie County, New York. Though Truth was about seventy-one years old at the time, one listener reported that she sang this song "in a steady, clear voice, which we know fell like a sacred baptism upon all hearts present."[21]

Speaking in Detroit in the campaign for the reelection of President Grant in 1872, when she was about seventy-five, she "sang several of her original songs, all of which," according to a newspaper, "were received with applause." When she was speaking in a small Pennsylvania town in

1874, a newspaper reported she sang "right sweetly a negro melody . . . giving just enough of the southern negro double-demi-semi-quaver to it, to make it interesting." Speaking in Chicago in 1879, she concluded a lecture by singing her old favorite Ulster County hymn, "There Is a Holy City"; a newspaper reported that it "was very well received, although it was very long and not specially interesting as a rhythmic production." On the same visit to Chicago, when she was being interviewed by a reporter in a private home, she sang for him another of her old favorites, "I Am Pleading for My People"; she sang it, the reporter wrote, "in a not unpleasant though quivering voice." After she spoke in Lansing in 1881, when she was about 84 years old (but believed to be 106), she "sang a hymn in strong musical tones."[22]

Of the songs that she sang, fourteen can be named by their title, or by their first lines, or at least by some snatch of their lines. Most of these fourteen were not well known, suggesting her taste in songs was eccentric. These fourteen are as follows, arranged by the date and place that she first sang or published or quoted them, as far as known:

"Washington's Ball"	1807? Kingston, NY[23]
"There Is a Holy City"	1827, Esopus? NY[24]
"It Was Early in the Morning"	1844? Northampton, MA[25]
"I Bless the Lord I've Got My Seal"	1844? Northampton, MA[26]
"I Am Pleading for My People"	1852, New Lisbon, OH[27]
"We Are Going Home"	1852, flyer, referring to New
(Chorus: "Beautiful Home")	Lisbon, OH[28]
"I'm on My Way to Canada"	1852, flyer, referring to New
	Lisbon, OH[29]
"O Glory, Glory, Glory"	1853, Andover, MA[30]
"I Pity the Slave Mother"	1853, Old Kennett, PA[31]
"Hail Ye Abolitionists"	1854? Abington, MA[32]
"Judah" (Juba?)	1860–1863? Battle Creek, MI[33]
"We Are the Valiant Soldiers"	1863, Detroit, MI[34]
"Free, Free, Free, Indeed"	1864? Washington, DC[35]
"We'll Take the Parting Hand"	1874, West Chester, PA[36]

Among these fourteen songs, the one she sang, or quoted, or published most often is "I Am Pleading for My People," with nine documented instances. This was an antislavery song of eleven verses (we have already quoted some of them in this chapter and earlier), whose words she had composed herself, and which she sang to the tune of "Auld Lang Syne." She sang it to audiences both before and after the Civil War, in antislavery meetings and in meetings where she was telling the story of her life. A Topeka newspaper called it "very beautiful and pathetic."[37] Other songs she sang moderately often are: "There Is a Holy City," her old favorite Ulster County hymn, with five instances, and three instances each for "We Are Going Home," "I'm on My Way to Canada," "It Was Early in the Morning," and "We Are the Valiant Soldiers."

Among her fourteen songs, only three were known to have been printed on flyers, presumably for her to sell. Two of these were primarily antislavery songs, "I Am Pleading for My People" and "I'm on My Way to Canada"; the third was a religious song, "We Are Going Home." Among her fourteen songs, there are nine for which the words of at least one apparently complete verse have been preserved.

The words of some of the songs she herself composed are not known. Speaking at a black church in Topeka in 1879, she was tantalizingly reported to have sung "a song, the music and poetry of which was composed by her some thirty years ago, which delineated the oppressions of her race," but the words of the song were not reported.[38] However, songs she sang that can be named and are believed to have been composed by her at least with respect to the words are:

"I Bless the Lord I've Got My Seal"

"It Was Early in the Morning"

"Hail Ye Abolitionists!"

"I Am Pleading for My People"

"We Are the Valiant Soldiers"

Of the nine of her songs whose words she probably did not compose, some indication about the origin of the words of three of them seems reliable. The words of "I Pity the Slave Mother" were taken from Garrison's *Liberator,* and were republished in an 1844 antislavery song book. The words of "There Is a Holy City" were as she remembered them being sung at a Methodist meeting in Ulster County, New York.[39] The words of "We Are Going Home" were those of an old revival song. Long after Truth is known to have printed the words of this song in an 1852 flyer, its words appeared in a collection of Methodist-related revival songs, called *The Revivalist,* published in 1869 in Troy, New York, though in a somewhat different version. For instance, while Truth gave these lines:

> Where the brow celestial gems shall crown
> And waves of bliss are dashing round,

The Revivalist gave the same lines as:

> Where the brow with sparkling gems is crown'd
> And the waves of bliss are flowing round.[40]

For others of the songs that Truth sang, it is possible to give at least hints on the origin of the words. In regard to "Washington's Ball," although no "famous" song of the time is identifiable by that precise name, it may have been a version of the well-known "Washington's March" (in various versions of words and music called also "President's March," "Washington's Grand March," "Washington Guard's Quick Step," and the like), with the music composed by the 1790s. However, none of the words for various available versions of "Washington's March" fit Truth's summary of the words of "Washington's Ball." Other of the songs Truth sang may have been black folk songs. "I'm on My Way to Canada" may have been one because Harriet Tubman as well as Truth sang it— Tubman sang it while guiding fugitive slaves to Canada. When Truth sang "We'll Take the Parting Hand," it was called a "negro melody."[41]

The subjects that may be said to have appeared in her fourteen songs most frequently (counting several of the songs as having more than one subject), were religion in eight songs, and antislavery in six. Appearing in two songs each were women's rights, patriotism, and dancing, while pro-war argument, antiwar argument, and the subject of parting appeared in only one song each. None of her known songs has temperance as a theme. Also absent were such popular themes as romantic love, fond recollection of a particular place, or the beauty of nature. In neither her singing nor her speaking was Truth known to have dwelt on these themes.

Among the songs she sang, the tunes of five are known, most of them popular tunes in her time:

"I'm on My Way to Canada"	Tune: Stephen C. Foster's "Oh, Susanna" (probably first sung in Pittsburgh in 1847)
"I Am Pleading for My People"	Tune: "Auld Lang Syne" (an old Scottish tune that had become popular in America by the 1790s)
"I Pity the Slave Mother"	Tune: "Araby's Daughter" (composed by the English musician George Kiallmark, born 1781)
"We Are Going Home"	Tune: a revival song, published at least in 1869
"We Are the Valiant Soldiers"	Tune: An eighteenth-century English tune (later called "John Brown's Body," and still later called "Battle Hymn of the Republic")

Other tunes she sang, including "We'll Take the Parting Hand," may have been traditional black folk tunes.

Truth sang not only in meetings, but also on visits to neighbors as in Harmonia where, according to one of her neighbors, she sang both "anti-slavery and religious songs." She also sang when working for the Merritts in Battle Creek, looking after their children. As one of the family later recalled, when some of the Merritt children were small, she would rock them to sleep, "while she sang quaint Negro lullabies." Another of the Merritt family recalled that when Truth "would sing and clap Judah" for one of the Merritt baby boys, he "would stop his play" to come dance for her.[42]

"Judah" may have been the Merritts' rendering of Truth's pronuncia-tion of "Juba," originally an African dance that became, in many varia-tions, a traditional African-American dance, accompanied by singing, clapping, patting the hands on the thighs, and patting the feet on the ground. As with other black songs and dances, the Juba's words and motions were often improvised, and appeared at different times and places in many different versions, including versions for children.

As one version of Juba was sung in New York by 1848, it included these lines:

> Juba dis, Juba dat,
> Round de kittle ob possum fat

As sung for dancing on a Maryland plantation in 1832, the Juba included:

> Juber forrud, Juber back;
> Juber dis way, Juber dat;
> Juber in, un Juber out;
> Juber, Juber, all ubbout.
>   Juber!

At the end of this verse, the dancers, pretending to be tripped up by each other, collapsed into a "struggling heap" on the ground, laughing.[43] If Truth, after singing such a song and clapping her hands for a little child to dance, encouraged the child to conclude by falling on the floor, it is small wonder that the child would stop what he was doing to dance for her.

According to Elizabeth Cady Stanton, Truth said once: "Life is a hard battle anyway, and if we can laugh and sing a little as we fight the good fight of freedom, it makes it all go easier."[44]

Truth is not known to have sung what became known as black spirituals. These spirituals were likely to be of Southern origin, and so perhaps not familiar to her from her early years. It was only in the 1870s, when the Fisk University Jubilee Singers made black spirituals popular, that many American whites first found themselves deeply moved by them. Truth became incidentally associated with one of these spirituals in 1879, when according to the Chicago Times, as she arrived to speak at a white Chicago church, "supported by her faithful cane, the excellent choir present struck up 'Swing Low, Sweet Chariot,' a well-known and popular negro melody, and continued singing while the old lady hobbled her way to the rostrum."[45]

About a year before Truth died, when a visitor called at her house, she

sang, "without a moment's hesitation" over either the words or the air, a
song she remembered from her childhood, "Washington's Ball." The
visitor reported that she sang it "with spirit," and that her voice was
"strong" and "masculine," but not "coarse."[46]

A few weeks before Truth died, Frances Titus visited her one morning, after she had a wretched night. But Titus reported that she managed
to smile and sing "in a sweet, low voice" one of her own "home-made"
songs:

> It was early in the morning,
> It was early in the morning,
> Just at the break of day,
> When He rose, when He rose, when He rose,
> And went to heaven on a cloud.[47]

21

Talking with God

God "is a great ocean of love, and we live and
move in Him as the fishes in the sea."

Truth liked to say that once she had converted to Christ, she never "changed" her religion.[1] While certainly Truth always retained much of her early religious perspective, over the years she opened herself to a surprising variety of religious experiences. She shaped her own religion to be not only unworldly, but also, in seeming contradiction, to be concerned, as she said, to turn the world "right side up."

In New York City she joined various churches, tried being a missionary to prostitutes, and tried fasting. She took part in revival meetings that included shouting and jumping. She came under the spell of the clamorous prophet Matthias who called himself a Jew. But she left New York as an evangelist with considerably traditional Christian beliefs.

She seemed to have contradictory needs in regard to associating with religious groups: On the one hand she chose to live in three intentional communities with distinctly different religious styles, and on the other hand once she left New York she seemed to shy away from tying herself to any one church.

Over the years she continued the direct communication with God that she had begun while still a slave. In her middle years she still said, "I talks to God and God talks to me." But her conception of God seemed to move from the more concrete to the more abstract. When she was converted, she claimed that she saw God directly and felt overwhelmed by

His presence. In her old age, in a letter to a Chicago newspaper, she seemed to reject the idea that we could see God directly, saying instead, "We shall never see God only as we see Him in one another." When she was near death, and a friend, visiting her, expressed grief at her suffering, Truth replied in a way suggesting that she had come to have a loftier, more inclusive view of God than she once had: "Oh, I suffers, chile, of course I do; but I hain't been thinkin' o' that; I've been thinkin' all day of the Infinite. The Infinite, chile! Think on it—what a word it is! The Infinite, and you and I are in it; we're part on't."[2]

Similarly, over the years she moved away from a literal interpretation of the Bible. Soon after she had been converted, when she said she first heard preaching from the Bible, she believed that devils literally were chasing her, and that hell literally was a place of flames. In time, however, in accordance with considerable Protestant tradition, Truth came to want to decide for herself what the Bible meant. She discovered that if adults read the Bible to her, they would invariably comment on what it meant to them, intruding on her own interpretation, while if she asked children to do so, they would not comment. So when she could, she asked children to read it to her.[3]

According to Olive Gilbert, by 1850 Truth had already worked out for herself views that differed from the literal text of the Bible, and were not in accordance with any existing system of theology. In listening to the creation story being read from Genesis, she thought that God, if He is a spirit, did not need to rest, as the story says He did, and that therefore there was no sound basis for the establishment of the Sabbath as a day of rest. She believed that God "was to be worshipped at all times and in all places," not just on special days or in special places. She came to believe that "the spirit of truth" spoke through the Bible, "but that the recorders of those truths had intermingled with them ideas and suppositions of their own." Truth was afraid, however, that such views as these might be considered to be "infidel" views, and so, according to Gilbert, for a long time she did not reveal such views to others.[4] As Truth said herself in a speech in her old age, she used to believe in hell as she saw it once in a picture, as a terrible smoking, flaming "abyss," but "when I got older I found out there wa'n't no such thing as hell," and that the mind that conceived that picture was "narrow." But she continued to believe, she said enigmatically, that "God's brightness . . . is hot enough to scorch all the sinners in the world."[5]

Although she continued all her life to have the Bible read to her, urged others to study it, and frequently cited it in support of various public positions she took, she believed that it was not the only source of God's truth. In the early 1850s, when a theology professor asked her why she seemed so sure about her belief in heaven, she replied not because the Bible told her so but because "I got such a hankerin' 'arter it in here," indicating herself. Similarly, when people said to her that she ought to learn to read the Bible, her reply was, as she reported it in 1881, "I have a Bible in me." She said, like many evangelicals, that God revealed Himself to her in many ways. For instance, in 1879 she said that newspapers, or at least certain newspapers, provided texts about life through which "she could see God's workings and evident purposes." She shocked some people when on a Sunday in Kansas she asked to have read to her not the Bible but the current Chicago newspapers. Newspapers are "the last gospel," she wrote in 1881, and claimed she had believed so for many years. At about the same time she said in a speech that she wished someone would write a new Bible that would discard the old Mosaic "eye for an eye" laws, and give us new "spiritual doctrines" to keep pace with the "wonderful inventions" of our time.[6]

While once she had seemed afraid to acknowledge "infidel" influences in her life, in her old age she was willing to say that if any of her associates in the Northampton community "were infidels, I wish the world were full of such infidels. Religion without humanity is a poor human stuff."[7]

Like Truth, the leading white abolitionist-feminist women of her time, in becoming leaders in reform, emancipated themselves in some degree from religious orthodoxy. But like Truth, many of these women—such as Elizabeth Cady Stanton, Lucy Stone, Susan B. Anthony, and Josephine Griffing—remained essentially religious in point of view. Like Truth, they felt God "called" them to the sacred mission of reform, and guided them in what they did. Like Truth, their religion was eclectic and nonconformist, often influenced by the Quaker emphasis on inner conscience. Also like Truth, they were inclined to be in transition from the earlier belief that the improvement of mankind depended primarily on individual regeneration toward the more modern belief that such improvement depended primarily on social and institutional change. They were not inclined to become bitter because of their failure to attain their visionary goals, but to remain romantic optimists, like Truth, with abundant faith that God would eventually carry the day for justice.[8] However, Truth remained all her life more Christ-centered in her beliefs and more evangelical in style than many of her white abolitionist-feminist colleagues.

Like many abolitionist-feminists, Truth was capable of severely criticizing churches and churchgoers. In regard to women's rights, she said that the church wrongs women as much as the state does. In a white church in New Jersey she said "there was no little heathenism in the very heart of the churches today." In a black church in New York City she said that many churches, surrounded by poverty, "were big, lumbering things, covering up costly space and doing good to no one." In a speech in Michigan she said that some people who go to church every Sunday all their lives "are like the door that swings in and out. They don't know any more when they go out than they do when they go in." In a letter she declared that the fashionable religious world was as "empty as the barren fig-tree."[9]

Black women before the Civil War, according to a recent historian, found special meaning in the promises embodied in Christian scripture for their "psychic survival and transcendence." This was undoubtedly true of Truth. But according to the same historian, for free black women who became leaders, the black church was often the training arena that provided them opportunity to develop leadership skills, control over their own lives, and commitment to freeing the slaves.[10] For Truth, however, it is doubtful that this was true; except for a brief membership in a black church in New York City—about which Truth herself told almost nothing—she was not known ever to have been active in a black church.

Yet she often spoke in churches. From 1850 on throughout her life, in the instances of her speaking for which the necessary information is available, 101 took place in churches (most of them white), 70 in public halls, and 38 in such other places as schools, court houses, or outdoors. Of the churches in which she spoke whose denomination is known, 72 were what may be called main-line churches (32 Methodist, 15 Congregational, 13 Presbyterian, 12 Baptist), and 19 were liberal churches (11 Quaker, 5 Unitarian, 3 Universalist). In no case was she known to have spoken in a Catholic, Episcopal, or Lutheran church. Perhaps these denominations were too afraid of even appearing to countenance the controversial reforms she advocated. Or perhaps they were too liturgical or dogmatic for her folksy, God-speaks-to-me style.

Like many abolitionists, Truth opposed racial segregation in churches as well as in other aspects of life. In Washington one Sunday in 1874, Truth attended the white Metropolitan Methodist Episcopal Church, and according to a next day's newspaper, was the first black to have taken communion in that church.[11]

Before the Civil War it was difficult for churches to let Truth or other abolitionists speak in their buildings because within the churches opposition to abolitionism was often virulent. In 1851 in Brecksville, Ohio, near Cleveland, both of the churches there, Methodist and Presbyterian, refused to let Truth and Parker Pillsbury use their buildings to speak because they were "promulgating Infidel sentiments under the guise of abolitionism." In 1861 in Steuben County, in northern Indiana, churches voted by small majorities to refuse to let her and her friends hold meetings there, so that they were forced to hold the meetings outdoors instead.[12]

When she spoke in churches, sometimes she was given the use of a church free; at other times she or others who were arranging a meeting for her were just renting space in the church building the same as they would in a hall. In a rare instance in 1871, she was invited to preach in a Methodist church in Rochester during a regular Sunday worship service as if she were a clergyman. The pastor, in introducing her, said that he had invited her to "occupy the pulpit." But she chose instead to speak below the pulpit, explaining to the congregation, "I prefer to be no higher'n what you are."[13]

Yet in a sense she was a preacher, and had been ever since she had been converted. She sometimes called herself a preacher. When Harriet Beecher Stowe introduced her to her father, the famous preacher Lyman Beecher, according to Stowe, Truth said to him condescendingly: "De Lord bless ye! I loves preachers. I'm a kind o' preacher myself." In 1878, in a newspaper interview, in effect she called herself both a lecturer and preacher. She said that when she gave "lectures," "De Lo'd just puts de words into my mouth, and I go to hear myself as much as any one else comes to hear me." That, she explained, "was her idea of genuine preaching."[14] But she is not known ever to have sought formal recognition as a preacher through any church. In the 1850s Quakers had already long been accustomed to having women ministers, and both Congregationalists and Free Will Baptists were beginning to ordain a few. By the 1870s Universalists and Unitarians were beginning as well. But Truth's illiteracy alone would presumably have made her ordination impossible.

Like many abolitionists and feminists, Truth was capable of criticizing preachers at large. She said they spent too much time "spouting" and too little listening. She said they spent too much time talking "about what happened thousands of years ago, but quite forgot that the living present around them teemed with the sternest realities." She also said fiercely that preachers were "big Greek-crammed, mouthing men, who, for many a long century, had been befogging the world, and getting its affairs into the most terrible snarl." At another time she scolded women for rushing to hear the evangelists Moody and Sankey preach. "What you specs?— dat dose two men goin' tote all you women to hebben? . . . I tell you it's the doers of the word, not the hearers, God wants." [15]

She sometimes had confrontations with individual clergymen. Once when a young revivalist called on her, begging her to be reconciled to God, she replied, "Reconciled to God! Why, I hain't got nothin' agin' God. What should I be reconciled to him fer? God's allus been mighty good to me; he called me out of slavery, and has took good care of me ever since, when you ministers would 'a' kep' me in bondage. Why, I haven't got nothin' agin' *him*." Once at an antislavery meeting, when abolitionists were attacking the church for its reluctance to fight slavery, a clergyman said he was afraid God might knock him down at any moment for listening to such blasphemy. In response, according to a friend, Truth told the clergyman, with withering force, "Don't be skeered. . . . I don't speck God's ever hearn tell on ye!" At another antislavery meeting, as Lydia Maria Child remembered it, an orthodox clergyman who was visiting the meeting protested that the antislavery speakers were "women and jackasses." Truth replied that in a Bible story, another minister, Balaam, also got "mighty mad" at a jackass, the one he was riding on, because it carried him off the road. But the reason the ass went off the road was that God had sent an angel to direct them not to go any farther, and only the ass, not the minister, was able to understand what the angel was directing them to do. [16]

On the other hand, Truth often found it natural to associate with clergymen. When she went to Providence to speak in 1870, she sought opportunities to do so by placing a notice in a newspaper that she would be "particularly pleased" if clergy would "favor her with a call." [17] In some places she visited she was invited to stay with ministers, as in Detroit (1869), Mount Pleasant, Iowa (1870), and in Topeka (1871). Several clergymen whom she knew wrote sympathetic articles about her, as did

Gilbert Haven (Methodist), Richard Cordley (Congregationalist), and Samuel Rogers (Reformed), all whites. Among the black churches where she spoke were J. T. Raymond's Abyssinian Baptist church in New York (1853), Henry Highland Garnet's Presbyterian church in Washington (1864), Leonard Grimes's Baptist church in Boston (1871), and William. F. Dickerson's African Methodist church in New York (1879). All four of these black ministers were significant leaders in black protest activities. But Truth is not known to have been close to these or any black pastors anywhere, at any time in her life.

Despite her outward appearance of naivete, she understood how churches could help pull people along toward what she considered to be the necessary remaking of both individuals and society. Once in a discussion among Michigan Progressive Friends, the radical abolitionist Henry C. Wright insisted on attacking churches bitterly for their usual cooperation with slavery, urging they be termed "so-called" Christian churches. Disagreeing, Truth said, as reported in an antislavery paper, "We ought to be like Christ. He said, 'Father, forgive them, they know not what they do.' If we want to lead the people we must not get out of dere sight." [18] She apparently believed that in approaching the public, reformers—though they often had reason to be sorely grieved with churches—might better not denounce churches bitterly, but rather keep a hopeful attitude toward them, and use widely acceptable, noncontroversial Christian teaching in their public appeals.

In her feminism Truth did not follow Elizabeth Cady Stanton and many Spiritualists in addressing God as Mother as well as Father—most people at the time were likely to find this offensive. The religious language she chose to use was considerably traditional, similar to what a vast number of Americans, black and white, used at the time. When arguing against racial prejudice, she could stress that both blacks and whites are the children of God. When arguing for the equality of the sexes, she could say, "God says: 'Honor your father and your mother.'" [19] When arguing against capital punishment, she could remind everyone that Jesus taught forgiveness and love. When arguing against greed, tobacco, whiskey, elaborate dress, and frivolity, she could say that Jesus called on us to come out of this world.

One of her white clerical friends was Gilbert Haven, who was so far ahead of his time that he declared he would never be satisfied until a black woman was president of the United States. Truth knew Haven as early as the mid-1850s when he was a Methodist minister in Westfield, Massachusetts, and one of her daughters worked for him there. In the fall of 1870, when Truth was in Massachusetts speaking in favor of land in the West for freedmen, Haven, then editor of the Boston Methodist weekly and soon to become a bishop, invited Truth to spend Christmas with him, and she eagerly accepted. While she remained in Boston, not only did Haven's paper endorse her campaign to settle blacks on land in the West, but he also arranged for her to stay for several weeks in the dormitory of the Boston Methodist Theological Seminary, where, according to Haven's paper, she "repaid" this "hospitality by her shrewd advice to the students." Haven once wrote: "The wisest, wittiest woman I know is Sojourner Truth. Wiser and wittier, of course, than any man."[20] All of this seems unlikely for one who was so insistent on theological orthodoxy as Haven was unless he interpreted Truth's theology to be similar to his own.

Yet in 1870 Haven scolded one of the clergymen whom Truth warmly admired, Henry Ward Beecher, for not believing in a literal hell of fire and brimstone. By this time surely Truth was less of a biblical literalist than that. In fact, long before this time, Truth had come to believe that God "appointed" religious liberals—with whom Haven was uneasy—to significant roles, as, during the Civil War, she said God "appointed" Thomas W. Higginson, a Unitarian pastor, to command black troops, and "appointed" Frances Gage, who found even her Universalist church too conservative, to care for Carolina blacks who had just been freed from slavery.[21]

Truth's religious evolution was in some respects parallel to that of Frederick Douglass. Both Truth and Douglass felt Methodist influences in their early years. Both, as reformers, were capable of being severe with the church for being too slow to move forward. Both were considerably independent in thought. But unlike Truth, Douglass, while still a slave, began to be seriously disillusioned with religion when he watched one of his slaveowners be converted to Christ but not therefore become willing to free his slaves. Later, Douglass came to emphasize that God, having given humans considerable ability, had committed the responsibility for human affairs to humans themselves, thus becoming remote from humans. But Truth emphasized that God was close to humans. (She once said, we needn't "go to amaginin' trouble aforehand. No matter what's a comin', Jesus will be thar when we git thar.")[22] She emphasized also that

God constantly intervened in human affairs. When the Southern slaves were emancipated, Douglass refused to thank God for it, angering many churchmen; Douglass instead thanked those humans who had used their God-given abilities to help free the slaves. By contrast Truth believed, as she told President Lincoln in her interview with him, that God was responsible for the emancipation and that God and the people had selected Lincoln to carry it out. It was not always clear, however, how Truth balanced God's ability to intervene in human affairs with the human obligation to help God accomplish His purposes.

Once she left New York, what were Truth's denominational connections? While she was a wandering evangelist, according to Olive Gilbert, Truth had no preference for one sect over another. At that time, however, she spoke against a paid ministry, as Quakers did and as her mentor Pierson had too. At that time also she deliberately exposed herself to Millerite Adventists, and considered joining the Shakers.

After she became a lecturer for reform, when she spoke about her early Christian experience, as she often did, she only occasionally specified that it had taken place in a Methodist context. Yet on the few occasions when she was introduced with a denominational tag, it was a Methodist tag: It was claimed in 1858 that she "is now, and has been, a member of the Methodist Episcopal Church for many years"; in 1871, that "she adheres . . . to the Methodist persuasion"; in 1872, that "she is a Methodist of the old John Wesley school." But it is questionable in her later years how appropriate it still was to call her a Methodist. In 1879 she explained, as reported in an interview, that "she had been a Methodist till that church outgrew her; it had changed and not she."[23] This suggests that she continued to identify herself with Methodists' old-time emphasis on experiential religion, which encouraged individuals to testify on their own personal experience of God, in their own colloquial language, but that if Methodists became more formal or doctrinaire, she grew uncomfortable.

When Truth lived in Ulster County, New York, Quakers had helped her recover her son from slavery in Alabama. Later in her antislavery agitation, of course she often met Quakers, or dissident Quakers. Many Quaker activists seemed to respect her inner experience, one saying, when she visited him, "She is rich native ore from the mountains of the Lord." When in 1853, some Pennsylvania Friends who were dissatisfied with the conservative Quaker hesitancy to agitate publicly for such reforms as blacks' and women's rights, formed a new Progressive Friends Yearly Meeting outside of the regular bodies of Friends, Truth spoke to them several times. Over a period of years she often met with Progressive Friends in Pennsylvania, New York, Ohio, and Michigan, as many reformers did. Moreover, one of the Merritt family recalled her once visiting the regular Quaker meeting in Battle Creek, where, in accordance with Quaker custom, there was no singing and no one was expected to speak unless "moved" to do so. But Truth rose and stated that she was "moved" to sing, and sang "a rousing Negro spiritual."[24] Although Truth sometimes wore Quaker-style garb, and was in more significant ways much influenced by Quakers, and may informally be called a Progressive Friend herself, still she is not known ever to have joined any regular Friends meeting.

After leaving the Spiritualist community of Harmonia, Truth continued to associate over many years with Spiritualists. In Washington in 1866, Truth visited the home of one of the most striking Spiritualist speakers in the nation, Mrs. Cora (Hatch) Daniels, then only in her midtwenties, whose custom was to make speeches while in a trance. Truth asked Daniels to write for her to their friend in common, Amy Post. Mrs. Daniels did so, commenting to Post: Truth "is a noble old hero and the world will long remember her when other names are forgotten."[25]

In 1868 on one of her frequent visits to the Posts in Rochester, Truth attended a national Spiritualist convention, and she did so, it was reported in the convention, as a "regularly elected delegate from Michigan." Truth herself spoke twice to the convention and was "frequently applauded," according to a Rochester newspaper, when she gave "an account of her experience with the spirit world, with which she says she has talked for more than forty years." The convention, illustrating the Spiritualist affinity for reform, declared itself in favor of equal rights for women and men, against the death penalty, against war, and against the use of tobacco and "intoxicating drinks," with all of which Truth was likely to sympathize. Among the leaders in the convention were Warren Chase, formerly of Harmonia, Rev. J. M. Peebles, formerly of Battle Creek, and the Philadelphia physician Dr. Henry T. Child, who was a sometime Quaker, an abolitionist-feminist, and a nationally known Spiritualist who had boasted that he had attended more than fifty seances. In the next few years when Truth visited Philadelphia, she sometimes stayed with Dr. Child.

While a few Spiritualist churches came to be scattered over the nation, and there were many Spiritualist "circles," Spiritualists generally remained, like the Progressive Friends, a loose, informal movement. They had no authoritative body to declare what Spiritualists must believe, there was no clear way to be a "member," and hence it was not easy to decide who was or was not a Spiritualist. However, the Rochester convention adopted resolutions declaring that Spiritualists champion "the sovereign right of every man and woman to judge in all matters of faith and conscience," which would certainly coincide well with Truth's insistence on the authority of her own religious experience. The convention also declared, in a statement with which Truth would also probably feel considerable congruence, that Spiritualists affirm that human happiness depends on personal "harmonization" with "universal and divine law"; that the spiritual world is "interblended with our present state of existence"; that "promptings from the spiritual realm" have not only occurred as miracles in past ages, but are "a perpetual fact" that continues to occur; that "the chain of causation leads inevitably upward or onward to an infinite spirit" who is "wisdom" and "love," and who is, in an expression that suggests the sympathy of many Spiritualists' for feminism, "father and mother" to all.[26]

In 1871 Truth spoke at the Spiritualists' Michigan state convention, held in Saginaw, along with her long-time friend Giles B. Stebbins of Detroit. In contrast to reports of her congenial participation in the Rochester convention, in this convention she was reported to have scolded those who attended "for talking so much about the good times they were going to have in the next world, and not doing anything to better the conditions of those living." She also was reported to have ridiculed Spiritualists for being the kind of people who changed often from one denomination to another, while she took pride that once God had converted her, "I nebber have changed." According to a Saginaw newspaper, she "convinced the convention" that she was "by no means an adherent" to spiritualism.[27]

In 1878, when asked if she had ever joined Spiritualists, Truth was reported to have replied enigmatically, "Why chile, there's nothing to jine." In that same year, however, when Truth and Frances Titus together visited New York City, they both stayed for several weeks at the home of the oldest of the "rapping" Fox sisters, Leah Fox Underhill, who had married into a Quaker family. While Truth and Titus stayed there,

Underhill held weekly evenings-at-home at which she honored Truth. When Truth held a meeting at Cooper Union to tell the story of her life, Underhill identified herself further with Truth by being the only person who appeared on the platform with her.[28] At this period Leah Fox Underhill was known as the most educated, stable, and reliable of the Fox sisters; she herself gave private seances, and was highly honored by Spiritualists. It was not until 1888 that the two younger Fox sisters, who had become alcoholics, confessed that their rappings were fraudulent and claimed that their older sister Leah knew it. They later recanted their confession, leaving many Spiritualists still believing that the Fox rappings were genuine.

Truth is never known to have clearly said that she was a Spiritualist, but when she died, a national Spiritualist weekly claimed, "Like nearly all others distinguished for what they have done for human progress, Sojourner Truth was a Spiritualist."[29]

Despite Truth's dalliance with spiritualism, she associated in Battle Creek with two conservative religious denominations. During the Civil War, Truth frequently visited the home of Samuel J. Rogers, a Dutch Reformed pastor who was called "orthodox," discussing with him her anxieties about the war. In 1863 when she was severely ill, she arranged that if she were to die, Rogers would preach at her funeral. The Seventh Day Adventists, who like Truth were strong believers in divine intervention in human affairs, had their world headquarters in Battle Creek, and established there a college, a publishing house, and a loosely affiliated "Sanitarium." Truth spoke at least once at the college. In her later years when the head of the Sanitarium, the Adventist Dr. J. H. "Corn Flakes" Kellogg, became her personal physician and friend, she occasionally spoke to the Sanitarium patients in their "great parlor." In 1875 Battle Creek Adventists offered to print a new edition of Truth's *Narrative,* and they printed it more than once.[30] Adventists say that she was a "familiar speaker" in their huge Tabernacle and probably "frequently attended services" there, and report a dubious claim that she was baptized into the Adventist Church. However, while Truth in her later years still believed in the second coming of Christ, she did not do so in a literal sense. "He's a-comin', chill'n," she said in a speech New York. "He ain't a-comin' flyin' in de air, de way dose Second Advent folks talk 'bout. . . . But he's a-comin' in de sperit, bress de Lo'd." In fact, she sometimes said it was not wise to emphasize the second coming. In a speech in Vineland, New

Jersey, she said, do not wait for the Lord to come to "clean up" this wicked world, but "take hold" and clean it up yourselves. Somewhat differently, in a speech in Lansing, Truth urged her listeners not to be "waiting for God to come. He is with you now, all the time, and what more can you want?" At the time of her death, Adventists may have tried to claim her as one of their own, for several newspapers announced that her funeral would be held in the Adventists' Tabernacle, with its minister officiating, but this proved to be mistaken.[31]

As her death approached, Truth lived quietly in Battle Creek in her modest little house on College Street—a visitor described it one summer as "a little dove cote of a house with a background of sunflowers and beds of quaint blossoms leading to the door."[32] Truth knew that her death was coming soon. She had had ulcers on one leg for years, and they were spreading. Dr. Kellogg and other physicians from the Sanitarium came to her home to help her as much as they could. Her two daughters who now lived with her, Diana and Elizabeth, cared for her. So also did her faithful friend Frances Titus, who visited often.

Truth died on November 26, 1883. Although she was commonly said to be over 100 years old, she was really about 86.

Before she died, Truth herself had decided that her funeral was to be held in Battle Creek in the Congregational and Presbyterian Church. She had also chosen—probably with the encouragement of Frances Titus—the two persons who were to speak at her funeral.[33] These two, Rev. Reed Stuart, the pastor of the church, and Giles B. Stebbins of Detroit, were both white and both conspicuously liberal. Stuart had been ordained a Presbyterian minister, but his views were sufficiently irregular—a local newspaper described him as caring "little for the iron-bound creeds by which religion has been fettered"—so that, shortly before Truth's death, when Presbyterians threatened to try him as a heretic, he withdrew from the denomination. His church, called the most popular in Battle Creek, sustained him, and itself withdrew from the Presbyterian denomination, becoming an independent church, unrelated to any denominational organizations, but still calling itself the Congregational and Presbyterian Church. Truth said of Stuart, a few days before her death, that "God is working a wonderful work" through him.[34]

The other speaker at her funeral, Giles B. Stebbins, had known Truth when, as a young prospective Unitarian clergyman, he and Truth both lived in the Northampton utopian community. He became, however, not a clergyman, but a lecturer and writer for black rights, women's rights, and spiritualism, and was active among Progressive Friends. Stebbins believed in downplaying such orthodox tenets as the wrath of God, miraculous revelation, and Jesus' atonement, affirming instead God, duty, the individual soul, and immortality. His popular book, *Chapters from the Bible of the Ages,* consisted not only of selections from the traditional Hebrew and Christian Bible but also from the ancient Egyptians and Hindus, as well as from such moderns as Tom Paine and Whittier. Writing about Truth shortly after her death, Stebbins praised her "moral worth and spiritual greatness."[35]

Perhaps it hints at the breadth that Truth had attained that this advocate of blacks could choose two whites to speak at her funeral, this advocate of women could choose two men, and this still evangelical Christian could choose two religious liberals.

In perspective, if in her early years Truth seemed somewhat extreme in her religion, and if she seemed to become even more so when she was a follower of Matthias, in her later years, she mellowed. Like many Americans, under the impact of the democratic exuberance of her time, she experimented with her religion, shaping it to meet her needs and what she perceived as the needs of others. After she moved out of New York, it has not been documented that she ever again affiliated with any church. She appeared to avoid fitting herself into any groove, religious or otherwise.

In part under the influence of her early black and Methodist religious traditions, she remained all her life evangelical, confident in the efficacy of prayer, in the love of Jesus, and in the long-range justice of God. In part under the influence of her reformist associates, she developed liberal inclinations, and was usually broadly tolerant of differences among those who worked for the coming of God's Kingdom on earth, no matter what their particular religious views. But if Garrison, Douglass, and Stanton emphasized that Christianity could be an instrument of oppression, Truth emphasized—more like Lucretia Mott, Gilbert Haven, and Frances Willard—that it could be an instrument for human rights and fulfillment.

In her later years she usually continued to speak in traditional Christian language, often in stories and epigrams, figuratively, so that she could easily be felt to be orthodox or liberal, literal or abstract, simple or profound, on many different levels. It was partly because of her broad, imprecise religious style that she reached large numbers of people, and that many of them, whatever their religion, could see in her something with which they could identify. This made it possible not only for Methodists but also for believers as different as conservative Adventists and progressive Quakers to feel that she was one of them, and to continue to do so into our time. This also made it possible for the American branch of the St. Thomas Christian Church—followers of the tradition of Christians in South India—to canonize her, in a ceremony in 1992 in Santa Cruz, California, as St. Sojourner Truth.

In keeping with the prevailing mood of her times, her faith was positive. She liked to say, God "is a great ocean of love, and we live and move in Him as the fishes in the sea." Her faith was not ritualistic or doctrinaire, but focused on how to live. "How can you expect to do good to God," she asked, "unless you first learn to do good to each other?" Similarly, she said that people "would never get to heaven by lifting themselves up in a basket, but they must lift those up below them, and then they would all go up together."[36]

If Truth was not all that mythmakers, past and present, claim, nevertheless she rose magnificently above the limitations imposed on her in her time as a slave, an illiterate, a black, and a woman. She insisted on applying her Christianity to help set the world "right side up," as she said; and with her whimsical illustrations, and her strange blend of the brash and the wise, she was often persuasive.

Her Kansas friends the Byron Smiths understood a good deal about her when they wrote that it was easy to detect in her "the spirit, however humble its garb, freed from the trammels of the world, party, or sectarianism. . . . Once a slave, now in the highest sense a freedwoman."[37]

Notes

1. Growing Up a Slave

1. *The Narrative of Sojourner Truth,* 1850, 13, says she was born a slave of Colonel "Ardinburgh," and identifies him as of "Hurley," but does not precisely say she was born in Hurley, and does not mention Swartekill at all. However, the 1790 U.S. Census lists "Johannis Hardenbergh" as living in the town of Hurley. According to the will of "Johannis Hardenbergh," May 15, 1799 (Record of Wills, bk. C, 164, Ulster County Surrogate's Office, Kingston), he lived in "Swarte Kill" in the town of Hurley. According to Miller, *Hardenbergh Family,* 60, Col. "Johannes Hardenbergh" lived at "Swartekill . . . a short distance north of Rifton." William Smith to Victor M. Hulbert, Jan. 29, 1884, BJ, reporting a conversation with one of the Van Wagenen family, says they believed she was born in the house of Col. "Hans Hardenbergh," in "Swartekill." Howard Hendricks, a Kingston journalist, in his "Sojourner Truth," 1892, 666, reporting an interview with the Dumont family, said that according to them she was born in "Swarte Kill," which by this time was known as Rifton. Town boundaries having changed, Swartekill is now in the town of Esopus.

2. Miller, *Hardenbergh Family,* 59–62; 1790 U.S. Census, town of Hurley.

3. Mohawk ancestry: Salem, OH, *Anti-Slavery Bugle,* Dec. 13, 1851; Boston *Liberator,* June 21, 1861. Appeared black: *Woman's Journal,* Dec. 1, 1883; Wyman, *American Chivalry,* 108.

4. *Narrative,* 13; Lansing *Republican,* June 4, 1881; *Sunshine at Home,* 91–92; New York *Globe,* Dec. 1, 1883.

5. Sources seeming to agree Truth was born about 1797: *Narrative,* 1850, 13, 17, 29; Vale, *Fanaticism,* pt. 1, 10–11, 17; Rogers, "Sojourner Truth," 6.

6. *Narrative,* 13–14. Johannes Hardenbergh died in 1799, sometime between his signing his will, May 15, and its being probated, Oct. 26 (Record of Wills, 172–73). Charles Hardenbergh was listed in the 1800 U.S. Census, town of Hurley, as having five slaves. After he died, when an "inventory" of his

possessions was made, they included four slaves: Isabella, her mother, her brother Peter (the inventory omits her father, perhaps because by this time, old and ill, he was monetarily worthless), and "Sam," who was not known to be of Isabella's family. ("Inventory," May 12, 1808, of possessions of Charles Hardenbergh, microfilm 17, sec. 10, Ulster County Surrogate's Office, Kingston.)

7. "Inventory" of the possessions of Charles Hardenbergh.

8. *Narrative,* 15–16.

9. *Narrative,* 17.

10. *Narrative,* 17–19, 26.

11. *Narrative,* 20–25; *Banner of Light,* May 2, 1863.

12. *Narrative,* 26–27 (which spells the name "Nealy"). An 1806 advertisement by "John Neely" is reprinted in *Olde Ulster,* April 1913, 108–9.

13. Chicago *Semi-Weekly Inter-Ocean,* Sept. 25, 1893.

14. In *Narrative,* 28–29, the name is spelled "Scriver"; in William Smith to Victor M. Hulbert, Jan. 29, 1884, BJ, "Martinus Schryver"; in the U.S. census (1800, 1810, 1820) town of Kingston or Esopus, spelled variously. Truth's steamboat recollection: Rochester *Evening Express,* July 25, 1878; Lansing *Republican,* July 30, 1881.

15. Squier, "Sojourner Truth," 17.

16. *Narrative,* 27, 59–62; Boston *Post,* Jan. 2, 1871.

17. *Narrative,* 29; Hendricks, "Sojourner Truth," 671. According to the U.S. census, town of New Paltz, in 1800 and 1820 Dumont had four slaves. The Dumont house is no longer standing. Its site is the only site where Truth lived as a slave which is agreed on by local scholars. It was on the Hudson River side of highway 9–W, opposite the present West Park Post Office, near where Floyd Ackert Road and a railroad line cross 9–W. The site is not marked because the owner does not want a marker.

18. *Narrative,* 31–33.

19. *Narrative,* 33–34; Detroit *Post,* Jan. 12, 1869; Boston *Post,* Jan. 2, 1871; Rochester *Evening Express,* Apr. 17, 1871.

20. On Charles Catton: Dunlap, *History of the Rise and Progress of the Arts,* vol. 2, 359–62; obituary, New York *Commercial Advertiser,* May 5, 1819. The 1810 U.S. Census, town of New Paltz, in the list near John Dumont, named "Charles Cating" with one slave; for 1820, also in the list near Dumont, named "Charles Catton," perhaps the artist's son of the same name, with five slaves.

21. *Narrative,* 34–36.

22. *Narrative,* 36–37. Gertrude Dumont recalled the names of Truth's four known children and added that the fifth did not live to grow up (Hendricks, "Sojourner Truth," 669). The one who did not grow up was James (Battle Creek *Daily Journal,* Oct. 25, 1904). Some commentators have supposed that Truth had a daughter named Hannah, but it seems likely that the "Hannah" after whom Peter enquired in a letter to his mother (*Narrative,* 77) along with enquiring after his sisters Sophia and Betsey (Elizabeth), was a misreading of his handwriting for "Dianah" (Diana).

23. New York *Daily Tribune,* Sept. 16, 1853; Salem, OH, *Anti-Slavery Bu-*

gle, Nov. 8, 1856; Battle Creek *Daily Journal,* Oct. 25, 1904 (the passage as printed seems to confuse names, but the thrust of it is clear).

24. *Laws of the State of New York,* vol. 4, Albany, 1818, chap. 137, passed 1817, 136.

25. *Narrative,* 73; William Smith to Victor M. Hulbert, Jan. 29, 1884, BJ; Hendricks, "Sojourner Truth," 668–69.

26. *Narrative,* 37.

27. *Narrative,* 29–31, 34, 38.

28. According to available evidence, not until 1938 was it hinted that any of Isabella's children might have been fathered by Dumont. Fauset, *Sojourner Truth,* 30, said that Tom was the father of her five children, but also said ambiguously that "considering Isabella's attitude toward Dumont, it seems likely that they were less the children of Thomas than of Dumont." This comment may have led Woodward, *The Bold Women,* 254, to say, "possibly he was her lover." Later claiming Dumont raped her: Pauli, *Her Name Was Sojourner Truth,* 29; Lerner, *The Female Experience,* 488; Hooks, *Ain't I a Woman,* 160.

29. *Narrative,* 30.

30. *Narrative,* 124–25.

31. *Narrative,* 81–82.

32. New York *Daily Tribune,* Sept. 16, 1853; "Inventory" of the possessions of Charles Hardenbergh. Unis Hardenbergh signed with "her mark" the deed of John E. and Unis Hardenbergh, to David Ackerman, for land in Swartekill, town of Hurley, June 12, 1809, Ulster County Record of Deeds, Kingston, vol. 19, 470–73.

33. Hendricks, "Sojourner Truth," 669.

34. Heidgerd, *Black History of New Paltz,* 48; Mabee, *Black Education in New York State,* chap. 3, 287; De Witt, *People's History of Kingston,* 218. The Quaker Alexander Young operated a "Boarding School" (1820 U.S. Census, town of Esopus). Quakers built a church in Esopus in 1813 (Clearwater, *History of Ulster County,* 479).

35. In their old age, Diana, Elizabeth, and Sophia all signed deeds with their marks. (Deeds, "Sojourner Truth, per heirs, to Frances W. Titus," Dec. 29, 1888, and "Sojourner Truth, per heirs, to William H. Clevenger," Sept. 15, 1896, Record of Deeds, Calhoun County Clerk's Office, Marshall, MI, bk. 127, 45; bk. 155, 571.)

36. Battle Creek *Daily Journal,* Oct. 25, 1904.

37. New York *Daily Tribune,* Sept. 7, 1853.

38. Douglass, *Life and Times,* pt. 1, chaps. 10–12; *Narrative,* 33–34.

39. *National Anti-Slavery Standard,* Sept. 10, 1853.

40. *Narrative,* 24.

41. Hendricks, "Sojourner Truth," 671.

42. Quotes: Saginaw *Daily Courier,* June 14, 1871; Chicago *Times,* Aug. 13, 1879. Story of her escape: *Narrative,* 39–43.

43. The Van Wagenens lived in Wahkendall *(Narrative,* 64). ("Waagendall" was identified as in the town of Hurley (Kingston *Ulster Sentinel,* Oct. 3, 1827).

Stowe, "Sojourner Truth," 475, in reporting what Isabella told her, says that the first house she came to was that of Quakers and there she stayed, but the *Narrative* makes it clear that she did not stay with the "Rowes" but at the second house, with the Van Wagenens. "Levi Roe" is buried in the Friends Cemetery, Tillson, his stone saying he died Oct. 19, 1826, age 33.

44. The Van Wagenens were called Quakers by Stowe ("Sojourner Truth," 475), who said she was reporting what Truth said, which is probably the origin of the claim. Stowe may have confused what Truth said about the Roes with what she said about the Van Wagenens. Truth did not call them Quakers in *Narrative*, nor did she in speaking about them at other times, as in New York *Daily Tribune*, Sept. 16, 1853, though it seems likely that she would have called them Quakers if they had been.

45. Both quotes, "good man" and "I can do that": West Chester, PA, *Daily Local News*, July 18, 1874.

46. *Narrative*, 43; Vale, *Fanaticism*, pt. 1, 10–11.

47. *Narrative*, 44. Gertrude Dumont recalled that Peter lived for a time with "Dr. Gedney, a neighbor" (Hendricks, "Sojourner Truth," 669). "Joseph Gidney" is listed in the 1830 U.S. Census, town of New Paltz, on the same page as John Dumont, and thus was probably living nearby.

48. *Narrative*, 63, 82; *Laws of the State of New York*, vol. 4, Albany, 1818, chap. 137, passed 1817, 136.

49. *Narrative*, 194; Warsaw, IN, *Northern Indianian*, Oct. 8, 1858.

50. Rochester *Evening Express*, Apr. 17, 1871; Salem, OH, *Anti-Slavery Bugle*, Nov. 8, 1856.

2. Slave Mother

1. Kingston *Ulster Sentinel*, July 11, 1827.

2. *Laws of the State of New York*, vol. 4, Albany, 1818, chap. 137, passed 1817, 136, 139.

3. Story of her recovery of her son: *Narrative*, 44–58.

4. "Ignorant": West Chester, PA, *Daily Local News*, July 18, 1874.

5. Vale, *Fanaticism*, pt. 1, 11.

6. *Narrative*, 51–58.

7. A plaque placed in 1983 in front of the Ulster County Court House, Kingston, commemorates Sojourner Truth's successful court case in this matter. However, in answer to the query if there were any court records available that would verify Truth's litigation, June Lee Davidson, Ulster County Chief Deputy Clerk, wrote Carleton Mabee (hereafter CM), Apr. 13, 1989, that the county clerk's office could not locate any such records. The records of the state circuit court, which sometimes met in Kingston, have been stored in the New York County Clerk's Office, but Bruce Abrams, Assistant Archivist there, wrote CM, Mar. 15, 1991, that no records about the case have been located there. James D. Folts, Archivist, Division of State Government Records, Albany, wrote CM, Apr.

2, 1991, that the most likely procedure lawyers would take in such a case would be for Truth to get a writ of habeas corpus to recover her son, which would not lead to any formal trial, and therefore records of the writ would not be likely to be preserved either locally or by the state. At any rate, the state, he wrote, has not preserved them.

8. Vale, *Fanaticism*, pt. 1, 17. "Judge Ruggles" was not yet a judge at the time Isabella was trying to recover her son. He was lawyer Charles H. Ruggles, who in 1828 was appointed Ulster County District Attorney (Kingston *Ulster Sentinel*, Apr. 16, 1828). "Squire Chip" is called "lawyer Chip" and "Esquire Chip" in *Narrative*, and doubtless was John Chipp, who was a justice of the peace in 1825 (Deposition by Daniel Osterhoudt et al., before John Chipp, Justice of the Peace, Ulster County, Dec. 14, 1825, HHS). "Lawyer Romain" is called "Demain" in *Narrative*, 50–51. But he is undoubtedly the lawyer identified as "Herman M. Romeyn" in the Kingston *Ulster Sentinel*, June 21, 1826. "Lawyer Hasbrouck" is Abram Bruyn Hasbrouck, law partner of Ruggles (obituary, New York *Daily Tribune*, Feb. 25, 1879).

9. Hendricks, "Sojourner Truth," 669–70.

10. New York *Daily Tribune*, Sept. 16, 1853; *National Anti-Slavery Standard*, May 2, July 4, 1863; West Chester, PA, *Daily Local News*, July 18, 1874; Chicago *Inter-Ocean*, Oct. 21, 1881.

11. *Narrative*, 55–56.

12. Vale, *Fanaticism*, pt. 2, 126.

13. Rochester *Evening Express*, Apr. 17, 1871.

14. Charles Hardenbergh had children baptized at New Paltz Dutch Reformed Church (Miller, *Hardenbergh Family*, 75; *Records of the Reformed Dutch Church*, 180, 186, 197). John Dumont had children baptized at Klyne Esopus Dutch Reformed Church, Esopus. Eventually Isabella's daughter Diana was affiliated there. About when Dumont moved away, the church dismissed both John Dumont and "Dinah" Dumont, called his "servant," Nov. 30, 1850 *(Vital Records of Low Dutch Church*, 8, 14, 129.)

15. New York *Daily Tribune*, Sept. 16, 1853; Stowe, "Sojourner Truth," 476; Chicago *Times*, Aug. 13, 1879.

16. *Narrative*, 64–65; Wyandotte, KS, *Gazette*, Jan. 25, 1872.

17. New York *Daily Tribune*, Dec. 7, 1878; Rochester *Evening Express*, Apr. 17, 1871; William Smith to Victor M. Hulbert, Jan. 29, 1884, BJ.

18. "Civilized" and "religion": Saginaw *Daily Courier*, June 14, 1871; "seed": Rochester *Evening Express*, Apr. 17, 1871; "lobe": Boston *Post*, Jan. 2, 1871.

19. *Narrative*, 1884, "A Memorial Chapter," 6. It provides some substantiation for Truth's recollection that Connelly, *St. James Methodist Episcopal Church of Kingston*, 41, says that in 1826 "Ira Ferris" was one of the two ministers of this church. At that period Methodist ministers in rural regions were likely to be more nearly circuit riders than established ministers.

20. West Chester, PA, *Daily Local News*, July 18, 1874; *Woman's Journal*, Aug. 10, 1878.

21. *Narrative*, 79.

22. De Witt, *People's History of Kingston,* 218; Connelly, *St. James Methodist Episcopal Church,* 5, 11. The church was originally located at approximately Pearl and Fair Streets, and at present is still on that site, and is known as St. James United Methodist Church. Its early membership records have not been preserved.

23. William Smith to Victor M. Hulbert, Jan. 29, 1884, BJ; *Narrative,* 73.

24. *Narrative,* 86, Vale, *Fanaticism,* pt. 1, 18.

25. *Narrative,* 73; Hendricks, "Sojourner Truth," 668, 670.

26. *Narrative,* 71.

3. Monstrous Kingdom

1. New York *Daily Tribune,* Sept. 7, 1853.

2. *Narrative,* 79–80.

3. New York *Daily Tribune,* Sept. 7, 1853.

4. Mabee, *Black Education,* chap. 4, 293.

5. A Phoenixville, PA, paper, ca. July 29, 1874, in *Narrative,* 222.

6. Vale, *Fanaticism,* pt. 1, 18–19; pt. 2, 21, 126; New York *Daily Tribune,* Sept. 7, 1853.

7. Stone, *Matthias,* 68–78; Vale, *Fanaticism,* pt. 1, 9–10; New York *Journal of Commerce,* Apr. 22, 1835.

8. *Narrative,* 96–97.

9. Vale, *Fanaticism,* pt. 1, 18, 40–42; *Narrative,* 90–93.

10. *Memoirs of Matthias,* 2.

11. Stone, *Matthias,* 6, 65.

12. Traubel, *With Walt Whitman,* 140; Vale, *Fanaticism,* pt. 1, 5, 13; pt. 2, 7. A significant run of Vale's *Citizen of the World* is not known to exist.

13. Stone, *Matthias,* 140, 142; Vale, *Fanaticism,* pt. 1, 53–54.

14. Vale, *Fanaticism,* pt. 1, 49–51; Stone, *Matthias,* 139.

15. *Memoirs of Matthias,* 5.

16. Vale, *Fanaticism,* pt. 1, 60; Stone, *Matthias,* 200, 218.

17. Vale, *Fanaticism,* pt. 1, 61–62.

18. Stone, *Matthias,* 179.

19. Stone, *Matthias,* 119–22.

20. Schroeder, "Mathias the Prophet," 65.

21. *Memoirs of Matthias,* 10; Vale, *Fanaticism,* pt. 1, 59; pt. 2, 9–10.

22. Vale, *Fanaticism,* pt. 1, 61–63.

23. Vale, *Fanaticism,* pt. 1, 68–70.

24. Vale, *Fanaticism,* pt. 1, 72.

25. Vale, *Fanaticism,* pt. 2, 17, 32.

26. Vale, *Fanaticism,* pt. 1, 82.

27. Vale, *Fanaticism,* pt. 2, 74–78; New York *Journal of Commerce,* Apr. 22, 1835.

28. Vale, *Fanaticism,* pt. 2, 81–82.

29. Vale, *Fanaticism,* pt. 2, 94–95, 107–8.

30. Vale, *Fanaticism,* pt. 2, 96, 108; Albany *Evening Journal,* Sept. 25, 1834; New York *Times,* Sept. 27, 1834.

31. Vale, *Fanaticism,* pt. 1, 10–12; pt. 2, 110, 112, 116–17.

32. Vale, *Fanaticism,* pt. 1, 12.

33. New York *Journal of Commerce,* Nov. 15, 1834.

34. New York *Courier and Enquirer,* Apr. 15, 1835.

35. Vale, *Fanaticism,* pt. 2, 83, 118–20; Stone, *Matthias,* 251–66; New York *Courier and Enquirer,* Apr. 17, 18, 20, 1835.

36. New York *Courier and Enquirer,* Apr. 20, 1835; New York *Journal of Commerce,* Apr. 22, 1835.

37. Albany *Argus,* Apr. 23, 1835; New York *Daily Advertiser,* Apr. 21, 1835.

38. New York *Times,* in Albany *Argus,* Apr. 23, 1835; Albany *Argus,* Apr. 23, 1835; *Memoirs of Matthias,* 13.

39. Joseph Smith, diary, 1835, in *Latter-Day Saints' Millenial Star* 15 (June 18, 25, 1853): 396–97, 422.

40. Vale, *Fanaticism,* pt. 2, 3, 93, 110, 112–13.

41. Vale, *Fanaticism,* pt. 2, 123, 126.

42. New York *Times,* in Albany *Argus,* Apr. 23, 1835; Schroeder, "Mathias the Prophet," 65.

43. Vale, *Fanaticism,* pt. 1, 5.

44. Vale, *Fanaticism,* pt. 1, 62–63.

45. Vale, *Fanaticism,* pt. 2, 127.

46. *Narrative,* 122.

4. New Missions

1. *Narrative,* 98–100.

2. *Narrative,* 98. According to Peter's letters, as presented in *Narrative,* 76–79, Peter sailed away in 1839 on the whaling ship "Done," of Nantucket, with Capt. "Miller." According to Kaplan "Sojourner Truth's Son Peter," 34, citing ship records, its correct name was "Zone," its captain was "Hiller," it left Nantucket in 1839, and returned there May 8, 1843, with whale oil. But whether Peter returned with the ship is unknown.

3. *Narrative,* 100.

4. Humez, *Gifts of Power*; Andrews, *Sisters of the Spirit.*

5. *Narrative,* 99–100.

6. Stowe, "Sojourner Truth," 478.

7. The seven accounts (of varying believability): Vineland, NJ, *Weekly,* Dec. 25, 1869; Kalamazoo *Daily Telegraph,* June 14, 1877; Rochester *Evening Express,* July 25, 1878; *Woman's Journal,* Aug. 10, 1878; New York *Herald,* Dec. 16, 1878; Chicago *Times,* Aug. 12, 1879; Chicago *Daily Inter-Ocean,* Aug. 13, 1879.

8. Chicago *Daily Inter-Ocean,* Aug. 13, 1879.

9. Vineland, NJ, *Weekly,* Dec. 25, 1969.

10. Chicago *Daily Inter-Ocean,* Aug. 13, 1879; *Narrative,* 101.

11. Truth seems to say she arrived in "Cold Springs," Long Island, on July 4, 1843, where the temperance meeting was held (*Narrative,* 105). On that day, according to the Huntington *Long Islander,* July 7, 1843, county temperance societies held a temperance festival in Cold Spring, with a procession from the Methodist church to a grove, where they provided music, orations, and dinner.

12. *Narrative,* 114.

13. *Narrative,* 105.

14. *Narrative,* 114.

15. Northampton Association: *Narrative,* 114–15, 120–21; Noyes, *History of American Socialisms,* 154–60; Sheffield, *History of Florence,* chaps. 8–9; Mabee, *Black Freedom,* 82–85.

16. Sheffield, *History of Florence,* 130–32.

17. Chicago *Daily Inter-Ocean,* Aug. 13, 1879.

18. *Narrative,* 115–20.

19. *Narrative,* 120–21.

20. Support herself: *National Anti-Slavery Standard,* Sept. 10, 1853; New York *Daily Tribune,* Nov. 8, 1853.

21. *Narrative,* 1850, 144.

22. *Narrative,* 121; Chicago *Daily Inter-Ocean,* Aug. 13, 1879; Hampshire County Record Book, vol. 133, Register of Deeds, Northampton, MA, deed, 106–7; mortgage, 124–25.

23. *Narrative,* 269.

24. New York *Daily Tribune,* Oct. 26, 1850.

25. New York *Herald,* Oct. 25, 26, 28, 1850.

26. Resolution: Woman's Rights Convention, held Worcester, 1850, *Proceedings,* 16. Claim: Benjamin Quarles, "Truth, Sojourner," *Colliers Encyclopedia,* New York, 1986, vol. 22, 501. It has also been claimed that Truth was the only black woman at the convention (Schneir, *Feminism,* 93; Ravitch, *American Reader,* 86). But the New York *Herald,* Oct. 25, 1850, reported, "several dark colored sisters were visible in the corners."

27. *National Anti-Slavery Standard,* Nov. 28, 1850.

28. Boston *Liberator,* Jan. 3, 1851; Lasser and Merrill, *Friends and Sisters,* 99–100.

29. Claimed: Bennett, *Pioneers in Protest,* 123; Levinson, *First Women Who Spoke Out,* 51. Stewart: Boston *Liberator,* May 4, 1833.

30. Truth to Garrison, Apr. 11, 1864, BPL.

31. Boston *Liberator,* Feb. 28, 1851; *National Anti-Slavery Standard,* Mar. 6, 1851.

32. Boston *Liberator,* Apr. 4, 1851.

33. On the Posts: Boston *Liberator,* Sept. 23, 1853; Rochester *Union and Advertiser,* May 13, 1872; Jan. 30, 1889; Colman, *Reminiscences,* 83–86.

34. Salem, OH, *Anti-Slavery Bugle,* May 17, 1851.

35. Colman, *Reminiscences,* 65.

36. James Brown Yerrington was the printer of the Boston *Liberator.*

37. Truth to Garrison, Aug. 28, 1851, BPL.

5. Why Did She Never Learn to Read?

1. Saginaw *Daily Courier,* June 11, 1871.

2. Chadwick, *A Life for Liberty,* 80; Stowe, "Sojourner Truth," 480.

3. New York *Daily Tribune,* Sept. 7, 16, 1853; Chicago *Daily Inter-Ocean,* Aug. 13, 1879.

4. Chicago *Daily Inter-Ocean,* Aug. 13, 1879; Salem, OH, *Anti-Slavery Bugle,* Nov. 8, 1856.

5. "Stiff": Redding, *Lonesome Road,* 78; Pauli, *Her Name Was Sojourner Truth,* 181 (Neither Redding nor Pauli documents this story; when I wrote Redding asking if he could cite a source for this story, he replied [May 16, 1986] that though he checked his notes, he could not). Cordley, "Sojourner Truth," 65.

6. Pennsylvania Yearly Meeting of Progressive Friends, held 1874, *Proceedings,* 17; Cordley, "Sojourner Truth," 65; Kimball House Museum, Battle Creek, to CM, July 14, 1986; Lansing *Republican,* June 7, 1881.

7. Chicago *Daily Inter-Ocean,* Aug. 13, 1879.

8. New York *Daily Tribune,* Nov. 8, 1853; Carter, "Sojourner Truth," 479.

9. Boston *Post,* Jan. 2, 1871; Springfield *Daily Republican,* Feb. 24, 1871.

10. New York *Daily Tribune,* Sept. 7, 1853; Tomkins, *Jewels in Ebony,* 6; Chicago *Times,* Aug. 12, 1879; Chicago *Daily Inter-Ocean,* Sept. 5, 1881; Stewart, *Holy Warriors,* 138.

11. Douglass, in Sheffield, *History of Florence,* 132; New York *World,* May 11, 1867; Boston *Post,* Jan. 2, 1871.

12. Colman, *Reminiscences,* 66; New York *World,* May 11, 13, 1867.

13. New York *Sun,* Nov. 24, 1878; New York *Herald,* Dec. 16, 1878; *National Anti-Slavery Standard,* July 4, 1863; Detroit *Advertiser and Tribune,* Nov. 23, 1863; Stone, in *Woman's Journal,* Aug. 5, 1876, 252.

14. Truth to Amy Post, Aug. 25, 1867, UR; Sojourner to Mary K. Gale, Feb. 25, 1864, LC.

15. New York *World,* May 13, 1867; Stone, in *Woman's Journal,* Aug. 5, 1876, 252; Douglass, in Sheffield, *History of Florence,* 131–32; Stowe, "Sojourner Truth," 473.

6. Her Famous Akron Speech

1. *Narrative,* 131–35; Stanton, Anthony, and Gage, *History,* vol. 1, 115–17.

2. Fauset, *Sojourner Truth,* 131.

3. In 1871 Truth was reported—whether accurately or not—to have warned,

in an illogical, humorous statement, that accounts of her life published in the period in which Gage's account was published were not reliable: "Of the published accounts of her life . . . 'what Mrs. Stowe writ was true, but since that it had growed and growed, and now it was a great book, and there wasn't a word of truth in it, and what there was that was true was all hind side afore' " (Washington *New National Era*, Apr. 20, 1871).

4. Stowe, "Sojourner Truth." We have two contemporary testimonies, if not impressive ones, that Stowe's article was accurate. One was by Truth, as quoted in the previous note. The other was by editor Oliver Johnson, who, in reprinting Stowe's article in his *National Anti-Slavery Standard*, Mar. 28, 1863, wrote: "Mrs. Stowe's picture is by no means exaggerated." By contrast, we have available no such contemporary endorsements of Gage's article. However, Stowe's article, like Gage's, was published many years after the events it described. Both Gage and Stowe claim to report what Truth said in lengthy, direct quotations, which in themselves inevitably suggest doubts about accuracy. Moreover, Stowe's article, like Gage's, contains significant factual errors about Truth's life, for example that she was born in Africa, that the Van Wagenens were Quakers, that Mrs. Dumont's daughter took Peter to Alabama, that the "Is God Dead?" incident took place in Faneuil Hall, and that Truth was already dead. But Stowe's article does not lend itself to checking for accuracy as well as Gage's does in that Stowe's recounts a private rather than a public meeting.

5. For this purpose, a "description" of the convention must be at least seven sentences long. If an article is signed, and is continued in a later issue, it is still considered as only one description. If a publication has more than one article on the convention that is unsigned, and they are short, they may be considered as one description. The twenty-seven descriptions, all published in 1851, arranged alphabetically by place of publication, are: Akron, OH, *Summit Beacon*, June 4; Boston, *Liberator*, June 13; Chillicothe, OH, *Daily Scioto Gazette*, June 5, 10, 13; Cincinnati *Daily Gazette*, June 2, 4, 9; Cincinnati *Daily Commercial*, June 3, 6 (by Celia M. Burr); Cincinnati *Daily Nonpareil*, June 2, 3, 5 (by Lucius A. Hine); Cincinnati *Enquirer*, June 6; Cincinnati, Woman's Rights Convention, held Akron, May 28–29, 1851, *Proceedings* (official); Cleveland *Daily Plain Dealer*, June 2; Cleveland *Herald*, May 30 (by "Observer"); Cleveland *Herald*, June 11 (by "Constance"); Cleveland *True Democrat*, May 30 (by "B"); Cleveland *True Democrat*, June 6 (by "Looker On"); Columbus *Ohio Cultivator*, June 15 (by Hannah M. Tracy); London, England, *The People*, July 19 (by Joseph Barker); New Lisbon, OH, *Aurora*, June 18; New York *Daily Tribune*, June 3, 6; New York *Home Journal*, June 21; Pittsburgh *Saturday Visiter*, June 7, 14, 28 (by Jane Swisshelm); Pittsburgh *Saturday Visiter*, July 19 (by Celia M. Burr); Pittsburgh *Saturday Visiter*, July 26 (by Gage); Ravenna *Ohio Star*, June 4; Ravenna *Portage County Whig*, June 4, Aug. 13; Rochester *Daily Democrat*, June 4, 9; Salem, OH, *Anti-Slavery Bugle*, June 7 ("Proceedings," but not the same as the official *Proceedings* cited earlier); Salem, OH, *Anti-Slavery Bugle*, June 7 (editorial by Marius Robinson); Salem, OH, *Anti-Slavery Bugle*, June 21 (unsigned report of Truth's speech).

6. Akron, OH, *Summit Beacon,* May 28; Salem, OH, *Anti-Slavery Bugle,* June 7; Cleveland *Herald,* June 11; Pittsburgh *Saturday Visiter,* June 7, 1851.

7. New York *Home Journal,* June 21; Cincinnati *Gazette,* June 2, 4; Gage in Pittsburgh *Saturday Visiter,* July 26, 1851. Similarly, Gage denied that "woman's rights women are so very unpopular" (*Lily,* Seneca Falls, NY, June, 1852, 50). Roseboom, *Civil War Era,* 238, described Ohio newspapers in the 1850s as not usually deriding the woman's rights movement, "perhaps from a sense of chivalry," but rather devoting small space to it, and damning it with faint praise.

8. Columbus *Ohio Cultivator,* June 15; Boston *Liberator,* June 13; New York *Home Journal,* June 21; Cleveland *Herald,* May 30; Burr, in Cincinnati *Daily Commercial,* June 6; Pittsburgh *Saturday Visiter,* June 7, 14, 1851.

9. National Women's Rights Convention, held Cleveland, 1853, *Proceedings,* 7.

10. Salem, OH, *Anti-Slavery Bugle,* Apr. 27, 1850; *National Anti-Slavery Standard,* May 22; Boston *Liberator,* May 23; Pittsburgh *Saturday Visiter,* Apr. 5; Salem, OH, *Anti-Slavery Bugle,* May 10, 1851.

11. Salem, OH, *Anti-Slavery Bugle,* Mar. 30, 1850.

12. Flexner, *Century of Struggle,* 90–91; Hine, in Hine, *State of Afro-American History,* 232; Rosalyn Terborg-Penn, in Harley and Terborg-Penn, *Afro-American Woman,* 20; Allen, *Reluctant Reformers,* 134–35; Davis, *Women, Race, & Class,* 62–64; Kerber and Mathews, *Women's America,* 202. "One recent": Hooks, *Ain't I a Woman,* 128, 159–61.

13. Swisshelm: *Saturday Visiter,* June 7, 14, 1851; Hannah Tracy Cutler: *Woman's Journal,* Sept. 26, 1896.

14. Truth to Amy Post, ca. June 1, 1851, UR.

15. The four reports, arranged from shortest to longest, are: Swisshelm, in Pittsburgh *Saturday Visiter,* June 14; Boston *Liberator,* June 13; New York *Daily Tribune,* June 6; Salem, OH, *Anti-Slavery Bugle,* June 21, 1851.

16. Gage's 1863 report spelled Truth's expression as "Ar'n't." *Narrative,* 1875, 134, in reprinting Gage's report, also gave it as "Ar'n't." However, Stanton et al., *History,* vol. 1, 1881, 116, gave it as "a'n't." In the Detroit *Post,* Nov. 29, 1883, it appeared as "ain't." By the 1970s, "ain't" had become the most commonly used form in publications about Truth, and it has remained so since.

17. The motto "Am I not a Woman and a Sister?" was a reversed sex version of the motto, "Am I not a Man and a Brother?" which was used as early as 1787 in Britain by the Society for the Abolition of the Slave Trade (Honour, *The Image of the Black in Western Art,* vol. 4, 62). The motto "Am I not a Woman and a Sister?" appeared in 1832, along with a picture of a female slave in chains, as the heading of the Boston *Liberator's* Ladies Department.

18. *Narrative,* 114. For New York: New York *Daily Tribune,* Nov. 8, 1853.

19. "Jessamines": Boston *Liberator,* Mar. 20, 1863. "Rhythm": Roseboom, *Civil War Era,* 241. The "Ain't I a Woman?" passage has been recognized as poetic, and printed in poetic format, as in Stetson, *Black Sister,* 24–25, with attribution of course to Truth, not Gage.

20. Truth to Post, ca. June 1; Gage, in Pittsburgh *Saturday Visiter,* July 5, 26. Columbus *Ohio Cultivator,* June 15; *Lily,* Seneca Falls, NY, Nov. 1851.

21. Akron, OH, *Summit Beacon,* June 4; Salem, OH, *Anti-Slavery Bugle,* June 7; New York *Daily Tribune,* June 3, 6; Boston *Liberator,* June 13, 1851.

22. *Woman's Journal,* July 2, 1881; Springfield *Daily Republican,* Nov. 27, 1883; Detroit *Post and Tribune,* Nov. 29, 1883.

23. Salem, OH, *Anti-Slavery Bugle,* June 21, 1851.

7. Confronting Douglass

1. Stowe, "The President's Message," 1. Stowe, "Sojourner Truth," 480; Rochester *Evening Express,* Nov. 27, 1883; *Crisis* 7 (Nov. 1913): 341; Detroit *Free Press,* Apr. 17, 1942.

2. Walter M. Merrill and Louis Ruchames, in Garrison, *Letters,* vol. 6, 538n.

3. Five newspapers: *National Anti-Slavery Standard,* Sept. 9, 23; Pillsbury, in Boston *Liberator,* Sept. 10, 17; Salem, OH, *Anti-Slavery Bugle,* Aug. 28, Sept. 4; Johnson, in *Pennsylvania Freeman,* Sept. 4; Douglass et al., in *Frederick Douglass' Paper,* Sept. 3, 1852.

4. Johnson, in *Pennsylvania Freeman,* Sept. 4, 1852, and Orange, NJ, *Journal,* July 29, 1876; Douglass, in Wyman, "Sojourner Truth," 63.

5. Stone, in *Woman's Journal,* Dec. 1, 1883; "American," letter to editor, in New York *Globe and Commercial Advertiser,* Apr. 16, 1918; Terry, "Sojourner Truth," [438].

6. New York, *Principia,* Dec. 29, 1860.

7. Douglass, *Life and Times,* 275.

8. *Pennsylvania Freeman,* Sept. 4, 1852.

9. Milly is based on Truth: *Banner of Light,* May 2, 1863; Rochester *Evening Express,* Nov. 27, 1883; Foster, *Rungless Ladder,* 72.

10. *Narrative,* 73, 75.

11. Mabee, *Black Freedom,* 23–25, chap. 6; Pauli, *Her Name Was Sojourner Truth,* 10.

12. On this song, "I Am Pleading for My People," see chap. 20.

13. Cleveland *Herald,* Sept. 10, 1852.

14. Woman's Rights Convention, held New York, 1853, *Proceedings,* 76.

15. Truth's recollection of this incident (*Narrative,* 140–41) is considerably substantiated in Angola, IN, *Steuben Republican,* May 18, June 1, 8, 15, 1861; Boston *Liberator,* June 21, 28, 1861.

16. Boston *Liberator,* June 21, 1861.

17. *National Anti-Slavery Standard,* Apr. 25, 1863; Detroit *Advertiser and Tribune,* Nov. 23, 1863; Truth to Mary K. Gale, Feb. 25, 1864, LC.

18. Mabee, *Black Freedom,* chap. 19.

8. Northampton to Battle Creek

1. U.S. Census, 1850, Northampton, p. 108, lists "Isabella Vanwaggener," Sophia, and Diana together. On Truth's descendants at large: Lowe, "The Family"; Battle Creek *Enquirer and News,* Nov. 26, 1981.

2. Samuel Banks's obituary: Battle Creek *Daily Journal,* Mar. 8, 1875.

3. *Narrative,* 125 ("Deanna Dumont" was a Hyde Park, NY, Reformed Dutch Church member from Nov. 23, 1849, to Nov. 18, 1851, according to its "Vital Records, 1810–1899"); Diana Corbin's obituary: Battle Creek *Journal,* Oct. 25, 1904.

4. Truth to Gale, Apr. 14, 1853, LC.

5. Truth to "Dear Friend," May 12 [1855? 1856?], LC.

6. Hampshire County Record Book, County Court House, Northampton, MA, vol. 133, 124–25; vol. 175, 11–12.

7. Salem, OH, *Anti-Slavery Bugle,* Nov. 8, 1856; George T. Garrison to Henry C. Wright, May 2, 1857, SC.

8. Deed, Hiram Cornell to Sojourner Truth, in Record of Deeds, Calhoun County Clerk's Office, Marshall, MI, bk. 46, 264. Later, date unknown, Truth purchased additional adjoining land, giving her a total of two acres (Truth's will, probated Nov. 10, 1888, Records of Probate Court, Calhoun County; deed, "Sojourner Truth, per heirs," to William H. Clevenger, Sept. 15, 1896, Records of Deeds, Calhoun County Clerk's Office, bk. 155, 571.) Truth's Harmonia house is no longer standing; the whole village was swept away to make room for the military Camp Custer in 1917.

9. "Follow": Chicago *Daily Inter-Ocean,* Aug. 13, 1879; Stone, "Sojourner Truth," 124. Delia Cornell Stone's mother was Dorcas, the daughter of the Quaker "minister" Alexander Young. In 1820 Young operated a "boarding school" in Poppletown, Esopus, NY. Dorcas Young married Reynolds Cornell, also a Quaker. Reynolds and Dorcas Cornell and their family left Ulster County in 1823 for Rensselaer County, NY (Anson, *Plains Monthly Meeting,* 12–13, 32, 84–85; U.S. Census, Ulster County, 1800, 1810, 1820). It was from there that the Cornells moved to Battle Creek. After their daughter Delia became a teacher in the Cornells' Seminary, she married another of its teachers, William B. Stone, with a Spiritualist minister officiating (Battle Creek *Journal,* June 17, Sept. 2, 1859).

10. Deed, Hampshire County Record Book, vol. 175, 31–32.

11. Battle Creek *Daily Journal,* Mar. 8, 1875; Chase, *Life-Line,* 203, 250–51; Chase, *Forty Years,* 51, 78.

12. Ford, *Heroes and Hero Tales,* 103–4.

13. Salem, OH, *Anti-Slavery Bugle,* Aug. 28, 1852; Nov. 8, 1856; Lowe, "History is Legend and Truth."

14. Salem, OH, *Anti-Slavery Bugle,* May 3, 1851.

15. *National Anti-Slavery Standard,* Oct. 31, 1857.

16. Braude, *Radical Spirits,* 59.

17. *Banner of Light,* Aug. 22, 1863; Battle Creek *Journal,* Aug. 5, 1859; *Narrative,* 258–59.

18. *Banner of Light,* May 2, 1863.

19. Syracuse *Standard,* in Battle Creek *Journal,* Apr. 12, 1871; New York *World,* May 13, 1870; Stone, "Sojourner Truth" (in both 1875 and 1876 it was rumored that Truth was dead); Colman, *Reminiscences,* 65.

20. 1860 U.S. Census, town of Bedford, 308–9 (apparently James Caldwell [or Colvin] is listed twice, once living with Truth and once living with a neighboring blacksmith); Lowe, "The Family."

21. Battle Creek *Evening News,* Jan. 1, 1918.

22. Henry B. Graves, "Sojourner Truth," statement dated Dec. 30, 1939, WL; Battle Creek *Daily Journal,* July 2, 1879.

23. Truth to Amy Post, Aug. 25, 1867, UR.

24. Battle Creek *Daily Journal,* Aug. 3, 1872; *Christian at Work,* Sept. 28, 1882; Coldwater *Republican,* Apr. 19, 1878; Michigan Department of Social Services to Mrs. Stanley T. Lowe, June 11, 1975, WL.

9. Underground Railroader?

1. Chicago *Daily Inter-Ocean,* Aug. 13, 1879.

2. Blockson, *Underground Railroad,* 1; Pease and Pease, *They Who Would Be Free,* 39; Gornick and Moran, *Woman in Sexist Society,* 490; *Ebony,* Feb. 1987, 3.

3. Sheffield, *History of Florence,* 165–67.

4. Salem, OH, *Anti-Slavery Bugle,* Oct. 25, 1851.

5. Bradford, *Harriet Tubman,* 49–50; Stowe, "Sojourner Truth," 479.

6. Amy Post's recollections of the Railroad, in Peck, *Semi-Centennial,* 458–62; Colman, *Reminiscences,* 83–86.

7. Lowe, "Michigan Days," 127–28; Detroit *News and Tribune,* Feb. 14, 1915.

8. Henry J. A. Wiegmink, "Early Days of Battle Creek," MS, ca. 1940, 653–72, WL; Battle Creek *Enquirer,* Oct. 15, 1916; Lambert, in Detroit *Tribune,* Jan. 17, 1886; Lowe, "Michigan Days," 127–28.

9. *Narrative,* 1884, "A Memorial Chapter," 26.

10. Redding, *Lonesome Road,* 77; Pauli, *Her Name Was Sojourner Truth,* 161, 240.

11. *Narrative,* 139–44.

12. *National Anti-Slavery Standard,* July 4, 1863.

13. New York *Sun,* Nov. 24, 1878; Saginaw *Daily Courier,* June 14, 1871; Chicago *Daily Inter-Ocean,* Aug. 13, 1879.

10. Romanticized: Libyan Sibyl

1. Stowe, "Sojourner Truth," 480–81.
2. James, *William Wetmore Story,* vol. 2, 70–71.
3. Yellin, *Women & Sisters,* 84; James, *William Wetmore Story,* vol. 2, 70–71.
4. Stowe, "Sojourner Truth," 473–81.
5. Sheffield, *History of Florence,* 129–32; New York *Evening Telegram,* Nov. 27, 1883.
6. *Athenaeum,* in Stowe, "Sojourner Truth," 481.
7. *Harper's Magazine* 27 (June, 1863): 133; Jarves, *Art-Idea,* 224; Boston *Liberator,* Jan. 20, 1865; James, *William Wetmore Story,* vol. 2, 76–80.
8. Detroit *Advertiser and Tribune,* Jan. 11, 1869.
9. Stanton: New York *World,* May 13, 1867; Tilton: *Independent,* Sept. 30, 1869; Pillsbury, *Acts of the Anti-Slavery Apostles,* 487; Truth: Rochester *Evening Express,* Mar. 13, 1867.
10. Springfield *Daily Republican,* Feb. 22, 1871; New York *World,* May 12, 1870; Vineland, NJ, *Weekly,* Dec. 25, 1869.

11. With President Lincoln and the Freedmen

1. Truth to Mary K. Gale, Feb. 25, 1864, LC.
2. *National Anti-Slavery Standard,* July 4, 1863.
3. Battle Creek *Journal,* Dec. 12, 1883; *National Anti-Slavery Standard,* Apr. 25, July 4, 1863; Truth to Gale, Feb. 25, 1864, LC.
4. *Narrative,* 172–73.
5. Detroit *Advertiser and Tribune,* Nov. 23, 1863.
6. *Narrative,* 126.
7. Wood, *White Side,* 247–48.
8. Detroit *Advertiser and Tribune,* Nov. 25, 1863; Jan. 11, 1869; Truth to Oliver Johnson, Feb. 3, in *National Anti-Slavery Standard,* Feb. 13, 1864; Truth to Mary K. Gale, Feb. 25, 1864, LC.
9. Boston *Commonwealth,* Aug. 12, 19, 1864; Conrad, *Harriet Tubman,* 183–84; Holt, "A Heroine in Ebony," 462.
10. Truth to Amy Post, Nov. 3, 1864, UR.
11. *National Anti-Slavery Standard,* Dec. 17, 1864.
12. Orange, NJ, *Journal,* July 29, 1876; Harlowe, "Sojourner Truth," 173.
13. Tomkins, *Jewels in Ebony,* 3.
14. Colman, letter, in Rochester *Evening Express,* Nov. 10, 1864; Colman, *Reminiscences,* 66–67.
15. Derby, "Sojourner Truth," 169; Colman, *Reminiscences,* 52, 65; Tomkins, *Jewels in Ebony,* 1–2.
16. Battle Creek *Journal,* Apr. 9, 16, 1868; Ypsilanti *Commercial,* Sept. 14,

1872; Blue Rapids, KS, *Times,* July 18, 1878; New York *Herald,* Dec. 16, 1878; Chicago *Daily Inter-Ocean,* Aug. 13, 1879; Chicago *Semi-Weekly Inter-Ocean,* Sept. 25, 1893.

17. *Narrative,* 178.

18. Orange, NJ, *Journal,* July 29, 1876.

19. Eppse, *The Negro,* 174–75; White, "Sojourner Truth," 17; Mabee, *Black Freedom,* 337; Martin, *American Sisterhood,* 102; Davis and Redding, *Cavalcade,* 78.

20. Detroit *Post,* Jan. 12, 1869; *Narrative,* 178 (Truth continued to tell the tale: New York *Herald,* Dec. 16, 1878; Chicago *Daily Inter-Ocean,* Aug. 13, 1879); Pauli, *Her Name Was Sojourner Truth,* 9.

21. Cordley, "Sojourner Truth," 65; Fairbank, *Rev. Calvin Fairbank,* 177–78.

22. Woonsocket, RI, *Patriot,* Aug. 5, 1870; *Narrative,* 275; Detroit *Tribune,* Nov. 4, 1885.

23. *National Anti-Slavery Standard,* Nov. 27, 1869; Detroit *Advertiser and Tribune,* Jan. 11, 1869; Northampton *Hampshire Gazette,* Feb. 21, 1871; Topeka *Kansas State Record,* Oct. 11, 1871; *Narrative,* xi; Chicago *Daily Inter-Ocean,* Aug. 13, 1879.

12. Riding Washington's Horse Cars

1. New York *World,* May 13, 1867.

2. Mabee, *Black Freedom,* chaps. 7–8.

3. [U.S.] *Statutes at Large,* vol. 13, 536–37.

4. *Narrative,* 184; *Congressional Globe,* 38 Cong., 1st sess., 1864, 553–54.

5. Washington *Weekly National Republican,* Mar. 17, 1865.

6. *Narrative,* 185.

7. *Narrative,* 184–85; Battle Creek *Journal,* Apr. 12, 1871. Other sources on her ride-ins: New York *Commercial Advertiser,* Mar. 22, 1865; Washington *Weekly National Republican,* Mar. 31, 1865; *National Anti-Slavery Standard,* Oct. 14, 1865; Detroit *Post,* Jan. 12, 1869.

8. Truth to Amy Post, Oct. 1, 1865, UR.

9. *Narrative,* 185–86.

10. *Narrative,* 186.

11. Truth to Post, Oct. 1, 1865, UR.

12. Washington *Daily National Republican,* Sept. 22, 1865. (An almost identical article appeared in the Washington *Evening Star,* Sept. 22, Washington *Daily Morning Chronicle,* and Washington *Daily National Intelligencer,* Sept. 23, 1865.)

13. Tomkins, *Jewels in Ebony,* 8.

14. *Narrative,* 187; Springfield *Daily Republican,* Feb. 24, 1871.

15. Washington *Daily Morning Chronicle,* Mar. 11, Dec. 25; Washington *Daily Times,* June 12, July 13, 1865.

16. *National Anti-Slavery Standard,* Dec. 1, 1866.

17. Bliven, *Mirror for Greatness,* 162; Grant, *Black Protest,* 68; Detroit *Free Press,* Apr. 23, 1972.

18. Mabee, *Black Freedom,* chaps. 6–7, 359.

19. Battle Creek *Journal,* Apr. 12, 1871.

13. Moving Freed Slaves to the North

1. Detroit *Post,* Jan. 12, 1869.

2. *National Anti-Slavery Standard,* Apr. 27, 1867; Saginaw *Daily Courier,* June 14, 1871; Kalamazoo *Daily Telegraph,* July 8, 1879.

3. *Banner of Light,* Feb. 11, 1865.

4. Mott and Wood, *Narratives of Colored Americans,* 68.

5. Saginaw *Daily Courier,* June 14, 1871.

6. Tomkins, *Jewels in Ebony,* 3–4.

7. Truth to Amy Post, Oct. 1, 1865, UR.

8. *Narrative,* 183.

9. Richard B. Merritt to Freedmen's Bureau, Oct. 7, 1867, roll 3, item 290, FB. Available bureau records do not list her as an employee.

10. *Narrative,* 181–82; *National Freedman,* 1–2, Mar., 1865 to July, 1866, passim; *American Freedman* 1 (Dec. 1866): 139.

11. A. E. Newton to Truth, Apr. 2, 1867, UR; *National Freedman* 1 (May 1, 1865): 137; Colman, *Reminiscences,* 67–68.

12. Washington *Daily Morning Chronicle,* Dec. 27, 1865.

13. Truth to Amy Post, July 3, 1866, UR.

14. Josephine Griffing to Brig. Gen. C. H. Howard, Nov. 7, 1866, roll 7, 197, FB.

15. Garrison, *Letters,* vol. 4, 269; Miss J. E. Griffing to Col. W. W. Rogers, Feb. 20, 1867, vol. 138, no. 366, FB.

16. Battle Creek *Enquirer and Evening News,* May 29, 1929.

17. Battle Creek *Enquirer and Evening News,* June 18, 1922.

18. *Narrative,* 191.

19. *National Anti-Slavery Standard,* Oct. 19, 1867; Kalamazoo *Daily Telegraph,* July 8, 1879.

20. Haviland, *Woman's Life-Work,* 449–51.

21. W. W. Rogers to Frances Titus, Dec. 12, 1866, roll 1, 562, FB.

22. The class: Battle Creek *Journal,* Jan. 2, 1868, Jan. 7, 1869.

23. *Banner of Light,* Feb. 18, 25, 1865.

24. Phoebe H. M. Stickney to Truth, Apr. 10, [1867], UR.

25. Rochester *Daily Democrat,* Rochester *Evening Express,* Mar. 13, 1867.

26. Truth to Josephine Griffing, Mar. 30, 1867, UR.

27. Josephine Griffing to Truth and Amy Post, Mar. 26; James Milroy to Truth, Apr. 10; A. C. Van Epps to Truth, Mar. 19; H. F. McVean to Truth, Mar. 25; Ruth Andrews to Truth, Apr. 3, 1867, UR.

28. Rochester *Daily Democrat,* Mar. 15, 1867.
29. Rochester *Daily Union,* Mar. 14, 16, 1867.
30. Amy Post to "General J. M. Howard" (error for O. O. Howard?), Mar. 18, 1867, roll 8, 1266, FB.
31. Griffing to Truth and Amy Post, Mar. 26, 1867, UR.
32. Truth to Griffing, Mar. 30, 1867, UR.
33. *Narrative,* 275.
34. Truth to Amy Post, Apr. 25, 1867, UR.
35. Mary H. Thomas to Truth, May 13, 1867, UR.
36. Roll 17, 509ff., FB; "Endorsements" concerning Truth to bureau, Sept. 18, 1867, roll 3, nos. 290, 382, FB.
37. Detroit *Advertiser and Tribune,* Jan. 11, 1869.
38. Rochester *Daily Democrat,* June 7, 10, 1867.
39. Truth to Amy Post, Aug. 25, Nov. 4, 1867, UR; Frances Titus to Eliza Leggett, Nov. 13, 1867, DPL.
40. *Narrative,* 289.
41. *Narrative,* 229; Kalamazoo *Daily Telegraph,* July 8, 1879.
42. Boston *Post,* Jan. 2, 1871.

14. Western Land

1. *National Anti-Slavery Standard,* Nov. 27, Dec. 18, 25, 1869.
2. New York *Tribune,* Mar. 13, 1871.
3. Move to Canada: Detroit *Post,* Jan. 12, 1869. Truth and Stebbins report their visit to Grant: *Narrative,* 273–75, Detroit *Tribune,* Nov. 4, 1885.
4. Told to petition: Topeka *Daily Capital,* Oct. 16, 1879. Reception: unidentified Washington newspaper, in Orange, NJ, *Journal,* in Battle Creek *Journal,* June 29, 1870 (*Narrative,* 130, reprints this article but incorrectly dates it in Lincoln's administration). Celebrating: Washington, DC, *New Era,* Apr. 21, 1870. The reception may have occurred on Apr. 20, 1870 when several Senators signed her autograph book (*Narrative,* 297–99). It has been claimed (Boston *Daily News,* Dec. 30, 1870; *Narrative,* 130) that Truth "spoke" to Congress, perhaps meaning at this time, but no convincing evidence for the claim is available.
5. *National Anti-Slavery Standard,* Mar. 4, 1871; Detroit *Post,* June 26, 1871; Fall River *Daily Evening News,* Oct. 14, 1870; Providence *Evening Bulletin,* Oct. 26, 1870; Boston *Daily Journal,* Dec. 29, 1870; Boston *Post*; Boston *Daily News*; Boston *Daily Evening Transcript,* Jan. 2, 1871. There is no available evidence for Pauli's claim, in her fictionalized *Her Name Was Sojourner Truth,* 224, that Theodore Tilton helped her word her petition.
6. Boston *Zion's Herald,* Feb. 23; *National Anti-Slavery Standard,* Mar. 4; New York *Tribune,* Mar. 13; Detroit *Daily Post,* June 26, 28; Saginaw *Daily Courier,* June 11, 1871.

7. Rochester *Democrat and Chronicle,* May 5; Boston *Post,* Jan. 2; Detroit *Daily Post,* June 26, 1871.

8. New York *Tribune,* Mar. 13; Springfield *Daily Republican,* Feb. 24; *National Anti-Slavery Standard,* Mar. 4, 1871.

9. Wyandotte, KS, *Gazette,* Jan. 25, 1872.

10. Burlington, IA, *Hawkeye,* Mar. 9, 1872.

11. Kansas City *Daily Journal of Commerce,* Jan. 12; Wyandotte *Gazette,* Feb. 1, 8; Kansas City *Daily Times,* Feb. 8, 1872. Redding, *Lonesome Road,* 78, claimed, without supporting evidence, that she was "manhandled" in Kansas and "ever afterward needed the support of a cane." Others repeated the claim. However, Truth sometimes walked with a cane long before she went to Kansas.

12. Wyandotte *Gazette,* Feb. 1, 1872; Lawrence *Kansas Daily Tribune,* Oct. 6, 1871; Topeka *Kansas Daily Commonwealth,* Oct. 19, 1871.

13. Jackson, MI, *Daily Citizen,* Aug. 21; Detroit *Daily Post,* Sept. 25, 1872.

14. Boston *Zion's Herald,* Dec. 29, 1870; Niles *Republican,* Oct. 16, 1873; Topeka *Kansas State Record,* Oct. 11, 1871.

15. New York *Tribune,* Mar. 13; Battle Creek *Journal,* Apr. 12, 1871.

16. Kansas City *Daily Journal of Commerce,* Jan. 16, 1872; Truth to O. O. Howard, Dec. 23, 1873, BC.

17. Saginaw *Daily Courier,* June 11, 1871; Niles *Republican,* Oct. 16, 1873; Detroit *Free Press,* June 13, 1871; about 200: Monroe, WI, *Sentinel,* Sept. 20, 1871.

18. Truth to O. O. Howard, Dec. 23, 1873, July 28, 1874, BC; Cromwell, *Negro in American History,* 110; Washington *Chronicle,* Apr. 20, 1874; *Narrative,* 251–52.

19. Chicago *Daily Inter-Ocean,* Aug. 13, 1879.

20. Chicago *Daily Inter-Ocean,* Apr. 16, 1881; Topeka *Daily Capital,* Oct. 16, 1879; Chicago *Daily Tribune,* Aug. 13, 1879.

21. Chicago *Daily Inter-Ocean,* Aug. 13, 1879.

22. Peeks, *Long Struggle,* 96; Bontemps and Conroy, *Anyplace But Here,* 65; Cordley, "Sojourner Truth"; Chicago *Daily Inter-Ocean,* Oct. 25, 1879. Truth's Michigan friend, Catharine A. F. Stebbins, who did not go to Kansas, claimed in *Religio-Philosophical Journal,* Feb. 28, 1880, that Truth in helping the migrants, "was taking long journeys in open wagons." (Similarly Stebbins, in Stanton et al., *History,* vol. 3, 532.) However, Titus (to Mary K. Gale, Dec. 3, 1879, undated clipping, Boston *Journal?,* LC), says Titus made a round trip in Kansas of 175 miles "in an open wagon" distributing relief, but, though she was writing primarily about Truth, Titus in fact did not say that Truth went with her.

23. Topeka *Daily Capital,* Oct. 15, Dec. 2, 5, 1879.

24. Topeka *Colored Citizen,* Oct. 11, 1879.

25. Battle Creek *Nightly Moon,* Jan. 18; Battle Creek *Daily Journal,* Feb. 24, 1880.

26. Wood, *White Side,* 348; Redding, in *Notable American Women,* vol. 3, 481; Topeka *Daily Capital,* Oct. 16, 1879.

27. Topeka *Commonwealth,* Oct. 10, 14, 1879; Topeka *Daily Capital,* Oct. 6, 1879; Chicago *Daily Inter-Ocean,* Jan. 1, Apr. 16, 1881.

28. Aptheker, *Documentary History,* 648n.; Redding, in *Notable American Women*; Bernard, in *Dictionary of American Negro Biography.*

29. Fauset, *Sojourner Truth,* 175; White, "Sojourner Truth," 18; Pauli, *Her Name Was Sojourner Truth,* 223; Middletown, NY, *Times Herald Record,* Feb. 2, 1986.

30. Battle Creek *Daily Journal,* Apr. 5, 1873.

31. Athearn, *In Search of Canaan,* 78–79, 183; Waldron, "Colonization in Kansas," 128–31; Haviland, in Topeka *Commonwealth,* Mar. 21, 1880.

32. Cordley, "Sojourner Truth."

33. Topeka *Daily Capital,* Oct. 16, 1879; Chicago *Daily Inter-Ocean,* Aug. 13, 1879.

15. Women's Rights

1. Vineland, NJ, *Weekly,* Dec. 25, 1869.

2. New York *Times,* Sept. 8, 1853.

3. Stowe, "Sojourner Truth," 479; Rochester *Evening Express,* Dec. 13, 1866; July 25, 1878; Vineland, NJ, *Weekly,* Dec. 25, 1869.

4. Salem, OH, *Anti-Slavery Bugle,* June 21, 1851; Battle Creek *Michigan Tribune,* Sept. 19, 1877.

5. New York *Times,* May 10, 1867; Rochester *Evening Express,* July 22, 25, 1878; New York *Daily Tribune,* Nov. 8, 1853; May 12, 1870; Battle Creek *Michigan Tribune,* Sept. 19, 1877; West Chester, PA, *Daily Local News,* July 18, 1874; Burlington, IA, *Hawkeye,* Mar. 9, 1872.

6. Salem, OH, *Anti-Slavery Bugle,* June 21, 1851; *National Anti-Slavery Standard,* June 1, 1867.

7. American Equal Rights Association Anniversary, held New York, 1867, *Proceedings,* 68.

8. New York *World,* May 10, 1867; Rochester *Evening Express,* Dec. 13, 1866.

9. West Chester, PA, *Daily Local News,* July 18, 1874; Detroit *Daily Post,* June 28, 1871; New York *Herald,* May 11, 1867.

10. *Narrative,* 282.

11. Rochester *Evening Express,* Dec. 12, 13, 1866; Rochester *Daily Union and Advertiser,* Dec. 13, 1866.

12. Stanton to Truth, Mar. 24, 1867, UR.

13. New York *World,* May 10, 11, 13, 1867; New York *Evening Post,* May 9, 1867.

14. New York *Daily Tribune,* May 10, 1867.

15. New York *World,* May 10, 1867.

16. "Broke": Again illustrating the difficulty of knowing what Truth really said, the New York *Tribune* and *Sun* (both May 10) also reported the word

"broke," whereas the *National Anti-Slavery Standard* (June 1) and American Equal Rights Association (*Proceedings*, held New York, 1867, 20), probably trying to "improve" her speech, reported the more elegant "broken" or "cracked."

17. New York *Evening Post*, May 9, 1867.

18. New York *Daily Tribune*, May 10, 1867.

19. Giddings, *When and Where I Enter*, 65.

20. *National Anti-Slavery Standard*, Nov. 27, 1869; Philadelphia *Inquirer*, Dec. 23, 1869; Stanton, Anthony, and Gage, *History*, vol. 3, 457–58.

21. Washington *New Era*, Apr. 14, 21, 1870.

22. *National Anti-Slavery Standard*, Mar. 20, 1869; *Narrative*, 290.

23. *National Standard*, Apr. 15, 1871; Detroit *Post*, June 23, 26, 1871; *Narrative*, 285.

24. Battle Creek *Daily Journal*, Nov. 1, 1872.

25. Battle Creek *Daily Journal*, Nov. 13, 1872.

26. Washington *New Era*, Apr. 21, 1870; Fish, "Sojourner Truth: Crusader," 15; Foner, *Voice of Black America*, 375.

27. Geneva, NY, *Gazette*, Aug. 28, 1868; Rochester *Daily Union and Advertiser*, Aug. 29, 1868.

28. New York *Times*, May 10, 1867; New York *Herald*, May 12, 1870.

29. Stanton et al., *History*, vol. 1, 567; Rochester *Daily Democrat*, Dec. 13, 1866; *Narrative*, 290; Rochester *Evening Express*, Dec. 12, 1866; New York *Evening Telegram*, Nov. 27, 1883.

16. Goose Wings and High Heels

1. Stowe, "Sojourner Truth," 479.

2. Chicago *Times*, Aug. 13, 1879; West Chester, PA, *Daily Local News*, July 18, 1874.

3. *Narrative*, 114.

4. Stowe, "Sojourner Truth," 479.

5. New York *World*, May 10, 1867; Rochester *Evening Express*, Apr. 17, 1871; Chicago *Inter-Ocean*, Aug. 13, 1879.

6. Wyman, *American Chivalry*, 107; Detroit *Free Press*, June 13, 1871; Akron, OH, *Summit Beacon*, June 2, 1852.

7. Warsaw, IN, *Northern Indianian*, Oct. 8, 1858.

8. Boston *Liberator*, Oct. 15, 1858; *Narrative*, 137–39.

9. Woonsocket, RI, *Patriot*, Aug. 5, 1870.

10. Providence *Daily Journal*, Nov. 1, 1870; New York *Daily Tribune*, Nov. 4, 1870; *Narrative*, 245.

11. Syracuse *Daily Standard*, Mar. 25, 27, 1871.

12. Rochester *Evening Express*, July 25, 1878.

13. Battle Creek *Michigan Tribune*, Sept. 19, 1877; Chicago *Times*, Chicago *Daily Tribune*, Aug. 13, 1879; Topeka *Colored Citizen*, Oct. 11, 1879; Topeka *Daily Capital*, Oct. 16, 1879.

17. Drink and Smoke

1. Hendricks, "Sojourner Truth," 669.

2. *Narrative*, 63–65; West Chester, PA, *Daily Local News,* July 18, 1874.

3. *National Anti-Slavery Standard,* Dec. 26, 1868.

4. *Narrative*, 105.

5. *Whole World's Temperance Convention,* held New York, 1853, 110.

6. Pennsylvania Yearly Meeting of Progressive Friends, held Old Kennett, 1853, *Proceedings,* 7, 37.

7. Colman, *Reminiscences,* 65; Truth to Post, Jan. 18, 1869, UR.

8. New York *World,* May 13, 1867.

9. Joseph Goodrich, an early settler in Milton, advocated temperance, opposed slavery, and was a founder of Milton College where it was rumored that Truth spoke. (Milton Historical Society to CM, Jan. 21, 1991.)

10. Coldwater, MI, *Republican,* Mar. 7, 1868. This story was often retold, as in *Revolution,* Jan. 19, 1871, which describes it as happening to "Chloe," "an aged, pious negress," not Truth; and in *Narrative,* 1875, 304, which says that the incident took place in Iowa, not Wisconsin; neither of these sources mentions Goodrich. There is evidence that by 1868 Truth had already been in Wisconsin, but not in Iowa.

11. Chicago *Daily Inter-Ocean,* Sept. 5, 1881.

12. Rochester *Daily Union and Advertiser,* Aug. 29, 1868.

13. *National Anti-Slavery Standard,* Dec. 26, 1868.

14. Lydia Allen to Truth, Feb. 1, 1869, UR.

15. Truth to Amy Post, Jan. 18, 1869, UR.

16. *Narrative*, 304.

17. As much against tobacco: *Christian at Work,* Sept. 28, 1882. Indiana: Chicago *Daily Inter-Ocean,* Aug. 24, 26, 1881. Union's paper: Chicago *Signal,* Sept. 8, 1881.

18. Battle Creek *Michigan Tribune,* Sept. 19, 1877.

19. *Christian at Work,* Sept. 28, 1882; Chicago *Daily Inter-Ocean,* Sept. 5, 1881; Battle Creek *Michigan Tribune,* Sept. 19, 1877; Chicago *Tribune,* Aug. 13, 1879; *Narrative,* 311–12.

20. New York *Daily Tribune,* May 12, 1870; Pennsylvania Yearly Meeting of Progressive Friends, held 1874, *Proceedings,* 14; Lansing *Republican,* June 7, 1881; *Christian at Work,* Sept. 28, 1882; Rochester *Evening Express,* July 25, 1878; Chicago *Daily Inter-Ocean,* Apr. 16, 1881; West Chester, PA, Daily *Local News,* July 18, 1874.

21. Henry Wiegmink, "Early Days of Battle Creek," ca. 1940, 1136, WL; Lansing *Republican,* June 7, 1881.

18. Friend Titus

1. Truth to Amy Post, Nov. 4, 1867, UR.

2. Walker, after having been imprisoned for assisting fugitive slaves, settled in Muskegon, Michigan, where Truth visited him.

3. Titus to Eliza Leggett, Nov. 13–14, 1867, DPL.

4. *Narrative*, 196–97.

5. *Narrative*, 181.

6. *Narrative*, 256.

7. Titus to Mary K. Gale, Mar. 31, 1876, LC.

8. *Narrative*, 1850, 13; *Narrative*, 1878, xii, 13, 308.

9. Altered word: *Narrative*, 227, in quoting what it identified only as a Rochester paper (really the Rochester *Evening Express* of May 3, 1871) reported it as saying, "she speaks to crowded houses everywhere," when what it really said was "she speaks to crowded houses elsewhere." Mixed up dates: *Narrative*, 174–75, indicated Truth visited Brooklyn in 1864, and quoted what it identified as a Brooklyn paper of 1864, about that visit; actually the paper was the New York *Independent*, Sept. 30, 1869, speaking about her visit to Brooklyn in 1869. Identified wrong: *Narrative*, 223–24, identified a quotation as from a Philadelphia newspaper, of no date, which in fact appeared in the Baltimore *American*, Mar. 6, 1874.

10. Grand Rapids *Daily Times*, Mar. 14, 1873.

11. Titus to Mary K. Gale, Dec. 3, 1879, undated clipping, Boston *Journal?* LC.

12. Emily Howland, Journal, Aug. 21, 1878, FHL; Topeka *Commonwealth*, Sept. 29, 1879; Topeka *Daily Capital*, Dec. 3, 1879.

13. Titus to Mrs. John P. St. John, Oct. 29, 1879, KSHS.

14. Topeka *Daily Kansas State Journal*, Oct. 8, 1879.

15. Topeka *Daily Capital*, Oct. 6, 1879.

16. Titus to Mary K. Gale, Dec. 3, 1879, undated clipping, Boston *Journal?*, LC.

17. Chicago *Advance*, Dec. 18, 1879.

18. Mrs. J. J. Taylor to John P. St. John, Dec. 15, 1879, KSHS.

19. Streator *Monitor-Index*, Jan. 2, 1880.

20. Chicago *Daily Inter-Ocean*, Chicago *Daily Tribune*, Jan. 2, 1880.

21. Chicago *Daily Inter-Ocean*, Jan. 8, 12, 13, 19, 1880; Chicago *Religio-Philosophical Journal*, Jan. 17, 1880.

22. Adventist: *Good Health*, Feb., 1883, 52; Stebbins: *Woman's Journal*, Dec. 8, 1883; Perry, *Lucinda Hinsdale Stone*, 320.

23. Washington *Evening Star*, Jan. 3, 1885; Battle Creek *Moon*, Feb. 27, 1892; clipping, Battle Creek paper?, marked Oct. 17, 1901, WL; Battle Creek *Daily Moon*, June 4, 1902.

19. Friends and Supporters

1. *Banner of Light,* May 2, 1863; New York *World,* May 13, 1870.

2. *Pennsylvania Freeman,* May 12, 1853.

3. This "doctor," Mrs. Erastus C. Clark, although not claiming to have any medical degree, called herself an "electic" physician, apparently meaning one who draws on various systems of practice. She may have been in part a faith healer; she associated with Spiritualists. Truth paid Clark $33 for her treatment, but when Clark wanted Truth to pay more, Truth, believing that Clark had not cured her, refused. Several years later Clark sued Truth for more. When neither Clark nor her lawyers appeared in court as required, the suit ended. (Battle Creek *Nightly Moon,* May 19, 23, June 23, 1880; Battle Creek *Daily Journal,* June 5, 1880).

4. Truth to William Still, Jan. 4, 1876, HSP.

5. Philadelphia *Evening Bulletin,* July 28, 1876.

6. New York *Daily Tribune,* May 10, 1867; Battle Creek *Daily Journal,* May 8, 1874; Boston *Liberator,* July 14, 1854; Vineland, NJ, *Weekly,* Dec. 25, 1869; New York *Daily Tribune,* Sept. 7, 1853.

7. New York *Daily Tribune,* Sept. 7, 1853.

8. Dowagiac, MI, *Cass County Republican,* Sept. 7, 1876; Detroit *Free Press,* June 13, 1871; New York *World,* May 11, 1867.

9. Eliza Leggett to Amy Post, Feb.? 1869, UR; Stebbins, *Upward Steps,* 210–11; Henry J. A. Wiegmink, "Early Days of Battle Creek," ca. 1940, 1136, WL; *Narrative,* 257; *Independent,* Sept. 30, 1869.

10. Emily Howland, Journal, Aug. 18, 20–22, 1878, FHL.

11. Pillsbury, in Ellen W. Garrison to Maria M. Davis, Jan. 28, 1875, SC; Battle Creek *Daily Journal,* Feb. 18, 1876.

12. Garrison, *Letters,* vol. 6, 338.

13. *National Anti-Slavery Standard,* Apr. 4, 25, July 4, 1863.

14. Chicago *Daily Tribune,* Aug. 13, 1879; New York *World,* May 13, 1870; Saginaw *Daily Courier,* June 14, 1871; *National Anti-Slavery Standard,* Nov. 27, 1869.

15. *National Anti-Slavery Standard,* Apr. 25, 1863.

16. Chicago *Daily Inter-Ocean,* Aug. 13, 1879; Salem, OH, *Anti-Slavery Bugle,* Dec. 13, 1851; West Chester, PA, *Daily Local News,* July 18, 1874; *National Anti-Slavery Standard,* Apr. 27, 1867.

17. *National Anti-Slavery Standard,* June 27, 1863; Topeka *Daily Capital,* Oct. 8, 1879; *Narrative,* 290; Chicago *Times,* Aug. 12, 1879.

20. Singer

1. Squier, "Sojourner Truth," 17–18.

2. Hendricks, "Sojourner Truth," 669.

3. Stowe, "Sojourner Truth," 476–77; *Narrative*, 1884, "Memorial Chapter," 6; Chicago *Daily Tribune*, Aug. 13, 1879.

4. Eva Warriner, on Quakerism in Battle Creek, in Battle Creek *Enquirer and News*, Nov. 6, 13, 1921, excerpts, WL.

5. West Chester, PA, *Daily Local News*, July 18, 1874; Springfield *Daily Republican*, Feb. 24, 1871.

6. [Watson], *Methodist Error*, 28–31.

7. *Narrative*, 87.

8. Stowe, "Sojourner Truth," 479.

9. *Narrative*, 114.

10. Chicago *Daily Inter-Ocean*, Aug. 13, 1879; *Narrative*, 116.

11. Stowe, "Sojourner Truth," 476–77.

12. Chicago *Daily Inter-Ocean*, Aug. 13, 1879.

13. Providence *Daily Journal*, Nov. 1, 1870; Dugdale, in Burlington, IA, *Hawkeye*, Mar. 9, 1872; Marshall, MI, *Statesman*, Apr. 11, 1877.

14. New York *World*, May 11, 1867.

15. From "I Am Pleading for My People."

16. From "I Pity the Slave Mother."

17. From "There Is a Holy City."

18. Pennsylvania Yearly Meeting of Progressive Friends, held 1853, *Proceedings*, 8–9; Smedley, *History of the Underground Railroad*, 256.

19. Rochester *Evening Express*, Dec. 12, 13; Rochester *Daily Democrat*, Rochester *Daily Union and Advertiser*, Dec. 13, 1866.

20. New York *World*, May 10, 1867; New York *Daily Tribune*, May 11, 1867; song quoted from Truth's flyer, "Sojourner's Mirror," 1852, KHM (slightly different from version in *World*).

21. *National Anti-Slavery Standard*, Sept. 26, 1868.

22. Detroit *Daily Post*, Sept. 25, 1872; West Chester, PA, *Daily Local News*, July 18, 1874; Chicago *Daily Tribune*, Aug. 13, 1879; Chicago *Daily Inter-Ocean*, Aug. 13, 1879; Lansing *Republican*, June 2, 7, 1881.

23. Squier, "Sojourner Truth," 17–18 (words not given, but their content is summarized).

24. *Narrative*, 1884, "Memorial Chapter," 6. Stowe, "Sojourner Truth," 476–77, prints nine verses.

25. *Narrative*, 116, prints one verse.

26. *Narrative*, 119, prints one verse.

27. The New Lisbon, OH, *Aurora*, Mar. 3, 1852, reported that Truth was speaking in New Lisbon, and published eleven verses of a "mirror" version of this song by "Mary," written in the third person, reading, for example, "She pleadeth for her people," making it likely that Truth had just sung it in the first person and "Mary" had transformed it into the third person. Truth sang the song in the first person in 1853 (New York *Daily Tribune*, Nov. 8, 1853). *Narrative*, 302–4, prints eleven verses.

28. Undated flyer, headed "Sojourner's Mirror," KHM (prints four verses plus chorus), and heads the song "Sojourner's Favorite Song." Date: In introduc-

ing one of the songs, this flyer quotes, without saying so, the New Lisbon *Aurora,* Mar. 3, 1852.

29. Undated flyer (see n. 28), prints eight verses plus chorus.

30. Stowe, "Sojourner Truth," 479, prints two lines.

31. Pennsylvania Yearly Meeting of Progressive Friends, held 1853, *Proceedings,* 8–9, prints three verses.

32. *Narrative,* 310, prints only three words.

33. Henry Wiegmink, "Early Days of Battle Creek," ca. 1940, 1136, WL, prints no lines.

34. *Narrative,* 126, prints six verses plus chorus.

35. Detroit *Post,* Jan. 12, 1869, prints one verse.

36. West Chester, PA, *Daily Local News,* July 18, 1874, prints five words.

37. Topeka *Daily Kansas State Journal,* Oct. 7, 1879.

38. Topeka *Commonwealth,* Oct. 8, 1879.

39. Clark, *Liberty Minstrel,* 1844, 32–33; *Narrative,* 1884, "Memorial Chapter," 6.

40. Hillman, *The Revivalist,* 253.

41. Bradford, *Harriet Tubman,* 49–50; West Chester, PA, *Daily Local News,* July 18, 1874.

42. *Banner of Light,* May 2, 1863; clipping, Battle Creek paper, ca. May 30, 1929, in Berenice Lowe, "Sojourner Truth: Data Collected," 1964, sec. 4, UM; Wiegmink, "Early Days of Battle Creek," 1136, WL.

43. [White], *White's New Illustrated Melodeon Song Book,* 50; Hungerford, *Old Plantation,* 198.

44. New York *World,* May 13, 1867.

45. Chicago *Times,* Aug. 13, 1879.

46. Squier, "Sojourner Truth," 17–18.

47. *Narrative,* 1884, "Memorial Chapter," 7–8.

21. Talking with God

1. Saginaw *Daily Courier,* June 11, 14, 1871; Chicago *Daily Inter-Ocean,* Aug. 13, 1879.

2. *National Anti-Slavery Standard,* July 4, 1863; Chicago *Daily Inter-Ocean,* Jan. 1, 1881; Perry, *Lucinda Hinsdale Stone,* 323.

3. *Woman's Journal,* Aug. 10, 1878; *Narrative,* 108–9.

4. *Narrative,* 69, 106–9.

5. Lansing *Republican,* June 7, 1881.

6. Stowe, "Sojourner Truth," 479; Chicago *Daily Inter-Ocean,* Apr. 16, 1881; Jan. 2, 1880; Topeka *Daily Capital,* Oct. 16, 1879; Lansing *Republican,* June 7, 1881.

7. Chicago *Daily Inter-Ocean,* Aug. 13, 1879.

8. Hersh, *Slavery of Sex,* especially preface and chap. 8.

9. New York *World,* May 13, 1867; Vineland, NJ, *Weekly,* Jan. 22, 1870; New York *Daily Tribune,* Nov. 8, 1853; Lansing *Republican,* June 7, 1881; *Narrative,* 1878, xii.

10. Hine, in Hine, ed., *State of Afro-American History,* 228.

11. Washington *Chronicle,* May 4, 1874.

12. Salem, OH, *Anti-Slavery Bugle,* Nov. 1, 1851; Boston *Liberator,* June 28, 1861.

13. Rochester *Evening Express,* Apr. 15, 17, 1871.

14. Stowe, "Sojourner Truth," 474; New York *Sun,* Nov. 24, 1878.

15. Unidentified newspaper (Phoenixville, PA, about July 29, 1874?), in *Narrative,* 223; New York *Daily Tribune,* Nov. 8, 1853; Orange, NJ, *Journal,* Dec. 16, 1876.

16. Perry, *Lucinda Hinsdale Stone,* 320; *National Anti-Slavery Standard,* May 2, 1863 (other accounts of her using similar words of rebuke to a clergyman but under different circumstances: Fall River *Daily Evening News,* Oct. 14, 1870; Underhill, *Missing Link,* 97; Perry, *Lucinda Hinsdale Stone,* 318–19); Chicago *Daily Inter-Ocean,* Apr. 16, 1881.

17. Providence *Daily Journal,* Oct. 20, 1870.

18. Salem, OH, *Anti-Slavery Bugle,* Nov. 8, 1856.

19. Woman's Rights Convention, held New York, 1853, *Proceedings,* 77.

20. Boston *Zion's Herald,* Feb. 23, 1871; *Narrative,* 262.

21. *National Anti-Slavery Standard,* Apr. 25, 1863.

22. Pennsylvania Yearly Meeting of Progressive Friends, held 1874, *Proceedings,* 16.

23. Warsaw, IN, *Northern Indianian,* Oct. 8, 1858; Detroit *Free Press,* June 13, 1871; Mount Pleasant, IA, *Journal,* Feb. 9, 1872; Chicago *Daily Inter-Ocean,* Aug. 13, 1879.

24. Burlington, IA, *Hawkeye,* Mar. 9, 1872; clipping, Battle Creek paper, ca. May 30, 1929, in Lowe, "Sojourner Truth: Data Collected," 1964, sec. 4, UM.

25. Cora Hatch Daniels to Amy Post, Jan. 2, 1866, UR.

26. Rochester *Evening Express,* Aug. 26–29; Rochester *Daily Union and Advertiser,* Aug. 29; Rochester *Daily Democrat,* Aug. 27, 1868.

27. Saginaw *Daily Courier,* June 11, 1871.

28. Blue Rapids, KS, *Times,* July 18, 1878; New York *Tribune,* Dec. 7, 1878.

29. *Banner of Light,* Dec. 8, 1883.

30. Rogers, "Sojourner Truth," 6–7; Battle Creek *Journal,* Dec. 12, 1883; Feb. 4, 1878; *Good Health,* Feb., Dec., 1883; Frances Titus to William Lloyd Garrison, Feb. 21, 1875, BPL.

31. *Seventh Day Adventist Encyclopedia,* 1503–04; New York *World,* Dec. 7, 1878; Vineland, NJ, *Weekly,* Dec. 25, 1869; Lansing *Republican,* June 7, 1881; Battle Creek *Moon,* Nov. 26, 1883; Detroit *Post and Tribune,* Chicago *Daily Inter-Ocean,* Nov. 27, 1883.

32. Squier, "Sojourner Truth," 17.

33. *Woman's Journal,* Dec. 8, 1883; Battle Creek *Moon,* Battle Creek *Daily Journal,* Nov. 28, 1883; *Narrative,* 1884, "Memorial Chapter," 10–12. Stuart also preached at Titus's funeral (Battle Creek *Moon,* Apr. 21, 1894).

34. Battle Creek *Michigan Tribune,* June 5, 1880; Grand Rapids *Eagle,* Nov. 20, 1883.

35. *Woman's Journal,* Dec. 8, 1883.

36. Chicago *Daily Inter-Ocean,* Jan. 1, 1881; Kansas City *Daily Journal of Commerce,* Jan. 16, 1872; Detroit *Free Press,* June 13, 1871.

37. *Narrative,* 265.

Bibliography of Works Cited

Manuscript Collections

Symbol
BC Oliver O. Howard papers, Bowdoin College, Brunswick, ME
BJ William Smith papers, Beatrice Jordan, St. Remy, NY
BPL Boston Public Library, Boston, MA
DPL Leggett family papers, Burton Historical Collection, Detroit Public Library, Detroit, MI
FB Records of the District of Columbia region, Freedmen's Bureau, National Archives, Washington, DC
FHL Emily Howland papers, Friends Historical Library, Swarthmore, PA
HHS Huguenot Historical Society, New Paltz, NY
HSP Leon Garniner Collection, Historical Society of Pennsylvania, Philadelphia, PA
KHM Kimball House Museum, Battle Creek, MI
KSHS John P. St. John papers, Kansas State Historical Society, Topeka, KS
LC Sojourner Truth papers, Library of Congress, Washington, DC
SC Garrison Family Papers, Sophia Smith Collection, Smith College, Northampton, MA (with permission of David Garrison)
UM Michigan Historical Collections, University of Michigan, Ann Arbor, MI
UR Amy and Isaac Post papers, Rhees Library, University of Rochester, Rochester, NY
WL Willard Library, Battle Creek, MI

Convention Proceedings

American Equal Rights Association Anniversary, held New York, May 9–10, 1867, *Proceedings,* New York, 1867.

National Women's Rights Convention, held Cleveland, Oct. 5–7, 1853, *Proceedings,* Cleveland, 1854.

Pennsylvania Yearly Meeting of Progressive Friends, held Old Kennett, May, 1853, *Proceedings,* New York, 1853.

Pennsylvania Yearly Meeting of Progressive Friends, held Longwood, June, 1874, *Proceedings,* Philadelphia, 1874.

Whole World's Temperance Convention, held New York, Sept. 1–2, 1853, New York, 1853.

Woman's Rights Convention, held Worcester, Oct. 23–24, 1850, *Proceedings,* Boston, 1851.

Woman's Rights Convention, held Akron, May 28–29, 1851, *Proceedings,* Cincinnati, 1851.

Woman's Rights Convention, held New York, Sept. 6–7, 1853, *Proceedings,* New York, 1853.

Books, Articles, and Theses

Allen, Robert L. *Reluctant Reformers: Racism and Social Reform Movements in the United States.* Washington, DC: Howard University, 1974.

Andrews, William L. *Sisters of the Spirit: Three Black Women's Autobiographies of the Nineteenth Century.* Bloomington: Indiana University, 1986.

Anson, Shirley V. *Plains Monthly Meeting (Quaker Meeting), Ulster County, NY.* No place, 1987.

Aptheker, Herbert. *A Documentary History of the Negro People in the United States.* New York: Citadel, 1951.

Athearn, Robert G. *In Search of Canaan: Black Migration to Kansas, 1879–80.* Lawrence: Regents, 1978.

Bennett, Lerone. *Pioneers in Protest.* Chicago: Johnson, 1968.

Bernard, Jacqueline. *Journey Toward Freedom: The Story of Sojourner Truth.* New York: Norton, 1967.

Bliven, Bruce. *A Mirror for Greatness: Six Americans.* New York: McGraw-Hill, 1975.

Blockson, Charles L. *The Underground Railroad.* New York: Berkley, 1987.

Bontemps, Arna, and Jack Conroy. *Anyplace But Here.* New York: Hill and Wang, 1966.

Bradford, Sarah. *Harriet Tubman: The Moses of Her People.* 1961. Reprint. Gloucester, MA: Smith, 1981.

Braude, Ann. *Radical Spirits: Spiritualism and Women's Rights in Nineteenth-Century America*. Boston: Beacon, 1989.

Carter, Harriet. "Sojourner Truth." *Chautauquan* 7 (May 1887): 477–80.

Chadwick, John White. *A Life for Liberty: Anti-slavery and Other Letters of Sallie Holley*. 1899. Reprint. New York: Negro Universities Press, 1969.

Chase, Warren. *Forty Years on the Spiritual Rostrum*. Boston, 1888.

———. *The Life-Line of the Lone One*. Boston, 1857.

Clark, George W. *The Liberty Minstrel*. New York, 1844.

Clearwater, Alphonso. *History of Ulster County, New York*. Kingston: Van Deusen, 1907.

Colman, Lucy N. *Reminiscences*. Buffalo, 1891.

Connelly, Arthur C. *St. James Methodist Episcopal Church of Kingston, New York: Historical Account*. Kingston, 1923.

Conrad, Earl. *Harriet Tubman*. Washington, DC: Associated, 1943.

Cordley, Richard. "Sojourner Truth." *Congregationalist* 32 (March 3, 1880): 65.

Cromwell, John W. *The Negro in American History*. Washington, DC: American Negro Academy, 1914.

Davis, Angela Y. *Women, Race, & Class*. New York: Random House, 1981.

Davis, Arthur P., and Saunders Redding. *Cavalcade: Negro Writing from 1760 to the Present*. Boston: Houghton Mifflin, 1971.

Derby, Mary. "Sojourner Truth." *Opportunity* 18 (June, 1940): 167–69.

De Witt, William C. *People's History of Kingston*. New Haven: N.p., 1943.

Dictionary of American Negro Biography. New York: Norton, 1982.

Douglass, Frederick. *Life and Times*. 1892. Reprint. New York: Collier, 1962.

Dunlap, William. *History of the Rise and Progress of the Arts of Design*. Vol. 2, 1834. Reprint. Boston: Goodspeed, 1918.

Eppse, Merl R. *The Negro, Too, in American History*. Nashville: National Publication Co., 1943.

Fairbank, Calvin. *Rev. Calvin Fairbank During Slavery Times*. 1890. Reprint. New York: Negro Universities Press, 1969.

Fauset, Arthur Huff. *Sojourner Truth: God's Faithful Pilgrim*. Chapel Hill: University of North Carolina, 1938.

Fish, Beverly A. "Sojourner Truth: Crusader for Women's Rights." In *Historic Women of Michigan: A Sesquicentennial Celebration*, ed. Rosalie R. Troester. Lansing: Michigan Women's Studies Association, 1987.

Flexner, Eleanor. *Century of Struggle: The Woman's Rights Movement in the United States*. Cambridge: Belknap, 1959.

Foner, Philip S. *The Voice of Black America*. Vol. 1. New York: Capricorn, 1975.

Ford, Richard Clyde. *Heroes and Hero Tales of Michigan*. Milwaukee: Hale, 1930.

Foster, Charles H. *The Rungless Ladder: Harriet Beecher Stowe and New England Puritanism*. Durham, NC: Duke University, 1954.

Garrison, William Lloyd. *Letters*. 6 vols. Cambridge: Belknap, 1971–81.

Giddings, Paula. *When and Where I Enter: The Impact of Black Women on Race and Sex in America*. New York: Morrow, 1984.

Gornick, Vivian, and Barbara K. Moran, eds. *Woman in Sexist Society: Studies in Power and Powerlessness*. New York: Basic Books, 1971.

Grant, Joanne, ed. *Black Protest: History, Documents, and Analyses*. Greenwich, CT: Fawcett, 1968.

Harley, Sharon, and Rosalyn Terborg-Penn. *The Afro-American Woman: Struggles and Images*. Port Washington, NY: Kennikat, 1978.

Harlowe, Marie. "Sojourner Truth: The First Sit-In." *Negro History Bulletin* 29 (Fall, 1966): 173–74.

Haviland, Laura S. *A Woman's Life-Work*. 1887. Reprint. Miami: Mnemosyne, 1969.

Heidgerd, William. *Black History of New Paltz*. New Paltz, NY: Elting Memorial Library, 1986.

Hendricks, Howard. "Sojourner Truth, Her Early History in Slavery." *National Magazine* 16 (Oct., 1892): 665–71.

Hersh, Blanche Glassman. *The Slavery of Sex: Feminist-Abolitionists in America*. Urbana: University of Illinois, 1978.

Hillman, Joseph. *The Revivalist: A Collection of Choice Revival Hymns and Tunes*. Troy, NY, 1869.

Hine, Darlene Clark, ed. *The State of Afro-American History*. Baton Rouge: Louisiana State University, 1986.

Holt, Rosa Belle. "A Heroine in Ebony." *Chautauquan* 23 (July, 1896): 459–62.

Honour, Hugh. *The Image of the Black in Western Art*. Vol. 4. Cambridge: Harvard University, 1989.

Hooks, Bell. *Ain't I a Woman: Black Women and Feminism*. Boston: South End, 1981.

Humez, Jean McMahon, ed. *Gifts of Power: The Writings of Rebecca Jackson, Black Visionary*. N.p.: University of Massachusetts, 1981.

Hungerford, James. *The Old Plantation*. New York, 1859.

James, Henry. *William Wetmore Story and His Friends*. 2 vols. 1903. Reprint. London: Thames, 1957.

Jarves, James Jackson. *The Art-Idea*. 1864. Reprint. Cambridge: Harvard University, 1960.

Kaplan, Sidney. "Sojourner Truth's Son Peter." *Negro History Bulletin* 19 (Nov., 1955): 34.

Kerber, Linda K., and Jane D. H. Mathews, eds. *Women's America: Refocusing the Past*. New York: Oxford University, 1982.

Lasser, Carol, and Marlene Deahl Merrill. *Friends and Sisters: Letters Between Lucy Stone and Antoinette Brown Blackwell*. Urbana: University of Illinois, 1987.

Lerner, Gerda. *The Female Experience: An American Documentary*. Indianapolis: Bobbs-Merrill, 1977.

Levinson, Nancy Smiler. *The First Women Who Spoke Out*. Minneapolis: Dillon, 1983.

Lowe, Berenice. "The Family of Sojourner Truth." *Michigan Heritage* 3 (Summer, 1962): 181–85.

———. "History is Legend and Truth." *Up to Date* (Historical Society of Battle Creek) 17 (Jan., 1975).

———. "Michigan Days of Sojourner Truth." *New York Folklore Quarterly* 12 (Summer, 1956): 127–35.

Mabee, Carleton. *Black Education in New York State: From Colonial to Modern Times.* Syracuse: Syracuse University, 1979.

———. *Black Freedom: The Nonviolent Abolitionists from 1830 Through the Civil War.* New York: Macmillan, 1970.

———. "Sojourner Truth and President Lincoln." *New England Quarterly* 61 (Dec., 1988): 519–29.

———. "Sojourner Truth, Bold Prophet: Why Did She Never Learn to Read?" *New York History* 69 (Jan., 1988): 55–77.

———. "Sojourner Truth Fights Dependence on Government." *Afro-Americans in New York Life and History* 14 (Jan., 1990): 7–26.

Martin, Wendy. *The American Sisterhood: Writings of the Feminist Movement.* New York: Harper and Row, 1972.

Memoirs of Matthias the Prophet. New York: Office of the *Sun,* 1835.

Miller, Myrtle Hardenbergh. *The Hardenbergh Family.* New York: American Historical Company, 1958.

Mott, Abigail, and M. S. Wood. *Narratives of Colored Americans.* New York, 1875.

Narrative of Sojourner Truth. Boston: For the Author, 1850.

Narrative of Sojourner Truth. Boston: For the Author, 1875.

Narrative of Sojourner Truth. Battle Creek: For the Author, 1878. Reprint. New York: Arno, 1968 (unless otherwise indicated, all references to the *Narrative* are to this edition).

Narrative of Sojourner Truth. Battle Creek: For the Author, 1881.

Narrative of Sojourner Truth. Battle Creek: [Adventist] Review and Herald, 1884.

Narrative of Sojourner Truth. Chicago: Johnson, 1970.

Notable American Women. 3 vols., Cambridge: Belknap, 1971.

Noyes, John Humphrey. *History of American Socialisms.* 1870. Reprint. New York: Dover, 1966.

Pauli, Hertha. *Her Name Was Sojourner Truth.* New York: Avon, 1962.

Pease, Jane H., and William H. Pease. *They Who Would Be Free: Blacks' Search for Freedom, 1830–1861.* New York: Athenaeum, 1974.

Peck, William F. *Semi-Centennial History of the City of Rochester.* Syracuse, 1884.

Peeks, Edward. *The Long Struggle for Black Power.* New York: Scribners, 1971.

Perry, Belle McArthur. *Lucinda Hinsdale Stone: Her Life Story and Reminiscences.* Detroit, 1902.

Pillsbury, Parker. *Acts of the Anti-Slavery Apostles.* 1883. Reprint. Miami: Mnemosyne, 1969.

Ravitch, Diane, ed. *The American Reader: Words That Moved a Nation*. New York: Harper Collins, 1990.

Records of the Reformed Dutch Church of New Paltz, New York. New York, 1896.

Redding, Saunders. *The Lonesome Road: The Story of the Negro's Part in America*. Garden City, NY: Doubleday, 1958.

Rogers, Samuel J. "Sojourner Truth." *Christian at Work* (Oct. 26, 1882): 6–7.

Roseboom, Eugene H. *The Civil War Era* (History of the State of Ohio, vol. 4). Columbus: Ohio State Archaeological and Historical Society, 1944.

Schneir, Miriam, ed. *Feminism: The Essential Historical Writings*. New York: Random House, 1972.

Schroeder, Theodore. "Mathias the Prophet." *Journal of Religious Psychology* 6 (Jan., 1913): 59–65.

Seventh-Day Adventist Encyclopedia. Washington, DC: Review and Herald, 1976.

Sheffield, Charles A. *The History of Florence, Massachusetts*. Florence, 1895.

Smedley, R. C. *History of the Underground Railroad in Chester and Neighboring Counties of Pennsylvania*. 1883. Reprint. New York: Negro Universities Press, 1968.

Squier, Effie J. "Sojourner Truth." *Christian at Work* (Sept. 28, 1882): 17–18.

Stanton, Elizabeth Cady, Susan B. Anthony, and Matilda Joslyn Gage. *History of Woman Suffrage*. 3 vols., 1881–87. Reprint. New York: Source Book, 1970.

Stebbins, Giles B. *Upward Steps of Seventy Years*. New York, 1890.

Stetson, Erlene. *Black Sister: Poetry by Black American Women*. Bloomington: Indiana University, 1981.

Stewart, James Brewer. *Holy Warriors: The Abolitionists and American Slavery*. New York: Hill and Wang, 1976.

Stone, Delia Hart [Cornell]. "Sojourner Truth." *Woman's Tribune* (Nov. 14, 1903): 124.

Stone, William L. *Matthias and His Impostures*. New York, 1835.

Stowe, Harriet Beecher. *Dred: A Tale of the Great Dismal Swamp*. 1856. Reprint. New York: AMS Press, 1967.

———. "The President's Message." *Independent* (Dec. 20, 1860): 1.

———. "Sojourner Truth, the Libyan Sibyl." *Atlantic* 11 (Apr., 1863): 473–81.

Sunshine at Home. Battle Creek: Review and Herald, 1883.

Terry, Esther. "Sojourner Truth: The Person Behind the Libyan Sibyl." *Massachusetts Review* 26 (Summer–Autumn, 1985): [425–44].

Tomkins, Fred. *Jewels in Ebony*. London, 1866?

Traubel, Horace. *With Walt Whitman in Camden*. Vol. 3. New York: Rowman, 1914.

Underhill, Ann Leah [Fox]. *The Missing Link in Modern Spiritualism*. New York, 1885.

Vale, Gilbert. *Fanaticism; Its Source and Influence, Illustrated by the Simple Narrative of Isabella, in the Case of Matthias*. 2 pts. New York, 1835.

Vital Records of Low Dutch Church of Klyn Esopus, Ulster Park, New York. No place, 1980.

Waldron, Nell B. "Colonization in Kansas from 1861 to 1890." Ph.D. diss., Northwestern University, Evanston, IL, 1932.

[Watson, John F.] *Methodist Error or Friendly Christian Advice to Those Methodists Who Indulge in Extravagant Emotions*. Trenton, NJ, 1819.

[White, Charles.] *White's New Illustrated Melodeon Song Book*. New York, 1848.

White, Deborah Gray. *Ar'n't I a Woman? Female Slaves in the Plantation South*. New York: Norton, 1985.

White, Walter. "Sojourner Truth: Friend of Freedom." *New Republic* 118 (May 24, 1948): 15–18.

Wood, Norman B. *The White Side of a Black Subject: A Vindication of the Afro-American Race*. 1896. Reprint. New York: Negro Universities Press, 1969.

Woodward, Helen Beal. *The Bold Women*. New York: Farrar, 1953.

Wyman, Lillie Buffum Chace. *American Chivalry*. Boston: Clarke, 1913.

———. "Sojourner Truth." *New England Magazine* 24 (March, 1901): 59–66.

Wyman, Lillie Buffum Chace, and Arthur Crawford Wyman. *Elizabeth Buffum Chace*. 2 vols. Boston: Clarke, 1914.

Yellin, Jean Fagan. *Women & Sisters: The Antislavery Feminists in American Culture*. New Haven: Yale University, 1989.

Acknowledgments

For permission to republish in this book in revised form portions of my earlier articles on Truth, I thank *New York History, New England Quarterly,* and *Afro-Americans in New York Life and History* (these articles are cited in full in the Bibliography).

For permission to quote their manuscripts, I thank the relevant manuscript collections listed in the Bibliography.

For permission to publish illustrations, I thank the following: figure no. 1, State Office of Parks, Senate House Historic Site, Kingston, NY; 4, J. Clarence Davies Collection, Museum of the City of New York; 5, New York State Historical Association, Cooperstown; 8, Battle Creek Historical Society, Battle Creek, MI; 10, Historic Northampton, Northampton, MA; 11, Metropolitan Museum of Art, New York, Gift of Wolf Foundation (1979. 266); 12 and 17, State University College, New Paltz, NY; 14, Library of Congress; 15, State Archives of Michigan; 20, Ellen G. White Estate, Seventh-Day Adventist General Conference, Silver Spring, MD.

Index